Defining the
YIDDISH NATION

Defining the
YIDDISH NATION

The Jewish Folklorists of Poland

Itzik Nakhmen Gottesman

WAYNE STATE UNIVERSITY PRESS   DETROIT

ISBN-13: 978-0-8143-2669-5   ISBN-10: 0-8143-2669-2

Library of Congress Cataloging-in-Publication Data

Gottesman, Itzik Nakhmen.
Defining the Yiddish nation : the Jewish folklorists of Poland / Itzik
Nakhmen Gottesman.
p. cm. — (Raphael Patai series in Jewish folklore and anthropology)
Includes bibliographical references and index.
ISBN 0-8143-2669-2
1. Jewish folklorists—Poland—Warsaw—History—20th century.
2. Jewish folklorists—Lithuania—Vilna—History—20th century.
3. Jewish nationalism—Europe, Eastern—History—20th century.
4. Yiddish language—Political aspects—Europe, Eastern.   5. Yidisher visnshaftlekher
institut—History.   6. Yiddish imprints—Collectors and collecting—Europe, Eastern.
7. Folk literature, Yiddish—Publishing—Europe, Eastern.   I. Title.   II. Series.
GR196.2.J49G68 2003
398.092'39240438–dc21   2003014472

Grateful acknowledgment is made to the Koret Foundation
for its generous support of the publication of this volume.

IN MEMORY
of the Jewish folklorists of Poland
who died in the Holocaust

Contents

Acknowledgments

With gratitude I acknowledge the wisdom and advice of my teachers at the University of Pennsylvania, Dan Ben-Amos and the late Kenneth Goldstein. I would also like to thank Professor Barbara Kirshenblatt-Gimblett at New York University. It was she who first urged me to study Yiddish folklore, and both she and Dan Ben-Amos have been very encouraging. Also enthusiastic was the late Raphael Patai, the original editor of this series. All of these people gave helpful suggestions and criticism, which I was not always able to follow—but I tried. *A hartsikn dank* to Professor Mordkhe Schaechter, who shared his knowledge of Yiddish language and culture.

The resources of the library and archives of the YIVO Institute for Jewish Research were indispensable, as will become obvious to the reader. My thanks to Zachary Baker and Dina Abramovitch *z'l* of the library and Marek Web and Fruma Mohrer of the archives at YIVO. It was during my years as an archivist at YIVO that I first discovered many of the folklore materials discussed here. Discussions with Chana Mlotek and Bina Silverman-Weinreich at YIVO were also helpful, as were interviews with Oyzer Paz-Pipe (in Israel), S. L. Schneiderman, Khayim Sheskin, Carl Zlotnick, and Ezra Tolpin (in New York). During my research visit to Israel, Professor Avrom Nowerstern showed great generosity, as did the staff at the archives of the National Library in Jerusalem.

I wish to thank my mother, Beyle Schaechter-Gottesman. Without her commitment to Yiddish culture this work would not have been possible. My father, Dr. Yoyne Gottesman, died during the preparation of this work; his knowledge of Jewish life in Eastern Europe was an inspiration. Finally, thanks to my wife, Emily Socolov, for her patience, support, and technical assistance. She and my daughter Esther have made life a pleasure.

A Note on Yiddish Language Use and Translation

I have almost always followed the YIVO/Library of Congress system of transcription of Yiddish words. The few exceptions were allowed in the cases when a popular spelling for a name or word was known to all. In terms of place names, I have generally used the Yiddish names of Polish towns, so that the capital of Lithuania is spelled Vilne, as it is pronounced in Yiddish. I chose to use the names that the Yiddish folklorists themselves used.

I have translated all Yiddish words in the text and have therefore not included a glossary. Book titles are given first in Yiddish and, when necessary, translated into English.

Abbreviations

AVJHES S. Ansky Vilne Jewish Historical-Ethnographic Society

BDMYL *Biographical Dictionary of Modern Yiddish Literature (Leksikon fun de nayer yidisher literastur)*, 8 vols. New York: Congress for Jewish Culture, 1956–81

EC [YIVO] Ethnographic Commission

LYL *Leksikon fun der yidisher literatur*, 4 vols. Ed. Zalmen Reyzen. Vilne: Kletskin, 1926–28

YIVO *Yidisher visnshaftlekher institut* (Yiddish Scientific Institute)

Introduction

Defining the Yiddish Nation:
The Roots of Yiddishist Folklore in Poland

We are stepping out in the Jewish public in a difficult and sad moment. Jewish nationalism has achieved great victories over the last thirty years. Nevertheless, there still remains a deep abyss between the folk and its higher strata, its intelligentsia. While a large segment of the folk is greatly distanced from modern culture, a large part of the wealthier classes and the intelligentsia in general are alienated from the folk-soul, the deepest and purest source of culture, because they have been torn from the folk, from its quotidian way of life, from its enormous past and blossoming future. It's difficult to breathe in the confining atmosphere of the old Jewish house. The atmosphere of the new Jewish house is also ruined, far from every Jewish tradition, dry and commonplace [*vokhedik*] without the slightest elevation of that true poetry that hovers around folklife and folk customs.

> Editorial, *Di yidishe velt*, Vilne, 1912[1]

This epigraph, written on the eve of the First World War, reflects the dilemma of the East European Jew in search of a modern identity. Torn between "the confinement of the old Jewish house" and the "dry and commonplace" atmosphere of the "new Jewish house," he faced an "abyss" that divided the folk and the intelligentsia. If somehow the fervor for Jewish nationalism and an appreciation of "Jewish tradition" or Jewish folklore could be combined, it implies, the Yiddish-speaking Jew could enter a new era in which the two classes would form an organic whole again.

A result of the rise of Jewish nationalism in Eastern Europe in the second half of the nineteenth century was to produce not one vision of a Jewish nation, but several. In recent work on nationalism, Benedict Anderson's term, "imagined communities," has come to the fore. Anderson suggests that the concept of the "nation" is "an imagined political community," since members of that group will never know each other, yet still imagine themselves in "communion."[2] In general, Anderson and other observers of nationalism, such as Ernest Gellner and Eric Hobsbawm, imply that there is only one "imagined community" for each nationalist movement.[3] In reference to the Jewish case, Hobsbawm goes so far as to say: "as the example of Yiddish shows, and that golden age of dialect literatures, the nineteenth century, confirms, the existence of a widely spoken or even written idiom did not necessarily generate language-based nationalism."[4] Yet for the Jews, in fact, there were several different "imaginings." Anderson et al. have exclusively focused on the Jewish nationalism of Zionism, with that ideology's belief in a return to the land of Israel and a revival of spoken Hebrew. There were other major Jewish nationalist movements at the time, however, which did in fact have the promotion of Yiddish language and culture as a central tenet of their ideologies. These movements included diaspora nationalism, autonimism, territorialism, folkism, and Bundism. Each, to some degree, included Yiddishism (the belief that Yiddish language and culture occupy the center of Jewish identity) as part of its platform.

This study analyzes to what degree and in what way the study of folklore assisted in the formation of the "imagining" of a modern Yiddish-speaking Jewish nation in Eastern Europe between the World Wars. Who studied folklore, how, and why? How did those who collected and wrote about folklore represent the folk and the lore?

I. J. Trunk, one of Yiddish literature's outstanding interwar critics, wrote "the Yiddishist ideology is the most daring attempt at true humanism in Jewish life." He drew the comparison with the Italian humanists of the Renaissance. The Jews of Eastern Europe, he held, resembled the Italians, who lived with two languages, Latin and Italian. The Jews, too, were torn between two languages, Hebrew and Yiddish. Inspired by Jacob Burckhardt's classic work of 1860, *The Civilization of the Renaissance in Italy,* Trunk wrote that the choice of language was directly related to one's weltanschauung. In Trunk's terms, Hebrew, the textual language, represented the past and death; Yiddish, the vernacular, represented the future, the people, life.

Trunk's essay was intended to use humanism as a model for Yiddishism, a secular Jewish ideology that, he believed, essentially had to cut its ties with its ancient Hebraic past in order to posit a new kind of nation for the Jews. What made Yiddishism so daring and similar to Italian humanism, according to Trunk, was its "search for the human being in history." Once you found the human, then you would find the essence of his culture. The Zionists, he implied, were creating a nation without people. They made Jews "slaves of the past." The Yiddishists, on the other hand, recognized "the Jewish present as the strongest expression of Jewish national existence in history."[5]

The situation of the Polish Jewish folklorists had much in common with the state of folklorists in other nations. Yet, the Yiddish case is significantly different in a number of ways. As with almost all European folklore movements, the Yiddishist one was rooted in nineteenth-century romantic nationalism and the ideas of J. G. Herder on the *volk*.[6] However, while the "folk" became synonymous in Europe with the peasants, the Jews had no peasantry. They were the ultimate town and urban people. According to the Polish census of 1931, 76 percent of the Jews in Poland lived in urban areas.[7] This fact determined the kinds of materials the Yiddish folklorists would collect and what genres would be sought to represent the Jewish "folk." For example, the search for ancient survivals in custom and ritual, so prominent in British folkloristics at that time, was a low priority among the Yiddish folklorists. Rather, the Yiddish folklorists sought out oral folklore that would reflect the beauty of the Yiddish language.

In all studies of folklore history, scholars have emphasized the need for the folklorist (like the politician) "to discover 'historical' models on which to reshape the present and build the future."[8] This was a necessary act in situations of emergent nationalism. However, while the intelligentsia of other nations could look to a remote past as a model, the Yiddishists were prevented from doing so. Most, but not all, firmly opposed returning to a Hebrew-speaking past, to the land of Israel, and to becoming part of the Zionist ideology. They decried this model for it left out the "folk," the diasporic Yiddish-speaking folk of Eastern Europe. Greek folklorists could turn to their Hellenistic roots in their construction of the nation; the Germans to their Teutonic origins; the French to their Celtic roots; the Finns to the mythic era of the Kalevala. But to what past could the Yiddishist folklorists turn? Because of the contestation of several nationalisms among Jews at this time, the Yiddish folklorists did not seek much inspiration from the distant past. They connected the study of folklore to the present, not the past. Following Herder, they believed that language was a nation's greatest achievement and that the best that the folk had to offer in language was folklore. Trunk added that "language was the most nationalist in the nation and the most humane in the human."[9] The study of language and folklore put one in touch with the folk, and Trunk concluded that Yiddishism was the only way to "Jewish self-awareness."

Yiddish and Yiddishism

Yiddishists believed that "the Yiddish language was the cementing force that united the Jewish people and would ensure its continued existence."[10] Unfortunately, the term "Yiddishism" has often been used synonymously with a singular political ideology, an inaccurate description. Yiddishism as political term did not take hold until after the Chernovitz Language Conference of 1908, which was a cornerstone in the history of the struggle to gain respect for the Yiddish language. At the conference, the participants adopted a resolution that Yiddish was a national language of the Jews.[11] Though Yiddish was the spoken language of almost all of German Jewry until the eighteenth century, and of East European Jewry until the Holocaust, it had always been considered a "debased" form of German, a Judeo-German, rather than an independent, unique, language. This view was maintained by outside observers as well as by its speakers.

With the emergence of a Jewish Enlightenment or *Haskala* in Germany in the eighteenth century and in Eastern Europe in the nineteenth century, the *maskilim,* or adherents of the Jewish Enlightenment, looked to modern European ways and rejected many traditional Jewish values. They heaped scorn upon the Yiddish language, projecting all that they viewed as corrupt and ugly in East European Jewish life onto the language.[12]

Emanuel Goldsmith, who has written on the history of Yiddishism, chose the second half of the nineteenth century and the publication of the Yiddish newspaper *Kol-Mevaser* in 1862 as the starting point of the movement.[13] Indeed, I. J. Trunk's combination of Yiddishism and humanism was preceded by an essay by the Yiddish lexicographer Y. M. Lifshits (1828–78) printed in *Kol-Mevaser* in 1867 in which the term "humanism" is used.[14] Since Yiddishism was a secular ideology, it is only right to place its beginnings in the period when such ideologies began to form in Eastern European Jewish life; however, any one event or person cannot be claimed as the beginning of Yiddishism. Several interwar Polish and Russian Yiddishist scholars sought their ideological roots as far back as the beginning of literature in the sixteenth century.[15]

Zhitlovsky and Dubnov

Though we cannot say who or what began Yiddishism, we can say that the ideology's greatest theoretician was Khayim Zhitlovsky. He was born near Vitebsk, White Russia, in 1865 and began his political career as a Russian populist, and later helped found the Social-Revolutionary Party in the 1880s in Zurich. He was among the first of the Russianized Jewish socialists to "return" to his people, and in so doing placed the language of the people at the cornerstone of a new alliance of socialism and Jewish nationalism. Zhitlovsky envisioned this Jewish nation as a diaspora nation. Other alternatives, such as Zionism, were simply impractical.[16] Zhitlovsky wrote often on assimilation, and he believed the Yiddish language would replace the Jewish religion as a buffer against outside culture, allowing Jews to develop a new secular culture and ethical worldview.

After the Russian pogroms of 1903, Zhitlovsky turned to territorialism and became associated with the Seimists, a socialist Jewish group that sought some measure of cultural autonomy as part of its program, while arguing against any immediate territorial solution.

Zhitlovsky's arrival in the United States in 1904 was a crucial event in the formation of a secular Yiddish culture there. The earliest Yiddish schools in America, called "National-Radical" schools, were founded by Zhitlovsky's followers in the then-evolving leftist Labor Zionist party. In Eastern Europe, all Yiddishist intellectuals considered him their mentor.

Because of Zhitlovsky's communist leanings in the 1930s, toward the end of his life, he was later taken less seriously, which explains the virtual disappearance of his name from Yiddishist ideological discussions in Poland, though not in the United States. He died in 1943, acknowledged as a leading Jewish political thinker of the pre-First World War era, a man who placed Yiddish in the heart of nationalist discussion. Numerous nationalist Jewish parties incorporated aspects of his ideas on Yiddish and diaspora nationalism.[17] In terms of the history of Yiddish folklore, Zhitlovsky's views were key, for he held that to understand the *folkslebn,* the folklife, of the Jews, one needed to use, to study, and appreciate the language of the folk. Eventually, such qualities associated with socialism as truth, beauty, and justice were transferred to Yiddish, Yiddish literature, and Yiddish secular culture.[18]

A connection between Jewish socialism and Yiddishism is commonly emphasized, especially in the case of the Bund, officially known as the General Jewish Workers' Union in Lithuania, Poland, and Russia, founded in 1897 in Vilne. However, only one folklorist in the present study, Shmuel Lehman of Warsaw, identified himself as a member of the Bund for his entire life. Lehman was clearly sympathetic to the working class, and his agenda in folklore collection reveals this. Other folklorists in this study belonged to other parties. Shloyme Bastomski was a leading Bundist in Vilne but switched to territorialism in the 1930s. Max Weinreich was also a Bundist, but kept rather quiet about his politics. In fact, his directorship of the YIVO Institute in Vilne often antagonized the Bund. Party politics had no profound effect on any of the Yiddish folklorists, from Lehman's Bundism, Prilutski's folkism, Graubard's socialist Zionism, and J. L. Zlotnik's Mizrachi (religious Zionist) involvement.[19] What connected all of these disparate political views was a deep affection for the Yiddish language and the belief that the language revealed the ethos of the Jewish people.

The other major voice that opened up the path of secular modern Yiddish culture was that of Shimon Dubnov (1860–1941). Unlike Zhitlovsky, with whom he shared some views on diaspora nationalism, national and cultural autonomy, Dubnov developed a clear analysis of Jewish history and the diaspora. Dubnov was not only one of the greatest Jewish historians, but a political activist who founded the Folkist Party in Russia in 1907 to promote his autonomist agenda. Many of the key Yiddishists of the next generation, including Nokhem Shtif, the initiator of YIVO, were active in this party. Dubnov believed that the Jews were "the most historical people," and that the Jewish diaspora was the highest stage of development a nation could attain. In the diaspora, Jews maintained national unity without territory through the historical consciousness of the people. Non-Zionists, including Yiddishists, gladly accepted this view. Dubnovism was seen as an attempt to create a positive nationalism that would be inclusive for all Jewish people and would deal with the current reality of the people.[20] Dubnov's emphasis on autonomy, self-sufficiency, and national institutions surely inspired the founding of the YIVO Institute for Jewish Research in 1925. YIVO would direct the trajectory of Yiddish folklore studies until the Second World War.

The impetus for a language-based nationalism came from inside the Jewish intellectual community as well as from the surrounding non-Jewish world. The Jews found themselves surrounded by a vociferous Polish nationalist movement that began with the final partition of Poland in 1795 and steadily increased until the Second World War. The Poles, in turn, were part of a larger pan-Slavic nationalist movement during the nineteenth century.[21] Particularly in Poland, where the Jews made up a larger percentage of the population, this Slavic nationalism was often anti-Semitic, xenophobic, and economically self-destructive.[22]

The Polish language was a significant factor in Polish nationalism, just as Yiddish was key in the Yiddishist nationalist view.[23] Since Poland was divided among the Prussian, Austro-Hungarian, and Russian empires from 1795 to the First World War, oppression of the Polish language by these powers only increased the symbolic importance of the language for nationalist pursuits. The study of Polish folklore was an integral part of this language-based nationalism.[24]

The Roots of a Yiddishist Folklore Study

While Dubnov and Zhitlovsky laid the theoretical foundations for Yiddishism, the connection between the ideology and folklore was possibly first promoted by Yoysef-Yehude Lerner in his essay on Yiddish folksong, "The Jewish Muse: Yiddish Folksongs," published in Mordkhe Spektor's journal *Hoyzfraynd* (The housefriend) in 1889.[25] Lerner (1847–1907) was a pioneer in the fields of Yiddish theater, Yiddish folklore, and especially Yiddish literary criticism. He lived in Odessa and mysteriously converted to Christianity toward the end of his life.[26] The argumentative introduction to this essay assailed the "nationalists," who believed the "Jews could move to Palestine overnight," and the "assimilationists," who believed that the Jews should speak only the language of their land of residence. Both camps, Lerner wrote, had made Yiddish their punching bag.

It is remarkable how similar Lerner's attack would be to one launched thirty-four years later by M. Vanvild, in his "Editor's Comments" to the magnum opus of the Warsaw group of Yiddish folklorists, *Bay undz yidn* (Among us Jews), published in 1923. By then, the term

"Zionists" replaced the broader term "nationalists," and the terms "Yid-dishists" and "Yiddishism," which were unknown in Lerner's time, were in common use.[27] The terms may have changed (Lerner refers to Yiddish as *zhargon,* jargon), but the Yiddishist struggle was pitched against the same enemies for decades: the Hebraists on one side (Vanvild referred to them as *Ivritistn*) and the Polish/Russian assimilationists on the other.

Lerner sought to counter the frequent charge by anti-Yiddish *maskilim* that the Yiddish language was not capable of "lofty thoughts" and "profound feelings," and was therefore unusable for creating po-etry. He considered this accusation one of the most important leveled against Yiddish and defended the language against this charge in his ar-ticle. The songs he presented would dispel any such notion, for "these ignored songs are the pearls of the crown."[28] Lerner then, in a footnote, defined the term "folksong" for his reader: "For the most part, the au-thors of these songs are not known; the songs stem directly from the folk, and are therefore called 'folksongs.' Every song was created by the folk over a number of years."[29] This was a necessary clarification, for, at this time, dozens of works by Yiddish poets included the word "folks-lider" in their titles. Included among these writers were the most popu-lar Yiddish *maskilic* writers of the day: Avrom Goldfaden, I. I. Linetski, and Eliakum Zunzer. The confusion about the concept of a "folkslid" in Yiddish culture continued for some time, culminating in a famous interchange between the writer Sholem Aleichem and the musicologist Joel Engel in 1901. Sholem Aleichem believed that all songs written for the folk in Yiddish were folksongs. Engel countered with a more folk-loristic view, similar to Lerner's.[30] Lerner, by beginning his explanation with the phrase, "for the most part," acknowledged that the border be-tween the two views was permeable. In fact, one of the prime examples which Lerner cited at length, apparently unknowingly, was a poem by his contemporary, Mikhl Gordon (1823–90).[31]

The directness of the folksong is what drew Lerner to the genre. Herder and the Grimms influenced Lerner's sensibilities, which equated "the folk" with "nature."[32] The directness of the folk poetry made it all the more truthful. Lerner also removed the folksong from the folk performer, giving it a superorganic life of its own. This approach, also an inheritance from the Grimms, would influence most Yiddish folkloristic discourse to follow.

Lerner made two crucial points on the intersection of Yiddishism and folklore. The first was that these songs were valuable. The second was that they reflected the thought of a unified people. The folksongs proved that there was a single "folk" of Yiddish-speaking Jews. "They reveal that a people feels and thinks exactly as an individual; even a group can have a head that thinks, a heart that feels."[33] Before one could develop a Yiddishist nationalism, one first had to demonstrate that a nation exists. Lerner was one of the first to use Yiddish folklore for that purpose and thereby define a Yiddish nation.

Lerner probably collected the songs used in this essay in Odessa in the 1880s. He brought examples of love songs, *rekrutn* (recruit) songs that described the drafting hardships in czarist Russia, and one nationalist song on longing for "home"—that is, Jerusalem. Lerner reiterated that the songs had nothing in common with the *maskilic* imagery of Yiddish-speaking women as "old wives who cast spells and pour wax."[34] This Yiddish folkpoetry possessed "an eternally youthful energy which [could] never be evaporated."[35] The love of the folk was great and pure. Lerner concluded that if the opponents of Yiddish were to read the poetry of the folk, they would throw off their shoes, for the place was holy.[36]

Mordkhe Spektor, the editor of the *Hoyzfraynd*, was himself a pioneer in the publication of folklore materials in Yiddish. Spektor printed a collection of proverbs in *Yidishes folksblat* in 1886 that was published separately in 1888–89.[37] In his own journal, Spektor gave folklore a prominent position. In the second volume of *Hoyzfraynd*, Spektor printed A. I. Bukhbinder's collection of Jewish omens.[38] This genre of folklore, which was not language based, was open to the same kind of criticism by its *maskilic* author that many earlier *maskilic* writers had leveled. This critique, called "anti-folklore" by Dan Miron, described in detail the customs and lifestyle of East European Jews in order to satirize them.[39] While Lerner exalted the Yiddish folk song in his collection, Bukhbinder's collection and analysis was determined to unearth the rational explanations for many of these beliefs and ultimately to ridicule them. In his comments on the *Shir hamayles* amulet which is placed in the newborn child's room, the author, after pointing out the Greek origin of many of the demons mentioned, concluded sarcastically, "Now, I think, every honest Jew can decide whether he should take in such a

Shir hamayles in a Jewish household and whether it would serve as protection."[40] Though this collection was a pioneering one, it represents a continuation of an anti-folkloric mindset parallel to the growing Yiddishist attitude that nurtured the oral forms of folklore.

In the fifth and final volume of *Hoyzfraynd*, published in 1895, Spektor printed the most impressive Yiddish folklore collection to date, more than two thousand proverbs collected by Ignaz Bernstein.[41] In his introduction to the collection, Spektor recalled his own appeal in 1886 in the pages of *Yidishes folksblat* to collect and to submit Yiddish proverbs, for they were hundreds of years old. He received a thousand letters within a few weeks, from around the world, from "doctors, engineers, writers, merchants, artisans, working class and even Jewish women."[42] This was perhaps the first such appeal in the Yiddish press. Spektor found that the simple working- and lower-class Jews sent in the good and juicy [*zaftike*] proverbs, while the intelligentsia, clearly alienated from the "folk," did not contribute valuable examples. "However, one also sees from their letters that they were, nevertheless, connected to the folk and enjoyed mailing in five or ten proverbs."[43] Spektor realized the importance of the wide spectrum of the reaction; even while distancing themselves from the "folk" in most other ways, the Jewish middle and upper-middle classes turned to Yiddish folklore as a means of remaining tied to their brethren.

By the 1890s, Jewish intellectual circles had incorporated Yiddish folksinging into their social gatherings. In Odessa, Dubnov and such other Jewish writers as Mendele, Shimon Frug, and Ben-Ami sang Yiddish and Hasidic melodies into the night.[44] In Warsaw, one of the most famous Yiddish writers of his time, I. L. Peretz, and his circle would meet on Saturdays: "Half of the time of those Sabbath gatherings at Peretz's was spent in singing the folksongs in a strange elevated mood. They were orgies of poetic ecstasy. They were the kind of experiences in which the spirit is shaped as metal in a flame."[45] Dr. Gershon Levin, Peretz's friend, remarked that the mood during the singing was "mystical," and Peretz seemed like a *rebbe* (Hasidic leader) encircled by his Hasidim.[46] In both Odessa and Warsaw, Yiddish folklore provided a means for acculturated and alienated intellectuals of the traditional *shtetl* to connect with lower-class and working-class Jews, and to empathize with the suffering of their "brothers" at the time. The songs revealed the creative potential of the Yiddish-speaking masses. The beauty of the people's language and folklore suggested that a Yiddish-speaking nation could be a nation like any other.

Peretz, because of his fame and influence, made Yiddish folklore respectable and brought it to the center of the Yiddish nationalist movement.[47] Peretz collected folk songs in the 1890s and urged others to collect as well.[48] Though, as we have seen, he was not the first to do so, his high status in Jewish intellectual society in Warsaw made the endeavor quite visible.

As a positive nationalist attitude toward Yiddish folklore spread among the intelligentsia at the turn of the century, two historians, Saul Ginzburg and Peysekh Marek, published 376 Yiddish folk songs in 1901 in one of the most comprehensive collections printed to date. *Yiddish Folksongs in Russia*[49] contained none of the strident tone that appeared in Lerner's essay. Polemics had been replaced with a positivist approach. They wrote (in Russian) that their collection of folk songs would, "lead us into the intimate world of folklife and present valuable material for the historian and the ethnographer."[50] A Yiddishist strand does emerge at one point in the introduction when the editors celebrate the rise of Yiddish poetry among the folk, and the struggle of the language "to exist side by side with Hebrew, the language of the prophets."[51] Unlike Lerner, Ginzberg and Marek were well aware of the growing literature on Yiddish folk song, especially in languages other than Yiddish, in such journals as *Mitteilungen der Gesellschaft fur judische Volkskunde* and *Globus*.[52] Compared to *Yiddish Folksongs in Russia*, previously published works on Yiddish folk song were scattered fragments.

The publication of the song texts in Yiddish along with the transliteration was a major breakthrough for Yiddish folklore studies: finally, a scholarly volume of Yiddish folklore with texts in the Yiddish alphabet (albeit with scholarly commentary in Russian). Yiddishist folklore scholarship still had further to go.

In 1908, Ignaz Bernstein published the second enlarged edition of his collection, *Yiddish Proverbs and Expressions*.[53] This impressive work was similar in layout to the *Yiddish Folksongs in Russia*, with Yiddish text and transcription appearing side by side. The German introduction explained the classification system used and concluded with a desire that the Jewish people enjoy the collection, which represented "an unknown treasure." Thus, Bernstein saw himself, as later Yiddish folklorists would see themselves, as a necessary intermediary in the Jewish people's growing consciousness of a national revival.[54]

The same year that Bernstein published his work, Peretz proclaimed, at the Chernovitz Language Conference, that the beginning of modern Yiddish literature could be traced to Hasidic folktales. Hasidim, the arch foes of the *Haskala* movement and of all secular ideologies, were no longer to be undervalued. Rather, they were to be respected as a source of Yiddish folklore, and this folkloric treasure was a cornerstone of Yiddish nationalism.[55] When Noyekh Prilutski published his first collection of Yiddish folk songs in 1911, consisting of religious songs, he was certainly under Peretz's influence.[56] Peretz likewise inspired the great Russian Jewish folklorist, S. Ansky (1863–1920), with whom he discussed folkloric matters.[57]

Peretz and Ansky both sought to elevate Yiddish folklore above the folklores of the Gentile nations.[58] At this same time, I. L. Cahan (1881–1937), in New York City, attempted to show that Yiddish folklore was equal to the other folklores of the world. Peretz and Ansky spoke for the romantic nationalist tradition of Herder, which asked that each tradition proudly proclaim its uniqueness. Cahan introduced a comparative approach fully aware of international folkloristic scholarship. He made textual parallels with other nations beyond co-territorial Eastern Europeans (i.e., Ukrainians, Germans, Russians, and Poles). He cited English and Indian versions, for example. Noyekh Prilutski would continue this kind of analysis among the Polish Yiddish folklorists.[59]

I. L. Cahan's two volumes of folk songs were the first book-length collections of Yiddish folk songs to include melodies.[60] He also introduced the notion of *ekhtkayt*, authenticity, into Yiddish folkloristic discourse and was well versed in German folklore literature in particular. His image of old songs that were as "fresh" as if they had been created yesterday echoed nineteenth-century German folkloristic writings that pictured folk songs and folktales spewing forth as from a spring.

Two events conclude this overview of the "roots" of Yiddishist folklore scholarship. They are the publication of *Der pinkes* (The chronicle) in 1913 and the Jewish Ethnographic Expedition, led by S. Ansky, in the name of Baron Naftali Horace Ginzburg, in 1912–14. *Der pinkes* was the first collection of scholarly essays in any language devoted to Yiddish philology.[61] It was the crowning achievement of the pre–First World War era of Yiddish scholarship and would not be matched until the second half of the 1920s, with YIVO's *Filologishe shriftn* series and the Soviet Yiddish academies' publications. *Der pinkes* shaped the direction of Yiddish philology by including folklore as a basic element.

The linguist, political thinker, and Yiddishist Ber Borokhov stated in his opening manifesto, "The Goals of Yiddish Philology," that "Of all the sciences, philology plays the greatest role in the national revival of the oppressed peoples."[62] Yiddish scholarship had, therefore, a nationalist agenda. This agenda became more crystallized as Poland attained independence and nationalist movements, strong in Eastern Europe since the second half of the nineteenth century, were validated by mandate of the Paris Peace Conference of 1919.

The three works on folklore included two collections of folk songs and one review of Noyekh Prilutski's first collection of folk songs by I. L. Cahan.[63] The fact that folklore was represented in this first Yiddish-language collection of scholarly essays legitimized the field's study for many intellectuals.

The second event, Ansky's expedition, was by no means the first such expedition by a Jewish folklorist or ethnographer.[64] The publicity, however, and the sheer amount of materials collected must have inspired budding Yiddish folklorists. Since Baron Ginsburg financed the expedition, the collection of folklore achieved the stamp of approval from a higher social class, one that had generally found Yiddish folklore embarrassing. Thus, by 1914, an increasing number of Yiddish scholars had turned to folklore, and an even greater number of nonscholarly Jews had become interested in finding these "gems." The major center of Yiddishist folklore scholarship where these treasures were collected was Warsaw.

PART I

Zamlers of Warsaw

CHAPTER 1

Almi, Vanvild, and Lehman

A small group of Yiddish folklorists in Warsaw including A. Almi (1892–1968), Shmuel Lehman (1886–1941), and Pinches Graubard (1892–1952) formed an informal circle before the First World War. The esteemed lawyer, politician, and journalist Noyekh Prilutski (1882–1941) served as its head.[1]

During the years 1909–12, the circle regularly met at Prilutski's home. Afterward, each went his own way, but they remained friends and continued to be supportive of each other's work and research. There were other Yiddish folklorists in or around Warsaw, working independently of each other and of Prilutski's circle of folklorists. They included "Hershele" Danilevitsh (1882–1941), Menakhem Kipnis (1878–1942), and Yehude Elzet (1887–1962). Judging by the number of folklore publications, one could say that Warsaw was indeed the Yiddish folklore capital.

In addition to Warsaw, Vilne was also a major Polish center for Yiddish folklore activity; yet, the two cities were hardly comparable. In 1897, Warsaw had a Jewish population of 219,141, 33.9 percent of the total population. Vilne had 63,831 Jews, which represented 41.5 percent of the total.[2] The Jewish population in Warsaw would increase during and right after the First World War and then decrease into the 1930s. It was the city with the greatest Jewish population in Eastern Europe, second only to New York in total size. With its large population, Warsaw

3

had many diverse Jewish cultural organizations, but ironically, none that occupied as central a role as those in the smaller Vilne.

At the turn of the century, Yiddish writer and Warsaw resident I. L. Peretz (1852–1915) emphasized that the study of folk materials was central to a modern Yiddish cultural identity. His reworkings of folktales, which he called *Folkstimlekhe geshikhtes* (Folksy tales), published in 1903–4, cleared the way for younger writers to search for the roots of their Jewish identity in the folk culture of Hasidism.[3] At the Chernovitz Language Conference in 1908, at which Yiddish was proclaimed a national language of the Jews, Peretz called the original tales of Nakhmen Braslover, the early-nineteenth-century Hasidic leader, the "genesis" of Yiddish literature. In later talks, he pointed out that while other world literatures developed "from the top down," Yiddish literature rose from the bottom up: from the folk to the intelligentsia.[4]

It is difficult to pinpoint what direct influence Peretz had on Yiddish folklorists of his time. Prilutski did not mention him as a mentor, although they participated together at the Chernovitz conference. Lehman probably never met him. Graubard was a close friend of Ansky, not Peretz. Hershele and Almi were friends of the writer, yet Almi gives no indication in his memoirs that he knew what folklore was before meeting Prilutski. Hershele was aware of Peretz's interest in folklore and, in fact, wanted Peretz to subsidize the printing of his large collection of folk songs; however, Hershele had been collecting folklore in Lodz before he ever met Peretz.[5]

While direct channels of influence may be hard to document, it is not necessary to acknowledge the importance of Peretz in the Yiddishist intellectual circles in Warsaw. His home was the center of the Yiddish intelligentsia in that city.[6] Dr. Alexander Mukdoni, the leading Yiddish theater critic of Warsaw in the interwar period and a close friend of Peretz, referred to him as the "high priest" of folklore. He recalled how collectors (*zamlers*) and folklorists, including the noted folklorist S. Ansky, came to Peretz for advice on their work.[7] Unfortunately, Mukdoni did not mention who these folklorists were, other than Anksy, though we know that the future leading Yiddish folklorist in America, I. L. Cahan, was among them.[8]

Peretz's interaction with the more assimilated Polish-Jewish folklorists who published in Polish has been well documented.[9] Regina

Lilienthal could often be found at the home of the writer, discussing folklore. Others associated with the Polish language journal *Wisla* sometimes translated for Peretz, but only Lilienthal seemed to have known Prilutski's group. She borrowed materials from Shmuel Lehman for one of her studies.[10] Prilutski, as coeditor of *Yiddish Philology*, published a translation of her work on the evil eye.[11]

With Peretz and Ignaz Bernstein as its forerunners in Warsaw, Prilutski's Yiddish folklore group rapidly developed the field of Yiddish folklore, expanding previous definitions of terms like "folk," "folk song," and "folklore" to incorporate ever widening segments of the population. They expanded the scope of research to incorporate previously excluded oral genres. The group achieved remarkable results in a short period of time.

Little is known about the origins and workings of Prilutski's Yiddish folklore circle in Warsaw. What we do know has been gleaned mainly from scattered mentions in the writings of A. Almi, who collected folklore for Prilutski from 1909 to 1911.

Noyekh Prilutski played host to one of four Yiddish literary salons in Warsaw between 1905 and 1915. I. L. Peretz's home was the most prestigious gathering place; it was not easy to gain entrance. Next in prestige was the literary home of Hillel Zeitlin. The third salon was run by the writer Y. Perle, who often invited the youngest of the Warsaw Yiddish writers to his home. Perle was also part of Noyekh Prilutski's literary scene.[12]

In addition to the aforementioned, Prilutski's apartment was also open to other folklorists, most notably Pinches Graubard and Shmuel Lehman. This Warsaw group of Yiddish folklorists had no outlined plan of action. They were united in their zeal for collecting Yiddish folklore. According to another occasional member of the group, Avrom Zak, Prilutski inspired Lehman and Graubard. He also enlisted everyone for his research in Yiddish linguistics and folklore:

> [He exploited] . . . the young writers who came to him for literary advice as well as the simple men and women from Warsaw and the area who sought him out for his skills as an attorney. He engaged them in discussions to draw out certain expressions and sayings for his collections. I was also one of his "victims" and supplied Noyekh with much material: nicknames of towns and cities from the Grodne area and many local proverbs. In this way Noyekh Prilutski's folklore collections grew and later appeared in book form.[13]

Prilutski's salon broke up in 1912, according to Almi, for quite a trivial reason. Prilutski required that his field collectors transcribe dialect accurately. His pedantic nature backfired when he, a Jew from the Ukraine, began telling the Polish collectors, including Almi, Lehman, and Graubard, how Polish Jews spoke Yiddish:

> The problem was that Noyekh was from Volynia and in his area, one said *iml un hert* instead of *himl un erd* [heaven and earth]. So in Poland he also heard *iml* and corrected our material so that he erased *himel* and replaced it with *imel*. The truth be told, Warsaw Jews say neither, they pronounce it *himu*. We protested against Prilutski's *imel* and only wanted *himel*. However, Prilutski was stubborn and did not want to concede. Other conflicts soon arose and the group fell apart.[14]

One can only assume that the other conflicts centered around Prilutski's stubbornness and egocentrism, traits often found in his writings. Lehman and Graubard went their own way; Almi and Perle remained with Prilutski. Both Almi and Perle eventually found enviable employment with the daily paper *Moment*, founded and edited by Noyekh's father, Tsvi Prilutski. Though the folklore group perhaps fell apart as a social unit, they published together into the 1930s. Their collecting continued until 1939, and in some cases, right into the Warsaw Ghetto.

The Collection *Bay Undz Yidn*

As a group, the highpoint of cooperation among the Warsaw Yiddish folklorists was the publication of *Bay Undz Yidn* in 1923.[15] This brazen work introduced an expanded notion of Yiddish folklore that shattered the rather conservative prevailing definition.[16] The editor's polemical introduction was like a manifesto of the Yiddish folklorists' group in Warsaw.

The editor went by the pseudonym M. Vanvild. He was the critic Moyshe-Yoysef Dikshteyn (1889–194?), more commonly known by another pseudonym, Shloyme-Leby Kava.[17] Though not a folklorist, he was well read in many areas, and was often satirized as a "know-it-all."[18] He earned his living by editing the works of other Yiddish writers, including Shmuel Lehman's 1921 collection of revolutionary songs.[19]

Vanvild's introduction to *Bay Undz Yidn* was a unique essay in Yiddish folkloristics. It reviewed the state of the field of folklore and the differences between folklore and philology ("the difference is only a formal one"). He pointed out that though folklore manifested "the national character in its entirety," the field received little recognition. The intelligentsia and the "folk," Vanvild wrote, believed folklore was worthless. The Hebraists, he believed, by not seeing any positive value in the Jewish diaspora, ignored great creativity. He countered that one folksong in Lehman's *Labor and Freedom* collection was of greater value than all of the writings of the Zionist-Hebraist philosopher Ahad Ha-Am (1856–1927) put together.[20]

In his review of the Yiddish folklore literature, the editor praised the efforts of the small group of folklorists, yet bemoaned the fact that all of the researchers had to work with their own funds. Unlike other nationalities, Jews had not been able to organize any serious folklore societies or academic institutions. Furthermore, in the one instance when an expedition had been organized (by S. Ansky), the materials collected were largely inaccessible to the public. Vanvild called for urgent action, for even those materials which had been collected over the years could be easily lost if not quickly published. For instance, bombing during the First World War had already destroyed Graubard's large collection in his hometown of Sokhatchev (in Polish: Sochaczew), Poland.

Shmuel Lehman emerged as the central figure in Vanvild's introduction. His collections dwarfed all previous collections; he was unequaled in his commitment to folklore collecting; and, most importantly, "he [was] himself a child of the folk and did not come to the folk as a stranger."[21] Whether Vanvild had Lehman's Bundist affiliation in mind, or simply believed that Lehman understood the folk better as a result of his upbringing is not clear.

Vanvild also underlined the urgency to collect before the older generation had died out. He acknowledged that Bastomski and Lehman had proven with their collections that the folk continued to create through the present day; yet, "the lovely world of yesteryear" was dying out with the older generation. In conclusion, Vanvild described the goals of *Bay Undz Yidn* as twofold: to spark intense folklore collection and to make folklore materials accessible in a systematic way. With numerous apologies for the material omitted: the melodies for Graubard's article, and Lehman's supplement, he ended with a plea that the critique of *Bay Undz Yidn* be fair.[22]

7

Though Vanvild was not part of the circle of Warsaw Yiddish folk-lorists, he had a reputation as a well-read intellectual and a competent editor. His introduction addressed several of the Warsaw group's concerns and reflected their thinking to some degree. With neither institutional nor popular support, the Yiddish folklorists were on their own in the collecting and publishing endeavors that followed. They shared Vanvild's passion for the Yiddish language and folklore, and his commitment to seeing its wrongful belittlement corrected.

A. Almi

Though not a contributor to *Bay Undz Yidn,* A. Almi was the chronicler of the Warsaw folklore group. He was born Elye-Khayem Sheps in 1892 into an indigent family in Warsaw.[23] He began to write ballads for street singers as a young teenager, and often witnessed his compositions "become" folk songs. His most popular poem was on the death of an old furniture peddler who succumbed to consumption in his apartment building. He wrote it when he was eleven or twelve, and an organ grinder composed a tune to it and played it all over the city. Living with the poorest Jews, Almi grew up in the Jewish underworld, with prostitutes and pimps a part of everyday life. When Prilutski's wife, Paulina, wrote a play about the seedy side of Jewish Warsaw, Almi was asked to edit it. He took it home and tried it out on "the real thing." Prostitutes read the roles of prostitutes, thieves read the roles of thieves. Jews from several courtyards came to see the fifteen-year-old Almi direct.

He published his first Yiddish poem in 1907 and was encouraged to write by I. L Peretz. Beginning in 1909, he became part of Prilutski's folklore group and collected songs and tales. In 1912 he emigrated to America, where he became an important journalist and poet. His memoirs of the literary scene in Warsaw, especially of I. L. Peretz, are unique.[24] He committed suicide in New York in 1968.

According to Almi, Prilutski asked him to collect Yiddish folklore for his collections. When necessary, Prilutski also paid Almi's informants for their texts. Almi's principal informants were in his own family. In Prilutski's first volume of folk songs,[25] Almi's mother, Reyzl-Gitl Sheps, contributed three songs, and his father's mother, Khaye Sheps,[26] contributed three songs. In the second volume,[27] Reyzl-Gitl contributed two songs, Khaye contributed six. In addition, one song is signed by Almi himself, "A. K. Sheps," in each of the two volumes. Prilutski made no distinction between collector and informant in his annotation.

Almi's most important work as a folklorist was a collection of Yiddish legends as told by his grandmother Khaye Sheps, about the Jewish participation in the 1863 Polish uprising. *1863: Jewish Tales of the Polish Insurrection*[28] originally appeared in the Warsaw daily newspaper *Moment* in 1910–11, where Almi was a contributing editor at the paper. In the book's introduction, Almi related the history of the tales. His grandmother was born in Nashelsk in 1836 and died in Warsaw in 1918. She had a great memory for songs and stories and told the young Almi these legends about the Jews in the Polish uprising, referred to as the "January Uprising."[29] His grandmother's first husband fought on the Polish side and eventually fled the country. She searched for him throughout Europe and found him finally in London, but, not wanting to live there, she obtained a divorce and returned to Warsaw.

Once his interest in folklore was sparked by Prilutski, Almi asked his grandmother to repeat the tales. He tried to recreate the orality of her performances when he published them. "I have tried, as much as possible, to remain faithful to her way of telling the stories, but have avoided her specific pronunciation since it was published in a daily paper where the plot was the main thing."[30] In his "Remarks," which accompanied the legend texts, Almi expressed the belief that the narratives had a "cultural historical" and "historical political" value, for, whether true or not, they demonstrated how the Jewish mind worked in Poland during the 1860s. He also drew a political connection between the events depicted from the nineteenth century and the situation in Poland in the 1920s. Now that Poland was independent, a book that described the Jews' efforts in Poland's struggle for independence was desirable. This was not a sign of Almi's Polish nationalist feelings, since many of the stories are anything but pro-Polish; rather, the publication, he thought, would aid in the scholarly analysis of Polish Jewish history.[31]

Almi was quite concerned about the legends' factuality and authentic style. He suspected that when his grandmother retold the tales to him for the newspaper, she "polished" them, so that they would seem "more beautiful to the world." Two of the legends were collected from Shloyme Hirsh Likerman, an acquaintance. Almi did not record a third legend from him, since it was similar to one of his grandmother's, and he regretted this at the time of the book's publication, for it would have allowed him to compare variants, and it might have illuminated the source of the other tales. This interest in variants stemmed from the work of his mentor, Prilutski.[32]

Almi concluded his preface with the hope that the "wonderfulness" of the tales would provide good material for the prose writer and artist. This hope echoed I. L. Cahan's call, in the introduction to his first collection of folk songs, for the "Jewish writer and musician to draw inspiration and invigoration from the pure folk-treasure."[33] Almi's writing reflected a seriousness about folklore studies which should have called attention to the book as a noteworthy addition to the small number of scholarly Yiddish folktale collections, but it received no such notice.[34] One possible reason for this lack of contemporary recognition was that Almi was very prolific and had published more controversial books. In the same year as his *1863: Jewish Tales of the Polish Insurrection,* he published his second work on the life and philosophy of Buddha, and his third collection of poetry.[35] The earlier printing in *Moment* also contributed to the lack of fanfare when the tale collection was reprinted as a book in 1927.

The dearth of reaction is unfortunate, since the work *1863* is a superb collection of Jewish legends. Almi's collection brought the Jewish legend historic and political context. In the interwar period, several collections of First World War legends, for example, would be published in Yiddish; but, Almi's original 1910 publication never received the credit it deserved.

These texts do not resemble the classic Jewish exempla. Few of the tales pit good against evil. Instead, one finds Jew versus Jew, or Jews caught between Poles and Russians. It is sometimes not clear who is on the side of good and who on the side of evil. In the first tale, "*Der roye-veeyne-nire* (The invisible man)," an old Jew who helps the Polish insurgents is alienated from both sides when he helps a wounded Russian soldier.[36] The narrative concludes with his disappearance, a disquieting resolution. The third legend recounts how a Jewish thief falsely testifies that a young cantor was a rebel and both are hanged. The fifth legend describes how a pregnant woman goes to a local witch to inquire whether her husband is alive or dead. In "*Reb Getsele Din* (Mr. Getsele Din)," through his cleverness a Jew saves a priest from execution.[37] Another relates how a young Jewish girl prefers to hang herself than be taken by the Russians. In another, a father goes mad when his sons join the insurgents. He is killed accidentally by his own sons, who then kill themselves. Several other legends involve Jews who go mad and kill themselves; brothers killing brothers, husbands abandoning their families, and the like. Many of the tales contain motifs from other Jewish tales, and Almi must have sensed this when he framed these historic texts in such a folkloric context.

Almi's work also implied new generic distinctions in Jewish folklore. One tale explains why the informant, Likerman, had a blind eye.[38] This legend was presented in quotation marks, in the first person, the only one printed in such a form. Almi treated this personal narrative no differently than the other third-person, legendary narratives in his collection. He thus expanded the definition of the Yiddish word "*mayses*" in the title from "tales" to "prose narratives." This definition was dependent upon the context in which the texts were heard. If the text were performed in face-to-face communication, in this case, by one's grandmother, then it was a *mayse*, no matter whether it was a tale or a personal narrative. Any narrative one heard in Yiddish directly from the teller was a *mayse*. If the narrative was not in Yiddish, it would not be from the folk, and therefore not folklore.

Almi did not publish any more folklore collections after this. He offered an occasional opinion on the subject in his extensive essays published over the next three decades. He was to be remembered as a poet and journalist, not as a folklorist. His importance in this study lay in his role as the historian of the Warsaw circle, and as the editor of a collection of legends that theoretically helped to shape the Yiddish folklorist's stance toward his material and his folk. The marking out of the boundaries of Yiddish folklore genres would be particularly addressed in the work of Shmuel Lehman.

Shmuel Lehman

Shmuel Lehman was the most prolific collector of Yiddish folklore between the wars. His publications, which exceeded in number those of his colleagues, were nonetheless a small percentage of what he had collected by the time of his death in the Warsaw Ghetto on October 24, 1941.

He was born on October 22, 1886, in Warsaw to a "well to do Hasidic family."[39] All who remembered him mentioned his silent devotion and humbleness regarding his folklore activities. He worked in various

11

businesses throughout his life, earning just enough to allow him to travel through Poland and collect folklore. According to the Yiddish writer Melekh Ravitch, his favorite line of work was as a bill collector, since he often came into contact with Jews who could "supply" him with folklore.[40] Others say he specifically sought out a line of work where he could record folklore during his workday, such as selling lottery tickets.[41] He often quit his job and spent his savings (and his wife's dowry) on these expeditions.[42] Once he had secured his Warsaw apartment for a few more months, he left for the *provints,* the countryside, away from the big cities. He had his "ambassadors" throughout Poland and knew where to go and with whom to speak.[43]

Lehman began to collect as a teenager, as young as thirteen, according to one source.[44] Since the Warsaw Yiddish intelligentsia celebrated Lehman's thirty years of folklore collection in 1932, the 1902 date, when he was sixteen, is probably the more accurate one. In 1910, Lehman traveled to more than fifty towns and cities, collecting folklore—one of the most extensive Jewish ethnographic expeditions. Much of his published material was collected at that time; however, Lehman collected his whole life, even until his death in the Warsaw Ghetto. Emanuel Ringelblum, the chronicler of the Warsaw Ghetto, noted in his diary, "Lehman, as was his way, was very active. He collected folklore of the war day and night—jokes, sayings, and so forth. Lehman always used to compare his enormous collection from the other World War to his collection on this war."[45]

Isaiah Trunk noted ironically that Lehman first received organizational support for his folklore work in the Warsaw Ghetto.[46] Otherwise, Lehman worked alone, unsupported, his whole life.

In his youth, Lehman joined the Yiddishist Socialist Workers' Party—the Bund—and remained a Bundist his whole life. He was among the founders of the Bundist Groser Club and the Groser Library, which eventually became the largest Jewish library in Warsaw. His younger brother, Volf, was a proofreader for the Bundist press in Warsaw.[47]

Little is known about where and how Lehman first met his fellow folklorists Noyekh Prilutski and Pinkhes Graubard. Graubard remembered meeting Lehman for the first time in 1910, when Lehman came to collect *Purim-shpiln* (Purim plays) in Graubard's town, Sokhatchev. The three worked closely, on and off, for twenty-five years. Prilutski or Graubard printed nearly all of Lehman's published materials.

LEHMAN'S WRITINGS

Lehman's first folklore material was printed in Prilutski's first *zamlbukh* in 1912.[48] Though Lehman is listed as a coeditor/publisher on the title page, Prilutski obviously put the collection together. Prilutski wrote the introduction and annotated most of the articles in the book. Lehman and Prilutski coauthored the first collection in the volume, "Yiddish Proverbs, Aphorisms, Expressions, and Nicknames about Countries, Areas, Cities and Towns."[49] This collection consisted of 1,061 items and was an early attempt to formulate a generic category for a heretofore unnamed body of material. It is not known whether it was Lehman's or Prilutski's idea to collect and publish them, or whether they independently collected the texts and pooled their materials together.

The eighty-page collection was devastatingly criticized by one of the leading Yiddishist ideologists, Ber Borokhov (1881–1917), in a review published in *Der pinkes*.[50] Borokhov leveled numerous criticisms specifically at Prilutski. First of all, he wrote, the collected material was not from a "collective folk creation. . . . Is this what you call 'folklore'? Is every expressive term that someone uttered out there to be called a folk-creation?"[51] Borokhov also chided the authors for not listing their informants or the recording locations. Secondly, he asked, why collect expressions from obscure towns and put them on the same level as "Odessa, or Warsaw, Lithuania or America"? The "Zhelekhover fools," he said, should not be compared to the "Chelm fools." The former nickname was a lesser-known local usage; the latter was known by Jews the world over as the legendary town of numbskulls. Borokhov failed to see any method or rationale in the collecting process. He criticized Prilutski for not explaining the items, or only explaining those that were self-evident. Finally, he asked, why did the collection not include folklore about entire peoples and countries, including the Jews themselves? This would have been of much greater value than the printed collection, which emphasized small towns and villages, Borokhov claimed.

Prilutski and Lehman never replied directly to Borokhov's sharp critique. Indirectly, however, they each showed the effect the critique had upon them. Prilutski printed a continuation in the next volume of his journal largely unchanged in method from the first installment, an obvious indication that Prilutski did not put much weight in Borokhov's article.[52] Lehman, on the other hand, also published a second installment on the genre (see following discussion), but this collection was well annotated, so that each item was a worthwhile contribution, not "trash to be thrown out," as Borokhov had characterized the first collection.[53]

Borokhov's point that the existing annotation was poor was certainly true. For example, in the phrase "*Bozinover kozes*" (goats of Bozinover), what does "goat" connote? Filthiness, stubbornness, stupidity? Perhaps different things in different locations. The same is true with the attribute "*parkhes,*" which can connote stinginess, filth, hubris, or ugliness. In this sense, much of the collection, perhaps half, is unusable. Even when a proverb is given, its meaning often remains a mystery to modern readers—and probably to contemporary readers as well. Nevertheless, the collection is valuable for the many anecdotes and legends that are included in the annotation. This was certainly Lehman's input since one sees the same kind of material added to his later collections and not to Prilutski's. The collection is also vital for the research of nicknames: even if one does not understand what a nickname means, one does learn about the repertory of appellations used among East European Jews. The fact that people were designated throughout Poland as "*khazerim*" (pigs), "*parkhes,*" and "*ganovim*" (thieves), but not "cats" or "rabbits," tells us something about Yiddish nicknames and their geographic distribution.

Borokhov does not mention the naivete on the part of the collectors in their belief that the attributes in nicknames were based on fact. After text number 366, "*Zvoliner tsibelefrsers*" (the onion gorgers of Zvolin), the authors added, "The Zvoliner Hasidim have a love for onions."[54] After text number 371, "*Zverzhnitser meydn*" (the girls of Zverzhnits), they added the comment that "More girls are born there than boys."[55] They did not present this as the belief of an informant, but as an ethnographic truth. After text number 405, "*Torbiner yalivkes*" (the barren cows of Torbin), they remarked, "The girls there are big and tall, and known for their stupidity."[56]

Lehman and Prilutski were drawn to this genre of folk speech for exactly the reasons Borokhov was not. Jews in every town and village in Eastern Europe created their own attributes and specific forms. The phenomenon of town and regional nicknames manifested the diversity, individuality, and dissemination of Yiddish creativity. Therefore, the annotation was not nearly as important as the presentation of a mountain of material to impress upon the reader the richness of the genre.

Borokhov, on the other hand, was interested only in those items that were extant among the greatest number of people. Borokhov criticized that the texts were not "geographic," but reflected "group ethnographic, psychological, and ethical characteristics."[57] His perception of the "collective" rendered Lehman and Prilutski's idiosyncratic collection irrelevant; Borokhov saw the forest, while Lehman and Prilutski saw the trees.

In 1912, the same year that this *Zamlbukh* was printed, Lehman was already reviewing the galleys for a collection of similes, but the World War ended the project and nothing more was heard of the book. Lehman's next publication was coauthored with Pinkhes Graubard. It was a collection of folk songs in a festschrift for the Hebrew-Yiddish writer Dovid Frischman (1860–1922).[58] The article, "Folkslider," contains eleven songs; nine "from P. Graubard's collections" and two "from S. Lehman's collections." They are presented as folk poetry to be admired as belles lettres. There is no annotation, or introduction, to give the article an air of scholarship. This was, perhaps one of the first attempts in Yiddish to print folk songs together with other Yiddish poetry in a literary, rather than a scholarly, context.[59] Since Graubard was the publisher of the festschrift, the idea was probably his.[60]

To enhance the literary "worthiness" of the songs, two of them, one in Graubard's collection and one in Lehman's, were titled as ballads. They are the only songs with titles. While other songs are lyrical love songs, the ballads tell of the deaths of lovers after unrequited love. The foregrounding of the ballad genre, marked here by the use of titles, indicates the influence of West European folk song scholarship, epitomized by the Child ballad collections.[61]

More directly connected to the Yiddish tradition was the German romantic tradition, which frequently adopted the folk ballad as suitable for belles lettres poetry, often publishing them together. Beginning with I. L. Peretz's "*Monish: A romants*" in 1891, the Yiddish writers began to write romances and ballads.[62] The vast majority of Yiddish folk songs are lyrical love songs, yet the ballad genre received much more attention as a result of the influence of German literature.[63]

Lehman's independence from Prilutski, and his emergence as a major Yiddish folklorist, came with his first book, published in 1921, *Arbet un frayhayt* (Labor and liberation), which included labor, strike, and revolutionary songs.[64] The publication of this work proved to be controversial among folklorists, for it contradicted several established notions held about Yiddish folk songs. Rejecting the romantic-nationalist notion that folk songs had to be old to reflect the national character, Lehman placed his socialist Yiddishist Bundist beliefs at the core of his folklore research, and implied that whatever the Yiddish-speaking folk creates is folklore. Time or topic, he felt, should not be factors in deciding what is folklore.

The work also contradicted S. Ansky's idealized notion that physical battle or combat were not themes in Jewish folklore.[65] The songs are replete with physical violence, often advocated by Jews. This work was a clear rebuttal of Ansky's position, although Ansky, himself once a radical, might have argued that the Jewish revolutionary movement represented a break from traditional Jewish values, and that therefore the folklore of that movement would necessarily be different and atypical.

In his review of *Arbet un frayhayt*, I. L. Cahan, who had become the leading Yiddish folklorist in the United States by this time, pointed out and applauded Lehman's careful avoidance of the word "folk song."[66] This pleased Cahan, no doubt, for the American folklorist stressed the "authenticity" of the Yiddish folk song and would have disputed the application of the term "folk song" in most of Lehman's corpus. Lehman's only words of introduction in his work are:[67] "Most of the material in the collection *Labor and Freedom* was recorded in the years 1903–1906,[68] which, for the most part, was the time of their creation. M. Vanvild edited the collection. H. Kumen was helpful in transcribing the notes."[69] Cahan chided Lehman for calling his publishing house "folklor-bibliotek," since only a few of the songs were folklore. Cahan's review was a lexical analysis of the songs to determine which were older, more authentic folk songs and which were "propaganda." He eliminated one song as a possible folk song because it used the word *"fabrike"* (factory), thus implying that folk songs could only have arisen in a pre-proletariat society. Therefore, the songs that describe a *varkshtat* (workshop) could be classified as folk songs. Along the same line of thinking, Cahan rejected as propaganda, rather than folk songs, those compositions that used the pronoun "we" instead of "I." Cahan's review was an example of the dean of Yiddish folklorists in his most purist mind-set, disqualifying songs as not *ekht* (authentic) on the basis of a single word.[70]

The Marxist Yiddish literary critic, Ayzik Rozentsvayg, in "Social Differentiation in the Yiddish Folksong," offered a similar word-by-word analysis.[71] Yet he praised the very words Cahan denigrated, for they reflected the changing consciousness of the Jewish working class. The songs in Lehman's collection that mentioned God and "help from above" were accepted by Cahan as folk songs, but rejected by Rozentsvayg as reactionary, and not part of the folk. Rozentsvayg wrote, "Yes, Mr. Cahan, the revolutionary folk songs are not really folk songs, because those that you call with that 'kosher' name are not 'folk songs'—such songs do not exist in this world! There are only folklore-songs of various social classes."[72]

Without doubt, Lehman's work led to much discussion and debate in the Yiddish folklore world, perhaps more so than at any other time. In another review, Jacob Shatsky called Lehman a "dilettante," since he "did not look at the connection between the text and other foreign language texts to see how much of the Yiddish folk song texts had been taken from others. Then one must look at the music of the songs and reveal what is purely Jewish and what is from foreign sources."[73]

In a second review, J. Shatsky noted that, textually, the revolutionary songs had created several new forms; melodically, however, nothing new was created.[74] It is not clear whether he meant this in a positive light or not, for the review underscored the concepts of "tradition" and "singability" (*gezanglakhkeyt*) in defining the folksong. Yet later in the article he praised S. Bastomski's collection of recent First World War songs as original.[75] For Shatsky, it seemed, newer creations could be considered folk songs; this was Lehman's point.

Shmuel Niger, the leading Yiddish literary critic, criticized Lehman's work in terms similar to Cahan's, pointing out that not everything the folk sings is a folk song, "As a child that suddenly begins to speak the language of an adult, it often doesn't know itself what it's saying; it doesn't feel any enjoyment in it. A minute later, it forgot what it was saying. Then you realize that it was not a brilliant remark but mere babbling. The folk can also babble things which are not deeply rooted in its heart."[76]

Lehman's work and the issue of the folksiness of revolutionary songs brought out feelings that were quite antifolk. These collectors were forced to come to terms with their own, usually hidden, attitudes toward the lower classes and the uneducated. Lehman in no way committed himself to any definition of the folk song except through his printed collections. While the debate raged around him, he continued to collect folklore in the widest possible sense. He never wrote a theoretical article.

Arbet un frayhayt is divided into eight categories, including: songs from the Russo-Japanese War and Russian Revolution; songs about the Russian czar; strike songs and "songs of struggle"; "songs of suffering"; songs about assassination and victims of struggle; agitation and parody songs; songs about arrest and jail; and lullabies and love songs. There are seventy-three songs with thirty-eight variants. Nearly every song is printed with the melody. Unlike Lehman's first publication with Prilutski, the informant and location for each text is given. Lehman added a large section of "comments" after the song texts.

The fact that the songs were printed in standard Yiddish and not transcribed according to dialect indicated the absence of Prilutski's influence. However, Shatsky, in his review, reminded the reader of the Lehman-Prilutski connection.

> It seems that he [Lehman] has imitated a well-known Warsaw pseudo-folklorist and philologist [Prilutski] and, where needed and where not needed, his comments are given. . . . The entire anecdotal material which is presented after the songs is extraneous. These are jokes which one can find in the humor journals of the years 1905–1907 and have no folkloric value. In general, Lehman has not considered the issue of what is folklore and where is its limit.[77]

Though several of Lehman's definitions of words and etymologies were either redundant or wrong, as Shatsky pointed out later in his review, the anecdotal material was by no means extraneous. Lehman sought to present the folklore of that period in a multigeneric presentation. The fact that the puns, jokes, and tales could be found in newspapers fifteen years earlier does not negate their folkloric value. These materials were the mark of Lehman's thorough collection process.

The commentary section is in itself an important collection of folk texts. In his comments on the second song, Lehman added ten anecdotes/jokes, one folk belief, two proverbs, and two puns. Lehman printed Polish and Russian expressions and jokes in their original language and in translation. If an older folk song served as a model for the revolutionary version, then Lehman provided the melody and text of that song. Cahan protested that many songs were parodies of known "composed" songs by Yiddish poets, and implied that Lehman did not know this. Cahan apparently did not read the comments carefully, for Lehman documented all the parodies in the collection. Except for Shatsky, who reacted negatively to Lehman's comments, the critics did not examine the work beyond the issue of whether these songs were folklore.

The commentary section also expanded the accepted genres of Yiddish folklore. Lehman printed two variants of recorded dialogue between a bully asking for protection money and his victim, asserting thereby that merely because these dialogues were formulaic, they could be included as folklore.[78] He believed everything the folk said in an artistic, performative manner was folklore. Lehman's book was new in this sense, but his concept was never developed or discussed beyond the initial short reviews.[79]

The multigeneric approach found in the commentary section of *Arbet un frayhayt* was a precursor to Lehman's next publication, "The European War: A Collection of Yiddish Folksayings, Anecdotes, Allusions, Letters, Rhymes, Songs, Tales and Legends, Which Were Created during the Time of the War."[80] This appeared as a major section in a special issue of *Lebn*, edited by Moyshe Shalit, one of the leaders of the S. Ansky Jewish Historical-Ethnographic Society in Vilne (see chapter 4). Lehman was the first Warsaw Yiddish folklorist to publish in Vilne, the other center of Polish folklore activity. He would eventually spend a number of years in Vilne as a student in the YIVO's *Aspirantur* (advanced study) program in the late 1930s.

With this publication, Lehman continued what he had begun a year earlier: the documentation of historically related folklore. This time, however, the folklore was based on an even more recent historical event. Again Lehman's work demonstrated that folklore need not be old. Moreover, by publishing two such works so close together, Lehman emphasized the newly created, underlining the fact that folklore is always in the process of creation. Given the utter destruction wreaked by the First World War, which annihilated so many shtetls, the "breeding ground" of Yiddish folklore, Lehman's piece could be seen as a life-affirming action: even amidst such horrors, Jews continue to create folklore.[81] His collection activities in the Warsaw Ghetto reiterated this view.

The materials themselves are typical Lehman texts: folk speech in any genre, irrespective of whether that genre had been previously discussed in the Yiddish folkloristic literature. The war had spawned new jokes in the form of letters and telegrams: letters from the czar to the kaiser or from a German general to a Russian general. A number of other jokes mocked the new technology of the airplane. Lehman had a clear sense of what was unique in the jokelore in the war context and collected appropriately.

Lehman's next publications were his contributions to *Bay undz yidn* (1923). His three collections dominated the folklore section of the volume. The first collection was "Thieves and Thievery: Folk Expressions, Proverbs, Questions, Rhymes, Anecdotes, and Tales."[82] Folk songs on a related theme (the underworld) were discussed in a subsequent article in the same volume by Graubard.[83] According to Vanvild's introduction, Lehman had prepared a supplement to Graubard's collection, including "two hundred new items, with one hundred and twenty with musical notation," which did not make it into the final version.[84] We can assume that this supplement was what was later printed as Lehman's *Thieves' Songs* in 1928.[85] The close cooperation and friendship of Lehman and Graubard can be seen in the fact that both made the Jewish underworld—a rather controversial topic—their specialty.

"Thieves and Thievery" is further divided into sixteen smaller collections by genre or theme, almost all of which were collected in Warsaw. The last subgroup comprises one of the best Yiddish tale collections printed by a folklorist up to that time in the original Yiddish. The classic collection by I. L. Cahan, *Yidishe folksmayses*, was still eight years away.[86] The collection includes seventeen tales and an additional two variants, as well as numerous international motifs from "Master-thief" tales.[87] They were printed in Polish Yiddish, though not overly dialectic. The oral quality of the tales was well captured, and Lehman's transcriptional ability could not be challenged.[88] There is also a photograph of Lehman's main informant, Noyekh Kubel (Noyekh Riz), who died in 1916 at the age of sixty-four. Shmuel Lehman recorded approximately one hundred tales from him.[89] The photograph expresses the idolization that Lehman had toward such a magnificent informant, as if to say, "here is what a great Yiddish storyteller looks like." This photograph, and the photograph of the *Purim-shpilers* in the same volume, were the only photographs ever published of folklore informants in a Yiddish folklore work.[90] The photographer was not credited—probably Lehman himself.

Lehman's next contribution to *Bay Undz Yidn* was "The Children's World: Rhymes, Songs, Gadgets and Games."[91] David Roskies notes that this collection must have seemed, "amoral at best, sacrilegious at worst."[92] Lehman transcribed the games with no holds barred. He presented the silly, the dirty, and the nonsensical. The first part consisted of counting out rhymes; the second part, of games. In his pioneering fashion, Lehman went beyond presenting just the texts, and included variants and vital contextual information.

This was Lehman's only collection that did not include primarily oral material. The oral component of the games was an important part of the materials, but not the central concern. His careful description of the genre disclosed a keen eye for ethnographic detail in addition to a keen ear for language. Compared to noted linguist Alfred Landau's similar collection, which included very few oral texts, Lehman's collection did indeed give much more importance to the rhymes and chants of the games.[93] Landau, in a private letter to Max Weinreich, lauded Lehman's children's collection above all other collections in *Bay undz yidn,* but bemoaned the lack of comparative analysis.[94] Lehman was not a comparativist like Landau. He was disinterested in the study of the origin of these texts. After all, such study would inevitably look to origins outside the Yiddish-speaking community, and Lehman was concerned only with this community and its creativity.

Lehman's third article, entitled "Treyfene skhoyre" (Unkosher goods), was a transcription of two *Purim-shpiln,* recorded in Sokhatshev and Loyvitsh (in Polish: Lowicz).[95] The two photographs of the *Purim-shpilers* were the first to accompany a text of a *shpil* (play). The three melodies provided were also rare in the publication of *shpiln.* The play is about Jewish smuggling during the First World War and its irreverence must have drawn Lehman to it. In his quiet way, he chose Jewish folklore that forced people to sit up and wonder, "this is folklore?"

In his review of Lehman's work in *Bay undz yidn,* Jacob Shatsky criticized Lehman's collections. He referred to "*Treyfene skhoyre*" as an "idiotic pseudo-*Purim-shpil*" without any explanation.[96] Shatsky did explain why Lehman's collection of games was faulty: Lehman should have analyzed the sources of the games to determine which games were originally Jewish. The collection on thieves had "a few interesting features," but the geographic names were of doubtful worth. Shatsky sharply criticized *Labor and Freedom* in the same review. His earlier negative review of the work was highlighted in Vanvild's introduction to *Bay undz yidn* as an example of an ignorant critic discussing a subject he knew nothing about. Lehman was caught in the middle of this feud between Vanvild and Shatsky. Having seen Vanvild's attack on him in the introduction, Shatsky was not about to offer positive criticism about the book.

Max Weinreich, in his review of the collection, was more favorable.[97] He pointed out that many of Lehman's collections were of high quality. He concluded, "Lehman's collection activity, which he has been doing for so long and with such devotion, is worthy of the highest praise. Maybe, yet, we can create the possibility to publish at least a portion of the mountains of materials, which he still possesses in his portfolio."[98]

Weinreich was one of many who called for the public to help publish Lehman's huge accumulation of materials. This crusade would extend even into the Warsaw Ghetto.

With the founding of the YIVO Institute of Jewish Research in 1925, a new era had emerged for Yiddish scholarship.[99] YIVO's first scholarly publication, *Landoy-bukh*, appeared in 1926.[100] Lehman's contribution of sixteen "Love Songs of Thieves" plus four variants is the festschrift's only collection of folk songs. Since the contributors were a "Who's Who" in Yiddish scholarship, Lehman's reputation as a master collector of Yiddish folklore, especially folk songs, was enhanced. These songs were a selection from a larger collection of thieves' songs in the collector's possession. This enlarged collection would be printed two years later, in 1928, in book form as *Ganovim-lider: mit melodyes*.[101]

The idea of selecting love songs was an ingenious one. What could seem more contradictory and curious than Jewish criminals singing love songs? Several reviewers of Graubard's collection in *Bay undz yidn* mentioned this incongruity. Though Jews were surely taken aback at the exaltation of Jewish criminals, a popular fascination with the underworld could not be denied. It is doubtful, though, whether any Jew would have gone as far as Heinrich Heine, who had no hesitation in referring to a roguish thief in a German folk song in Arnim and Brentano's collection *Das Knaben Wunderhorn* as "the most German character I know."[102] Lehman never made such nationalist claims for the thieves. The fact that they created folklore in Yiddish, however, did make them part of the Jewish character or folk.

When Lehman published the much larger collection in book form in 1928, he included all the songs he had published in the *Landoy-bukh*. He divided the work into three sections: "thieves', prisoners', and convicts' (sentenced to hard labor) songs"; "love songs"; and "comments and additions." The first two sections include 131 texts and 80 melodies. The volume was published by his good friend Pinches Graubard, who, together with Lehman, developed the folklore of the Jewish underworld in a scholarly context.[103] In Yiddish folkloristics, this was the first time that the folklore of a specific social class had been collected to such an extent.

This was another definitional expansion of Yiddish folklore. In *Arbet un frayhayt*, Lehman questioned, by implication, any time factor in determining what was folklore. With *Ganovim-lider*, he questioned any factor that involved a social boundary. The social class he had selected was a pariah in East European Jewish society. By placing such emphasis upon love songs, and by placing them in a context of variants found among any other Jews, Lehman suggested that the underworld's songs are similar in many ways to those of other Jews. Thieves just had different problems.

The songs were collected over a twenty-two-year span, from 1903 to 1925. Lehman's interest in the Jewish underworld must have begun with his earliest fieldwork and continued beyond his publication of the collection on thieves in 1923. The texts are printed in standard Yiddish rather than in dialect. The Vilne Yiddish folklorist Shloyme Bastomski criticized Lehman for this in his review of *Thieves' Songs*, calling this transcription the most glaring fault of the work:

> The majority of songs have been presented in the accepted literary orthography. In the mouths of the Warsaw thieves, the songs would sound different from S. Lehman's texts. Based on Lehman's collection, one could get the impression that most Polish thieves are Litvaks. Perhaps Lehman received the songs through a second hand. And perhaps the intention here was to make the collection acceptable to a wider audience? If so, then that's a large minus.[104]

It is likely that Bastomski was correct: Lehman wanted a larger readership for his works. Lehman, however, did not view this in a negative light. Perhaps inspired by the popular success of M. Kipnis's collections, Lehman wanted people to sing the songs and to read the tales that he had printed. He wanted to be considered both a good scholarly folklorist, on the one hand, and a widely read collector, on the other.

Lehman's next and penultimate publications were his five contributions to *Arkhiv far yidisher shprakhvisnshaft, literaturforshung un etnologye* (Archive for Yiddish linguistics, literary criticism and ethnology).[105] Publication efforts began in 1926, but it was finally published in 1933. Lehman and Prilutski were coeditors; the publisher was "Nayer

farlag," Prilutski's publishing house.[106] The *Arkhiv* cost Lehman and Prilutski seven thousand gulden—a small fortune at the time.[107]

Lehman's article "Elijah the Prophet in Folk Fantasy: Tales and
Legends" consisted of twenty-five texts, some quite lengthy.[108] Yiddish
folktale studies had still produced very little in Yiddish by 1933.[109] The
idea of collecting Elijah tales may not have been original, but many of
these texts were printed here for the first time.[110] Noteworthy, too, is
Lehman's fourth contribution to the volume, "Gazlen-shpil" (Bandit
play), not least because the informant was the collector himself, who
remembered the play from his childhood, when he performed it with
his sister Rive.[111] Sholem Aleichem had written about a similar play
in his autobiographical novel, *Funem yarid* (From the fair). Lehman
also included three melodies for the text. For the first time in Lehman's
writings, the folk and the folklorist had merged.

Lehman's final article in the *Arkhiv* of cante fables (tales that re-
volve around a melody) is entitled "Folktales and Anecdotes with Melodies."[112] Haim Schwarzbaum has written of this collection that it exem-
plifies "the genuine folk-psyche of Polish (and East European) Jewry."[113]
Reviewer Zelig Kalmanovitch said the tales were full of charm.[114] This
genre of narrative was largely ignored in Yiddish folkloristics[115] until
Lehman published this sizable body of material, containing fifty-six
texts.[116] Sixteen of them, as Kalmanovich rightly pointed out, did not
belong in a tale collection, for they were parodies of songs or prayers
and had no narrative component. The material had been collected from
1902 to 1927, from all over Poland.

LEHMAN IN THE 1930S

On the eve of the publishing of the *Arkhiv*, the Warsaw Yiddish cultural
world celebrated Lehman's thirty years of fieldwork in 1932. This was an
unprecedented honor for a Jewish folklorist at that time. Every important Yiddish cultural organization and newspaper in Warsaw sent greetings to mark this anniversary.

From February 11 to May 5, 1932, several cultural organizations
celebrated the event: *Fareyn fun yidishe literatn un zhurnalistn, Kultur-
lige, Varshaver arbeter-vinkl, Prager arbeter vinkl, Yidishe gezelshaft far
landkentnish*. Lehman's work was lauded by leading scholars and writers, including E. Ringleblum, Y. Shiper, Nakhmen Mayzel, and Noyekh

Prilutski, as well as by leading Bundists such as S. Mendelsohn and
V. Shulman.[117] At these events, Lehman spoke of his experience in the
field, and singers presented selections from his printed collections. At
one gathering, several folktales were dramatized. In the speeches and
greetings, several themes were reiterated: Lehman's devotion to collecting despite lack of funds; the physical difficulty of collecting among the
underworld; Lehman's humbleness; and Lehman as the protector of the
Jewish folklore treasure. To a great extent, Lehman had become synonymous with Yiddish folklore.[118]

In 1937, Lehman printed a selection from his graduate thesis,
which he was writing for the YIVO Institute in Vilne at that time. "A
Story with a Heroic Prince" was a unique graduate thesis, for it consisted
of just the tale, with no analysis.[119] Unlike the other graduate students at
YIVO, he was not in residence in Vilne, but lived in Warsaw. The YIVO
Aspirantur, or research program, accepted him in order to offer him
some financial assistance while he continued his fieldwork. Lehman had
plans to go on an expedition into Galicia and to complete his collection
of "geographic" folklore.[120] It is not clear whether he actually went on
the expedition.

In 1937, a collection of greetings and short memoirs from the
thirty-year anniversary celebration in 1932 was printed in book form to
help raise money for the publication of Lehman's materials. The book,
Shmuel Lehman: zamlbukh, was published, "not just to popularize folklore and the works of S. Lehman in particular—but with the distribution
of the book, we hope to help materially the continuation of his work, and
the publication of, at least partially, the folklore treasure collected by the
celebrity."[121]

A group formed to help Lehman called the "Committee to Enable
the Publication of the Collections of the Folklorist Shmuel Lehman." It
included the historians E. Ringelblum and Y. Shiper; fellow folklorist
N. Prilutski; writers and editors M. Vanvild and Y. M. Nayman; and
Yiddish cultural leaders Y. Giterman and S. Mendelson. The committee,
however, never realized its hopes to help publish Lehman's materials.
This did not stop Lehman from continuing to collect. As late as 1938, he
was in Lodz, working on "Lodz in Jewish Folklore."[122]

One article did appear in the prestigious Warsaw weekly, *Literarishe bleter,* "The social moment in the Yiddish proverb."[123] This was a
one-page compilation of Yiddish folklore on the topic of poverty. The

editor's introduction mentioned that Lehman was working on a "large work" on the social motif in Yiddish folklore. He and Prilutski had spoken on the subject at the *Yidisher gezelshaft far landkentnish* (the Jewish Geographic Society). As in much of Lehman's work, texts from various genres of folklore were employed around a certain theme. It was highly unusual for this journal to publish folk texts with no interpretation or explanation. This was a further sign that Lehman's name had become synonymous with folklore. M. Vanvild wrote that Lehman was not "a folklorist," but "*the* folklorist."[124]

In evaluating Lehman's lifetime dedication to folklore, one can turn to two autobiographical narratives included in the *Shmuel Lehman: zamlbukh* for some insight into the man and his work. These two episodes concerning his fieldwork reveal basic attitudes on the collecting of Yiddish folklore, the folk, and the folk texts themselves.

The first "episode"—"Gepakt a yold in kapelutsh" (Caught a guy in a brimmed hat red-handed)[125]—describes how Lehman, at the beginning of the First World War, heard a twelve-year-old girl sing a Yiddish love ballad and asked her to sing it for him. Since it was dark, she asked him inside a nearby apartment, which was not her home. When the landlady heard such words as "prison," "shot," and "bride and groom," she chased them out. The girl led him to her home, in a broken-down building. By the time they arrived, a large crowd of grown-ups and children had gathered to see, "some kind of fool, a nut who has come to write down songs." While he sat at a table transcribing her song, the room filled with people who wanted to see this amazing sight. While she sang, the bystanders nudged and poked him. The informant joined in and banged on his hat and began to sing a popular song,

> Where is the guy in the brimmed hat and his free meals?
> His hat gets banged up, and he's sent home for the Sabbath.
> Here is the guy in the brimmed hat with his jokes.
> When his hat gets banged up, he begins to sweat.[126]

When he finally was able to get up to leave, the whole gang mocked him with song and animal sounds. The girl asked him to return; she knew many songs but wanted chocolates to continue singing. He did return at a later date with the sweets, and recorded the girl and eventually many others in her house and courtyard.

In the narrative, Lehman does not have anything positive to say about the girl or the crowd, other than that they eventually provided folk texts. The relationship between the folklorist and informant, as presented, is a precarious one. The folklorist was in danger of physical harm. Lehman elaborated upon this relationship in his next episode: "[She] wanted to catch a sucker."[127]

In this incident, Lehman describes how he once remained alone with a prostitute in her home and recorded songs. He recalled one song that described how the pimps got rich at the expense of the prostitutes. The girl confided in Lehman that her boyfriend, a thief, was in prison. She had no one to look out for her and could not work, for she had no shawl. She asked Lehman to buy her one. After he gave her some money, she asked him to marry her. When he told her he was already married, she abruptly ended the dialogue: "In that case, there's nothing to discuss."[128]

Here again, Lehman portrayed the folk as duplicitous; the folklorist is the sucker.[129] There is no sympathy for the desperate girl, who obviously was willing to go to great lengths to escape her low standing. For Lehman, the folklore fieldwork process was one fraught with danger, not unlike the situation of the "ballad hunters" who went to remote areas to record old ballads in America.[130]

And what was the danger? The folk, the very idealized group whose texts Lehman wanted to use to show the world how profound and creative it was. The two episodes manifest the dispossession of the folk text from the folk. Perhaps Lehman intuited this (as did the prostitute) when he included her song, which metaphorically implied that Lehman's relationship to her paralleled a pimp's exploitation of a whore. If folklore was a treasure, then Lehman had appropriated the jewels. The folk gave him the treasure and got nothing in return, except for some chocolate and a little spare change.

Viewed differently, perhaps Lehman sensed that he was the "whore" and the academic world was the "pimp." After all, he spent every cent he owned to gather the folklore, and received no support at all. There are indications that some intellectuals were aware of Lehman's exploitation. In a letter to his brother, S. Z. Pipe, a young folklorist at the

YIVO Institute in Vilne, wrote: "In the first row, belongs the folklorist S. Lehman—himself the ideal of a man, warm and selfless. He serves everyone with his rich folklore treasure. Take, for example, Dr. Shiper, who relied primarily on his materials in his *Geshikhte fun yidishn teater* (did he, 'heaven forbid,' mention it in his work?) What Shiper did do, is to mention it openly at the Writers' Union."[131]

In his memoirs, the Yiddish writer I. Rappaport wrote: "And during the time that Shmuel Lehman had great troubles, many a philologist and scholarly folklorist used, without charge, his collected treasures which he had gathered with such great effort."[132]

Earlier in the article, Rappaport likened Lehman to the bee that gathered nectar from the wildflowers. Scholars then came to the beehive to use the honey that he had collected. Lehman was the middleman in the folklore process, and as such received very little honor: he was not the creator, nor was he the scholar.

Lehman's work augmented and broadened the field of Yiddish folklore; yet, he clearly had ambivalent feelings toward the folklore-collecting endeavor. The sheer volume of the material he accumulated reflected his single-mindedness and passionate commitment. This commitment was to the Yiddish language and to the creations of the Yiddish-speaking folk, but not to the folk itself. The lack of any interpretation of the collected texts bespeaks this complex allegiance as well. The texts were to stand on their own, apart from any discussion that would bind them to the people who performed them. Assuming that Lehman was indeed fond of the folk, the folk texts were a prism through which to admire them and remain at a distance.

CHAPTER 2

Graubard and Prilutski

Pinkhes Graubard

The folklorist Pinkhes Graubard was a close friend of Noyekh Prilutski and Shmuel Lehman. Their friendship began in 1910 and lasted until 1939. Though he did not publish nearly as much folklore as his two friends, Graubard played a significant role in the development of the field of Yiddish folklore. His financial support and his publishing house helped publish several crucial Yiddish folklore works, the most important of which was *Bay undz yidn*.

He was born in Sokhatchev, west of Warsaw, in 1892.[1] Early on, he joined the Poale-Zion, the Labor-Zionists, and remained faithful to that party. The party, though Zionist, supported Yiddish much more than did the mainstream Zionist groups. Their platform viewed Yiddish as the language of the working class, and thereby legitimate.[2]

In a short autobiographical sketch,[3] Graubard wrote how the workers' strike in his town had sharply divided Jew against Jew, resulting in assassination attempts on fellow Jews. His own relative, a strictly Orthodox Jew who resented the secularism of the Jewish socialists, informed on them numerous times. Eventually Graubard had to leave his hometown, and ended up in Antwerp.

In 1909, he returned and planned a journey to Israel as part of a pioneer group which included the Yiddish writers A. Almi and I. Trivaks.

Graubard was willing to pay the fare for a group of seven or eight. The trip was announced in the Warsaw *Moment*. En route to their port of departure, delegations of young admiring Zionists greeted them at train stations. Almi and Trivaks got so involved with a couple of girls that they missed the train and returned to Warsaw.[4]

Graubard did reach Israel, remaining there for one year. He then returned and lived in Warsaw, becoming a frequent visitor at the home of Prilutski. The Yiddish writer A. Zak wrote that Prilutski was the one who inspired Graubard to collect folklore.[5] The journalist Ber Rosen stated, on the other hand, that S. Ansky deserved the credit.[6]

However, according to Graubard's own brief recollections, Shmuel Lehman initiated him into folklore research.[7] One Purim afternoon, at home during the festive meal, a young man entered and introduced himself as a collector in search of a *Purim-shpil*. It was Shmuel Lehman. He and Graubard spent the next twenty-four hours collecting. This was the first, but not the only, field trip the two made together. Though Lehman was a Bundist and Graubard a Poale-Zionist, and they argued often and furiously, their common "passion for the primitive Yiddish folk songs" prevented any serious split between them.

Graubard earned good money in the lumber trade and was able to finance numerous publications, including his own collections. He was active as a folklorist from 1910 to 1923. In 1915, the Russians arrested him for collecting materials on atrocities committed by the Russians against the Jewish population. Graubard was by no means active only in the world of folklore; he was one of the founders and main patrons of an organization, *Di muze*, to promote the plastic and dramatic arts. He published two novels, *Oyfn vegn fun erets yisrol* (On paths from the land of Israel) in 1925, and *An ander lebn* (Another life) in 1928. He cherished his friendship with S. Ansky, which began when the elder writer and folklorist lived in Warsaw before the First World War. Graubard came to the United States at the outbreak of the Second World War and died in New York on December 23, 1952.[8]

Graubard's first collected songs were published in Prilutski's first volume of folk songs in 1911.[9] The close interaction between Prilutski and Graubard can be gauged by Prilutski's prefatory remarks, where he states that he began to collect folk songs in 1910, and a year later had already collected two thousand, half of them from the town of Sokhat-

chev. Not only Lehman, but Prilutski as well, frequently came to Graubard's town to collect, and Graubard undoubtedly hosted these field
trips.

The six songs that are attributed to Graubard in Prilutski's first
volume of folk songs included three from his hometown, two others
from Kalushin (in Polish: Kaluszyn), east of Warsaw, and one from the
village of Sentomin, outside of Warsaw. The six songs are printed in
standard Yiddish with few changes in spelling to indicate dialect. The
songs displayed Graubard's linguistic abilities typical of a Polish Jew at
that time: one is entirely in Polish and one in Russian. He and Lehman
both printed their songs almost entirely in standard Yiddish, unlike their
mentor, Prilutski, who transcribed the texts in dialect form.

As an indication of his independence, intellectually and financially,
Graubard turned to publishing. In 1912 he edited and published *Literarishe shriften: zamlbukh no. 1* in Warsaw.[10] Numerous writers of all ages
participated in producing this small, thirty-two-page literary pamphlet.
The editor concluded the publication with a collection of sixteen children's songs, preceded by a one-page excursus on "*Dos yidishe kinder-
lid*" (The Jewish children's song).

> The folksong is woven from the thinnest, quivering threads of the human
> soul. The simple, non-artificial, expression of plain people in which joys and
> troubles, longing and sorrow, love and pain are sung. No matter how sad the
> folk songs are among the normal peoples—one feels a sureness, a solidity
> with oneself and one's surroundings. One cries only at the moment when one
> feels sadness. With the Yiddish folk song, on the other hand, you feel such an
> abandonment, such deep loneliness, such an insecurity with the coming day,
> with oneself and with your surroundings—that it just pains your heart.[11]

Only a year earlier, in his introduction to his first volume of folk songs,
Prilutski had quoted Gogol, "A song is created when the soul quivers,"
and Prilutski then asked, "Whose soul quivers more than the Jew's?"[12]
Graubard borrowed this romantic imagery, but the contrasting of "normal" nations with the implied abnormal nation of the Jews stems from
his own Zionist ideology, which sought to normalize Jewish life by es-
tablishing a Jewish state in Palestine. There was little joy in the diaspora.
"Where does one find the only joyous songs among the Jews—among
the children's songs. . . . When one were to compare the songs of our

Jewish children with the songs of non-Jewish children, one could not refer to them as such. . . . It is a Jewish happiness!"[13]

Graubard's third point in this short essay is to question which children sing:

> Among other nations, even the children of the wealthiest homes sing—and among us? Among us, the wealthy children also sing. These children who do not see any troubles in their neighborhood and would be able to truly laugh heartily; but, they sing in foreign tongues, in those tongues in which their parents and educators raise them. Only the poor Jewish child sings! Blessed be the hands that collect the pearls of the pure childish hearts![14]

This short piece, Graubard's first folkloristic writing, contains all the vital elements of his ideology: the class consciousness of socialism, the Zionist view of the "sadness" of diaspora existence, and the elevation of the Yiddish language. This folkloric declaration was a bold one, coming so soon after Prilutski's volume on religious songs, which had been criticized for including songs only "elitist" religious Jews would sing. Graubard quietly established himself as an independent thinker, writer, and folklorist who wanted to distance himself from Prilutski.

In 1914, Graubard published a festschrift for the Yiddish-Hebrew writer, Dovid Frishman.[15] The fact that many of the leading Yiddish writers participated, including Sholem Aleichem and Mordkhe Spektor, is an indication of Graubard's rising status. In the small collection of nine folk songs he published with Lehman he added no footnotes or dialectic transcription.[16] As in Lehman's small collection, Graubard emphasized the ballad genre. In his view, it was the ballad form that deserved to be singled out in the literary context. Whereas Prilutski viewed folk song texts as linguistic materials, Graubard viewed them as literary "artistic" texts.

During the same year, 1914, Graubard edited and published another literary journal, *Fun nont un vayt: zamlung fun literatur un folklor* (From near and far: collection of literature and folklore).[17] The editor contributed a short travelogue to the first section of "Literature." The second section, "Folklore," consisted of Graubard's ample collection of *purim-shpiln*, nine texts in all. The texts were written in standard Yiddish and were not annotated at all, indicating the collector's preference that these texts be read as literature and not be deciphered in a scholarly frame.

As the ultimate sign of self-assurance as a folklorist, Graubard printed a call for materials,

> To my correspondents and assistants—who help me collect the folklore materials in Poland and Galicia, I want to express my best thanks for their love and devotion to the collection of old folk-creations. Please continue, my assistants, to let me know about every material that is relevant to folklore. Those few that know of such materials, please write me at my address.[18]

There were now two people in Warsaw, Prilutski and Graubard, who publicly sought Yiddish folklore materials from fieldworkers. It should be no surprise, then, that Graubard contributed nothing to Prilutski's second *Zamlbikher* in 1917.[19]

Graubard's next folklore project, the collection *Bay undz yidn,* was his crowning achievement as a publisher and a folklorist. Published by *Farlag Pinkhes Graubard,* the collection became an immediate classic of Yiddish folkloristics. Graubard dedicated the work to "his unforgettable friend S. Ansky" (Shloyme Zayvnil Rapaport). He included two photographs of Ansky, one taken in 1913 and one from 1919, and reproduced a letter from Ansky to himself, in which it is clear that Graubard had been Ansky's secretary in Warsaw for the previous few years. The letter details Ansky's physical problems and his attempt to get a visa to Germany, and he makes no mention of folklore at all. Graubaud's close relationship to Ansky could explain the inclusion of four woodcuts by Ansky's nephew, Shloyme Yudovin.

As a folklorist, Graubard's contribution, "Songs from the Abyss . . . Songs of Thieves, Convicts, and Prostitutes," was praised universally by the critics.[20] If the melodies to the songs had been printed, as promised (they never were), it would have been the first time Graubard had printed any musical notes with his texts.[21] That he apparently had the music reveals an interest in the musical side of the songs not previously displayed; since he stressed the literary quality of the texts, Graubard's effort to provide the music is laudable.

The title of Graubard's collection, "Songs from the Abyss," was an example of Graubard's flair for poetics. He viewed these songs as poetry, and as a book of poetry needs a poetic title, so did this body of texts.

The first section is entitled "The Song of the Thief" and includes thirty-one texts written in standard Yiddish, with few dialectic transcriptions. The second section, "The Song of the Convict," includes seventy-nine songs, and the third section, "The Song of the Prostitute," concludes the collection with twenty-two songs. The editor correctly noted at the beginning of this section that only the first two songs were by prostitutes; the others were about them.

The entire collection surely surprised the Yiddish reader at that time. The underworld had begun to be portrayed in Yiddish literature, but the songs and poetry of that world were not included. Graubard recorded and printed a folklore genre that, all agreed, was difficult to obtain.

The two reviewers of the volume were moved by Graubard's collection to state their belief in the uniqueness of the folklore of the Jewish thief. Jacob Shatsky wrote,

> this is the only collection of its kind in Jewish folklore literature. We find often very interesting forms. Textually one senses in these songs a certain peculiarity. The Jewish thief-songs have a regretful tone; a feature which is absolutely missing in the same kind of songs among other peoples. [22]

In a similar vein, Max Weinreich wrote, "Could you imagine that a thief of the gentile persuasion would lament so on his unlucky fate, that God made such a bleak profession for him?" [23]

After *Bay undz yidn*, Graubard turned to writing novels and stopped collecting folklore. He published Lehman's *Ganovim-lider* in 1928 and contributed a short autobiographical article to honor his friend in the *Shmuel Lehman: zamlbukh*, which revealed much about Graubard's attitude toward Yiddish folklore and the fieldwork process. Graubard compared Lehman and himself to "merchants looking for merchandise." [24] He mused: "One cannot deal with such 'merchandise' all the time. In Serotsk, for example, I had to escape in a row boat to the other side of the Narev, because an army of Jews attacked me with wild exclamations and yells, and I would have been cut up pretty badly if they had caught me. In another town, an elderly Jew who could not stand to see how his daughter sang for a strange man, drenched me entirely with water." [25] The triangular relationship between the folk, the text, and the folklorist discussed in regard to Lehman is valid here as well. Graubard, like Lehman, offered no sympathy for the folk who provided the folklore. The folk were not to be trusted. Ironically, when they first met, Graubard was the "folk" for Lehman, the supplier of folk texts. Both younger brothers of the folklorists were informants for

Prilutski's volumes of folk songs. Did they view their own families as dangerous?

Graubard quoted Lehman, who said, at the end of their first near-death adventure together, "He who goes to collect folk songs must feel like a soldier. He must be prepared for everything."[26] They were thus soldiers, bringing in folk texts by force. The thrill of collecting inspired Graubard and Lehman to collect from the seedy side of Jewish life.

Graubard regarded the texts he collected uniquely among his folklorist friends. In his two literary journals and the Frischman festschrift, he placed folk texts side by side with the works of well-known Yiddish poets and writers, equalizing them in terms of "literary value." In his recontextualization of the folk text, Graubard, as a member of the intelligentsia, claimed as his own, discourse originating among people he often viewed as adversaries.

When Graubard returned in 1909 to his hometown, which had been torn by inner strife, his Zionist-Socialist Party was nearly nonexistent. The *balabatim* (bosses) were in control, and no longer feared the workers.[27] It was at this precise moment that Graubard began to collect folklore. So while the collection of Yiddish folklore was a means for this alienated *shtetl* socialist to express his nationalism, it also provided the means to dominate a previously hostile social class through the recording of texts from these older, "traditional" Jews.

Noyekh Prilutski

Prilutksi was one of the leading Yiddish philologists before the Second World War and certainly the greatest Yiddish dialectologist. He was born in Berditchev in the Ukraine in 1882, but grew up in Kreminitz, northeast of Lvov. His father, Zvi-Hirsh, was a leading *maskil*, and later a leading Yiddish editor. Prilutski came to Warsaw to attend law school in 1900 but was expelled and imprisoned for two months for leading a nationalist Jewish student's group. By that time, he had written stories and articles in the Yiddish, Hebrew, and Russian press. He finished his law degree in St. Petersburg in 1907 and wrote reports on Jewish life there for the Yiddish press.

Prilutski attended the Chernovitz Language Conference in 1908 and became one of the seven on the committee to draft the resolution that Yiddish was a national language of the Jews.[28] The conference directed his life interest toward the development of Yiddish scholarship and the fight for Yiddish language rights. In 1908, he published a small book of erotic poetry, *Farn mizbeyekh* (Before the altar) dedicated to his bride, Paulina. In 1910, he opened his law practice in Warsaw and a year later cofounded, with his father and two others, the Warsaw daily *Der Moment*. This newspaper lasted until 1939 and was the second most popular in Poland.[29]

Prilutski was also a leading Jewish politician in Warsaw between the world wars. In 1916, he became a representative on the Warsaw City Council, where he defended the rights of Jewish schools and the Yiddish language. Some considered him the most popular Jew in Warsaw in the years following the First World War.[30] He organized the *Folkspartey* and was the party's representative in the first Polish *seijm* (parliament).[31] He traveled extensively throughout Poland as part of investigative subcommittees and in the course of his Jewish cultural work. On these travels he encountered Jews in settlements large and small, and collected materials for his folklore and philological works, as well as amassing the largest Yiddish library in private hands in Poland.

At the outbreak of war, he went to Soviet-occupied Vilne and took over the leadership of the YIVO Institute, which was then under the Soviet authorities. Right before the Nazis invaded, he was given a Chair at the University of Vilne. Soon after the Germans took control, Prilutski was tortured and shot by the Gestapo in July 1941.

He first became aware of folklore at the age of nine, outside of his grandfather's house in Kremenitz, where the neighborhood children came to play. One day he happened upon a young cobbler in the middle of a circle of children. He was telling them all manner of folktales in Yiddish, "with kings, princesses, witches, golden apples and so forth."[32] Prilutski had already read Afansiev's fairy tales, but this was the first time he had encountered the Yiddish tale. He wrote down several of the tales in Russian. Later, in high school in Warsaw, he came into contact with the poorer Jews of the city, and he began to collect proverbs in 1901. He filled a notebook in a few months' time with two thousand proverbs from Warsaw, Kremenitz, and Lithuania.

When he settled in Warsaw again in 1909, he intensified his collection efforts to include many genres of oral folklore. He also encouraged others to collect. "While collecting, I propagandized for Jewish folklore, for the interest in it, and called for others to collect through newspaper articles. At various times, I had devoted assistants outside of Warsaw who used to send me packages of materials. Unfortunately, there was no place to use them."[33] Prilutski asked young Yiddish writers to collect, occasionally paying them as well.[34] He also "exploited" the Jews who came to him from the countryside to ask for a lawyer's advice, and he recorded many proverbs, tales, and songs from his clients.[35] Almi evaluated the relationship between Prilutski and the young writers he recruited in the following way, "The truth is, that most of us collectors, did not really understand the value of folklore and also did not particularly like it (except with the possible exception of Pinkhes Graubard and later, Shmuel Lehman). But Noyekh assured us that it is important, very important, invaluably vital for Yiddish culture; so we believed in it and worked like bees."[36] Once a young man sought Prilutski's advice as a lawyer. He was in trouble, for he claimed that someone had lied and told the authorities that he was a pimp. When Prilutski refused to take the case, the man reminded him that when Almi had collected folk songs among the Jewish prostitutes, Almi had assured him that Prilutski, his boss, would be "good to them." Almi wrote an article about the incident years later in New York and nostalgically recalled his days collecting folklore among the Jewish underworld in Warsaw. The piece was reprinted in numerous newspapers around the world and caused Noyekh's father, Zvi-Hirsh, some embarrassment at the public knowledge that his son had sent friends to the red-light district.[37]

Prilutski's first book on any topic was his groundbreaking and controversial first volume of folk songs on religious and holiday themes, *Yidishe folkslider: ershter band—religyeze un yontifdike, ershte serye.*[38] This was the first scholarly collection of Yiddish folk songs in only the Yiddish alphabet. However, the material that Prilutski considered to be folklore caused quite a stir.

Prilutski began to collect folk songs in February 1910, and eight months later he claimed to have amassed two thousand Yiddish folk songs. "Is there a nation in the world that possesses such a treasure of folk songs as does the Jewish people? Whose soul quivers as much as the Jews'? Who is as lively, nervous, open, expansive? Who else feels as much as the Jew, in whom fear and hope, horror and joy, sadness and optimism are always playing in his heart, as the sun and the rain on a cloudy summer sky—that is why the Jewish life bathes in songs!"[39]

In the foreword, Prilutski discussed how the "Jews sing in every place and in many languages," and how the song texts displayed the multithematic nature of Jewish folklore. Jews sang of everything: of religious and secular subjects, of family, of poverty. To know the Jewish soul, one must know its folk songs. The history of the Jews could be found in the themes, motifs, and especially, in the language of the songs.

Why religious and holiday songs? They represented "original folk creations," while other genres of folk song were not "independent" of non-Jewish sources. The religious songs demonstrated the falsity of the "widespread judgment" that the Jew did not understand his Hebrew-Aramaic prayers. The truly religious Jew, "profoundly feels each word of the pietistic odes."[40]

Prilutski privileged the religious songs over other song genres from his earliest writings on folklore. In a 1910 article, he specifically chose to examine the Passover *Khad Gadye* song because of its old age. He wrote that the song gave one insight into the "young, full-blooded, healthy" period of the Jewish people, when such songs could be written that "objectify" the folk's "theological and philosophical ideas . . . in true poetic form."[41] Prilutski's connection of Yiddish folklore to the religious world reflected the influence of both Peretz and Ansky, who saw them as inseparable. Like them, Prilutski romanticized the traditional world and stressed the ecstatic nature of the Hasidic Jew as in this description of Hasidic singing, "With the hands and with the feet, with the head, the eyes, the lips, every muscle moves, every vein beats to the rhythm, absorbing the holy content of the words, forming throughout the whole organism the soulful mood which joins man with the divine."[42] Macaronic songs, he claimed, were a result of the mixing of languages that resulted from this wild ecstasy. This explained why so many Jewish songs were macaronic and why most of them were religious in nature. The macaronic songs created "bizarre" translations of the Yiddish which were sung as something new, and not just a translation of the old.

Prilutski's primary interest in the songs was a linguistic one. No other Yiddish folklorist, nor any other scholar, was as familiar with the Yiddish dialects as he. According to Prilutski, the exact transcription of the folk text was essential in folklore research. The most important part of the folklorist's research was to find the key to the folk-psyche, and the pronunciation was a vital element in this search. The pronunciation was a "complicated product of various relations among geographical, anthropological, and cultural forces."[43]

Two of the leading Jewish folklorists up until Prilutski's time, Leo Weiner and Alfred Landau, were also philologists, and their printed collections were accurately transcribed texts in dialect.[44] Prilutski greatly admired Landau's work, and Landau may have served as the inspiration for his view that the studies of philology and folk literature were interdependent. Much of philology was folklore, and vice versa, he felt: "As a scholarly field, language connects folklore to philology."[45] The folklorist thus provided important material for the scholar of language. Prilutski's foreword to this volume was one of the first essays on the importance of studying the Yiddish dialects. For Prilutski, dialect research was the study of the East European Jew in all his or her diversity.

In his conclusion to the foreword, he thanked those who had sent him materials or had collected songs for him, including P. Graubard, A. Almi, the Yiddish writer Y. Perle, and the veteran folklorist Benyumin Zev Segal, who had sent him a collection of a hundred songs from Eastern Galicia. He mentioned that Segel, due to external forces, had no way of expanding his activities in Yiddish and therefore published in German and Polish publications. This remark was appropriate, for it reinforced Prilutski's desire that the volume signal a new chapter in Yiddish folklore scholarship in Yiddish.[46]

The first section of the volume, "Religious songs," includes thirty-one songs plus thirty-five variants. After each song text, the place where it was recorded and the name of the collector or informant are given. There is no musical notation. Given Prilutski's linguistic emphasis, this was not unexpected. He made no mention of the melodic aspect of the songs in the foreword.

Prilutski's erudition emerged from his extensive footnotes. This annotation was concerned principally with the language of the text, variants, sources, and some performance directions, such as, "Repeat over and over." The term "variant" was very loosely applied.[47] The presentation of as many variants as possible, some already printed elsewhere, became part of Prilutski's methodology, one he probably inherited from German folklore studies. The German folkloristic literature appeared more than any other in his annotation.[48]

Prilutski included several variants published in the *Mitteilungen zur juddischen Volkskunde*, indicating how difficult it was for the Polish reader to obtain this journal. Prilutski, who had a large library, said that he could not get all the volumes of the Hamburger journal to check for variants. The *Mitteilungen* might have also influenced his decision to include twenty-two variants of the Yiddish prayer *Got fun avrom*, which Jewish women recite to end the Sabbath and greet the coming week. The German journal included this prayer in 1899 and 1901, and Prilutski reprinted them together with his collected texts.[49]

The numerous texts and comments on *Got fun avrom* comprised a short historic-geographic analysis of a very old prayer. In addition to the variants, Prilutski also printed two older texts from the eighteenth and nineteenth centuries as a possible ur-form.[50] He examined older Yiddish songs and was intrigued by comparisons of Geman and Jewish versions. He did not always assume the original text came from one group or the other. After reviewing all of the possible variants of the Yiddish *Khad Gadye* song, he asked, "What is the process of its dissemination? That is one of the many secrets of folk poetry."[51]

Other comments by the author were speculative. A widespread proverb, he wrote, stemmed from a song he had collected.[52] To justify lewd lyrics in a "Hasidic song," he reasoned that the Hasidim often got drunk on the holiday of *Simkhes toyre*, and this was the result. In his review, I. L. Cahan pointed out that this was not a Hasidic song at all, but a *maskilic, misnagdish*, or anti-Hasidic song.[53] Today's folklorist could possibly agree with both. The song was certainly written as anti-Hasidic, but it is possible that Hasidim did sing it. After all, the anti-Hasidic song "Kum aher du filosof" (Come here you philosopher), written by the *maskil* Velvl Zbarzher, has been interpreted in performance as praising the Hasidic rebbe.[54] The contextual information on who sang the song and how it was interpreted by singer and audience would have helped settle the dispute.

In the second section, "Holiday songs," Prilutski included a forty-two-verse "*Simkhes toyre* song" printed in a prayer book in 1891. He defended his inclusion of this text as a folk song in the following ways: (1) the longer text was composed of three smaller songs. The changing structure and the repetition of various themes pointed to this. "These are all developments which are possible only in a work which survived in the memory of the folk masses until the writing down of the texts";[55] (2) fragments of the song have "wandered" among the Jewish people and are very popular; (3) the incorrect order of the ten commandments is "naive-folkish"; and (4) several expressions are "profoundly folkish." I. L. Cahan sneered at the inclusion of this song, stating that it had just been born.[56] He ignored Prilutski's generally sound observations on why it should have been called a folk song. Prilutski's volume concluded with Purim and Passover songs, followed by a section of "comments and explanations," which included additional linguistic observations and supplemental variants.

Two leading Jewish folklorists, S. Ansky and I. L. Cahan, criticized the work sharply. Ansky particularly attacked the inclusion of the *Got fun avrom* prayers. They were songs for the folk, he said, but not by the folk. Ansky also berated Prilutski for his orthography, as well as for his ecstatic vision of religious folk song and the reprinting of songs from the *Mitteilungen zur juddischen volkskunde.*[57] Cahan basically had the same criticisms as Ansky. He added that the author's claim that "no one sings as much as the Jews" was very naive, since Jewish folklore had very little to show the world, and Prilutski's collection was very small indeed.[58]

Prilutski rebuked his critics in his next book, the first volume of his and Lehman's *Zamlbikher.*[59] The final contribution to the volume, Prilutski's "Polemic—A Reply to a Reviewer,"[60] was a point-by-point rebuttal of Ansky's criticisms. This was the most combative article ever written in Yiddish folkloristics, and must have been particularly startling since the critique was directed at S. Ansky, one of the most beloved Jewish writers and folklorists. Ber Borokhov wrote that, "Prilutski's reply is, in essence, correct. But the tone! Lord have Mercy!"[61]

Neither Ansky nor Cahan had considered the "*Got fun avrom*" prayer a folk song. Ansky called these prayers "unfinished creations." Cahan added that in every woman's prayer book, one could find a different variant, casting doubt on the orality of the prayers and implying that if one had an endless number of variants, then the text could no longer be folkloric. Prilutski countered that Ansky and Cahan did not understand the profound difference between the oral and written sources of the texts. The printed texts were prose; the oral versions were poetry. "On the contrary, those examples of the religious treasure of the fair sex, which are not trapped in the yellow page of prayerbooks; but, . . . like the various butterflies in the sun's rays, they hover in the hot breath of the gentle breasts, that rock from uplifted religious ecstasy."[62]

While printed texts remained the same for hundreds of years, the oral texts developed into variants, and the hundreds of variants of the *Got fun avrom* established its folk song identity.[63] What contributed to the development of the variants? The garrulousness of women and the "psychological moment"—the particular emotional context in which the woman who uttered the prayer found herself. Older women would produce longer "*Got fun avroms*," since they had to worry about the whole household and would have more on their mind.[64]

Prilutski then responded to the questioning of the prayer's poetic character by a line-by-line analysis of the rhyming pattern of all his texts. This yielded incontrovertible evidence of the poetic nature of the genre. To prove that these texts were for the people *and* by the people, Prilutski pointed out that variants and dissemination are signs of a folkloric process. Those songs that Ansky had doubted as folk songs had been collected in four different regions.

Prilutski described the birth of a song as "breaking out" of a "poetic soul" in a small town when it is soon picked up by friends and transferred to other towns and cities. The songwriter is forgotten and the song is transformed. The individual characteristics of the personality that created it fade away, and the song obtains a communal folk character.[65] This slight reworking of the "communal recreation" theory of folk song genesis was very close to I. L. Cahan's idea, published in his essay in 1912.[66] "The psychological moment" concept which Prilutski employed in his description of the creation of *Got fun avrom* and which implied a more individualistic and performance-oriented approach had been ignored in the conception of folk song creation up to that time.

However, in defending his highlighting of religious songs, Prilutski developed his own brand of "communal recreation." If the creator were a child of the masses, then the individual features "rubbed off quickly." If, however, the creator were one of the "higher" or "cultured" classes, then the creator's stamp would remain even after hundreds of years of wandering.[67] Prilutski did not deny that, for the most part, the higher "lamdonish," or traditional scholarly class, created the religious songs, but he felt that they must still be considered folk songs. He gave three reasons: the authors are unknown; the texts exist only in oral tradition; and the songs are deeply rooted among the folk masses.[68]

Prilutski staked out his own approach to folk songs in contradistinction to the leading folklorists (Ansky, and the emerging leading scholar, I. L. Cahan). In their criticisms of Prilutski, these men defined the folk song as emerging from the "folk masses." Cahan believed that the folk did not understand the *lomdish* songs, for they were too difficult. Prilutski, however, expanded the "folk" to include all classes of Jews.

His main criterion was not who wrote the songs, but whether they were sung by the folk. Prilutski set the tone for his fellow Warsaw collectors, Lehman and Graubard, who expanded the definition of folk to include revolutionaries, criminals, prostitutes, and pimps.

Ansky (and Cahan) complained about the excess of transcription in Prilutski's work. Prilutski replied that whether Mr. Ansky liked it or not, Polish Jews spoke in the exact way that he transcribed. It was the duty of the folklorist to record the unique and specific features of the works, and this he did. Prilutski printed a German example from *Am urquell* to demonstrate the precedence for his action.[69]

Ansky wrote that Prilutski had lost his "perspective" in his excitement to describe the religious songs, and had mixed up the song, the melody, and the accompanying dance. Prilutski retorted that he was not mixed up at all; he illustrated only the religious ecstasy at the moment of singing. Of course, he and the collectors would have preferred to record and study the melodies, but they were unable to read or write music. Nonetheless, he understood that the melodies were older than the words and were more characteristic than the texts. The melodies determined the words; "the hegemony always belongs to the melody."[70]

The final point in Prilutski's rebuttal explained why the author reprinted so many texts from *Mitteilungen zur juddischen Volkskunde*. Ansky had failed to mention that Prilutski credited the German journal as his source, thus giving the appearance that Prilutski was unethical. This outraged Prilutski. Prilutski argued that he had had to print the necessary variants, no matter whether published or not, in order to make his points of dissemination, of psychological differences between German and Polish variants, and to give the song a full analysis.

"Polemik" was to be Prilutski's fullest exposition of his understanding of folklore in essay form. Unfortunately, the strident voice was probably better remembered than the ideas expressed. These ideas were well thought out and should have influenced many, but Prilutski's large ego, it seems, could not nurture a large following in any of his fields, whether folklore or linguistics.

The title of the *Zamlbikher*, with Prilutski's name at the head, surely alienated possible admirers. Ber Borokhov, who reviewed this book, spent much of his critique deriding Prilutski's self-centeredness.[71] His name in the title was particularly irksome, since Prilutski was launching the first journal in Yiddish for philology, folklore, and cultural history.

The short introduction included a call to collectors:

We call upon the Jewish youth, particularly the teachers, male and female in the far-flung Jewish cities and towns. They, who live near the unchanging Jewish folklife; there where the old-time way of life has not disappeared, the old-style seders and customs, the patriarchal atmosphere and the prehistoric material culture, they can accomplish much for the young Jewish ethnology. We ask you to send us: (1) folk songs, folk tales, *purim-shpiln*, proverbs, expressions, sayings, charms against the evil eye, riddles and other such material; (2) folk narratives on historic events and figures; (3) old documents, letters from family archives, old pages from places of safe-keeping; (4) descriptions and photographs of old cemeteries, tombstones, houses, housewares, dishes and so forth. [72]

The call for help from teachers reflected the growing importance of the Yiddish cultural movement and the Yiddish school movement especially. The S. Ansky Vilne Jewish Historic-Ethnographic Society and the YIVO Ethnographic Commission would also rely on Yiddish teachers in the campaign to collect folklore at later dates. [73]

Prilutski's call for material was comprehensively inclusive. He sought material culture and narratives, as well as material on folk life and folk belief. Since the subtitle of the *Zamlbikher* includes *Kultur-geshikhte*, it is not surprising that documents were also sought. Prilutski did indeed study all three fields—folklore, philology, and cultural history—in his scholarly career.

The first contribution to the *Zamlbikher*, "Yiddish proverbs, sayings and expressions and nicknames on countries, areas, cities and towns," was coauthored by Priluktsi and Lehman. The texts were primarily Lehman's, the commentary, Prilutski's. [74] In the afterword printed directly after the article, Prilutski defended the article by virtue of the belief that the vast number of different attributes of the towns showed how they were "individualized," thus making them invaluable. [75] They also exemplified the wisdom of a folk who could so well describe its own and other towns. Prilutski even suggested that a "map of Jewish social-historic life" could be put together based on the texts. [76] He acknowledged that knowing the origin of the expression, or the accompanying legend or tale, was often the key in understanding the text. Yet, Prilutski and Lehman rarely provided any annotation. When they did, the texts were valuable; when they did not, the texts remained a mystery.

Priluktsi's next collection in the first *Zamlbikher* was three versions of the *purim-shpil* on David and Goliath.[77] The first was taken from a "cheap booklet—one of those that are sold in the street for 2–3 kopikes a piece and are quite popular among the masses."[78] Prilutski suggested that the fact that the booklet did not name an author indicated that the play was taken from local *purim-shpilers* in an attempt to make a profit. When compared to the other two variants, the oral nature of its origin became clear.

Prilutski's *shpiln* were the first to be published in the Yiddish alphabet and in a scholarly context.[79] Prilutski's endnotes for all three plays commented on the dialectical forms and on the citations used in the *shpil* from the appropriate biblical passages. The second *shpil* was sent in by P. Graubard, and the third one by Yekhil Meyer Platoy, who, we are told, wrote the play down while still a boy in *kheyder* (traditional elementery school). Prilutski made little comparative textual analysis, but he promised a more in-depth look at the plays in a future *Zamlbukh*. The rest of the materials in the *Zamlbikher* are linguistic and cultural historical materials, not folklore.

Prilutski's next work was his second volume of folk songs, containing ballads, songs "with and without a moral," and songs on the theme of death, published in 1913.[80] Unlike the first volume, in which Prilutski's introduction was a poetic and romantic ode to the wonders of Yiddish folk song, his introduction to the second volume was only three paragraphs long. It contained a description of the contents and another call to collectors to send him materials.

The numeration is a continuation of the first volume. The first volume ended with song number 102; this volume began with number 103. Perhaps Prilutski wanted to eventually show the skeptics that he had indeed collected two thousand songs in eight months. The first section, on death, contained sixteen songs and six variants. The second section of ballads and legends contained twenty-nine songs and forty-three variants. The numeration of texts reached one hundred ninety-seven. Though the title indicated "songs and tales," there were tales only in the second section.

As in his first folk song collection, Prilutski's analysis could be found only in the footnotes and endnotes, and the language was precisely transcribed according to dialect. Several collectors sent in texts in standard (*literarish*) Yiddish transcription, and Prilutski printed them in that way. However, since the transcription is so uniform on the other texts,

one can assume that he edited the dialect transcription. As in the first
volume, the strengths of the collection are the number of variants from
regions of Poland, Lithuania, and Russia. He again reprinted from other
journals. As if to spite Ansky on this point, Prilutski took one variant
that Ansky had published in *Evreiskaia Starina*. Prilutski also continued
his practice of printing variants from popular literature, "cheap booklets," of which he had a large collection. The more variants available,
he felt, the more accurate the determination of the song's folk character.[81] He also reprinted a German song in order to compare the two cultures. The Jewish version, in this case, he believed, was much stronger
emotionally.[82]

Prilutski printed a name and location at the end of each song. Yet
sometimes the name was the collector and sometimes the singer. At the
conclusion of one such published song, Prilutski elaborated on the "author," whom he met in the streets of Warsaw while the author was selling his pamphlet.[83] The encounter must have lasted quite a while, for
Prilutski learned much about the "author's" life and about the process
of putting together such a chapbook. It was the kind of brief narrative
that fills the six volumes of A. Litvin's *Jewish Souls*, but is rarely found
in the Yiddish folkloristic literature of Poland. Litvin, writing as a jour-
nalist/ethnographer, was able to describe the performer and the performance, and often was able to place the folklore in a historical context.
Litvin, however, was a journalist whose discourse was aimed at a different, more popular audience. Prilutski, in this one-page note, offered
the reader a brief life history of the folk composer, a short description
of his livelihood, including income, and a discussion of how the text
came to be published. The result is a unique account of how Jewish folk
literature was produced in Eastern Europe at that time. Compared to
other fieldwork narratives by Yiddish folklorists, this account is unusu-
ally sympathetic.

The second section, "Ballads and legends with and without a
moral," contain rare items in the older Yiddish repertory.[84] The first
song, "A song about a common man, who wanted to have the king's
daughter as his wife," begins nearly each verse with a spoken line in-
forming the listener who is talking. Two other songs in this section begin
with spoken tales. This phenomenon of an interplay between spoken and
sung elements in the Yiddish ballads is rarely seen today. Prilutski only
briefly noted that some songs, whose plots are not made clear by the

words of the songs themselves, must have once had an accompanying story to set the stage.[85]

He did, however, analyze the Yiddish riddle song and the comparative genre of riddle songs among the Germans, Poles, Celts, English, and Serbs.[86] Likewise, he compared the Yiddish version of the Elfin Knight with various other international versions.[87] Much of his information in this discussion came from the Polish journal of folklore and ethnography (*Visla*), but Prilutski based his comparisons on journals in other languages. His remarks on how the Jewish versions differed from the non-Jewish, particularly the German, were often illuminating. Rarely, however, would Prilutski ever concede that the Yiddish version had originated from the German, even in the light of strong hints to this effect. Though he often speculated on other issues, he did not like to speculate on origin. One must seek the roots to a song, he wrote, "in the most secretive darkness of ancient society."[88] Like other folklorists, Prilutski was fascinated with the oldest and most widely disseminated songs. The entire second volume of his collected folk songs is evidence of this.

The reviews of the volume were mixed. In the *Vokhenblatt*, the work was briefly reviewed and praised for printing unpublished materials and for including so many Polish Yiddish songs.[89] A second review was not printed until more than ten years later, in the second issue of *Yidishe filologye* in 1924.[90] The dean of Yiddish linguists, Dr. Alfred Landau, had sent the review article to Prilutski from Vienna in 1913. Though it dealt with both volumes of Prilutski's *folkslider*, the review emphasized the latter. Landau believed that many of Prilutski's texts "should not be considered Yiddish folk songs, but as German songs sung by Jews."[91] The highly Germanized language and the similar motifs indicated this. This was an extreme position, going beyond the claim that the songs originated in Germany. Landau cited numerous German variants to back up his claim. His immense knowledge of German dialects enabled him to specify from which area in Germany the songs traveled (usually from western Prussia, which bordered Poland). Landau praised Prilutski for transcribing the dialects, but found Prilutski's transcription inaccurate. Though Prilutski incorporated one of Landau's spelling suggestions in volume two of his *Zamlbikher*, he clung to his own orthography throughout his career, which put him at odds with the evolving Yiddish discipline of linguistics.

The second volume of the *Zamlbikher* was another important step in Prilutski's development as a folklorist.[92] The opening article on Doctor Moyshe Markuz established Prilutski as a scholar of old Yiddish and folk texts. Markuz's Yiddish guide to the ill, *Seyfer Refues* (Book of remedies), was a "discovery" that Prilutski revealed to the Yiddish world.[93] Prilutski's essay was entitled "A Yiddishist from the Eighteenth Century," and in it he called Markuz one of the first Yiddishists in Poland, if not the first.[94] The Yiddishism of Markuz's work consisted of his assertion, in the introduction to his work, of the right to print the work in Yiddish, since it was the language of the Jews in Poland. Because he wanted to influence the health practices of the Jews, he had to write in a language they understood.

Though Prilutski principally treated *Seyfer Refues* as a source for linguistic knowledge and Yiddishist ideology, he basked in its wonderful ethnographic details. He reprinted more than thirty pages of the most ethnographically detailed descriptions of the practices of the "old grandmothers," witches, and other folk healers whom Markuz had attempted to oust from their positions of power. At the heart of the Yiddish folklorist's ideological dilemma was the ambivalence encapsulated in a character such as Markuz. On the one hand he was a "Yiddishist"; on the other hand, he worked to put an end to those folkloric, traditional practices that Prilutski and other Yiddishists sought to study and to mystify as authentic, traditional Jewish folklife. This kind of paradox was noted by Dan Miron among the Yiddish writers of the *Haskala*, who wrote ethnographically detailed accounts of a life they dismissed, and in a language (Yiddish) they denigrated.[95] In later examinations of older Yiddish folk texts, Prilutski concentrated on their linguistic features, perhaps sensing that an emphasis on folk practice was inherently contradictory. He shifted away from folklore and toward linguistics after the publication of this volume.

The fourteen *Purim shpiln* that followed comprised the largest collection of *Purim shpiln* ever printed in any language up to that time.[96] They were recorded throughout Poland by fieldworkers and by Prilutski himself. Prilutski's comments focused mainly on linguistic features, though at one point he reinvoked a psychological approach to folklore analysis. Prilutski attributed the combination of two short dramas into one longer drama to the *"folksfantazye,"* which can bring together formally and psychologically similar texts.[97] Prilutski never explicated his uses of the "psychological" with folk texts and folkloric processes.

He was certainly one of the earliest Yiddish folklorists to use the term.

Prilutski linguistically annotated several *Purim-kidush*s and *Purim-toyre*s in the volume, and printed several variants, but he did not textually compare these variants, as he had in his earlier works. As his interest in linguistics grew, the folkloric discussions faded.

"Yiddish Folksaying About Lands and Settlements"[98] was a continuation of his collection in the first volume of the *Zamlbikher*, coauthored by Shmuel Lehman. "From Noyekh Prilutski's Collection" was the author given for the article, though many, if not most, of the texts had been collected by Lehman. Prilutski ignored many of Borokhov's criticisms. Once again, many texts were unexplained; however, enough proverbs, tales, and anecdotes were added in the annotation to greatly enhance the collection.

Apparently, the first collection of *abderitn* (attributes) brought many responses from readers, who sent in corrections and additions. Lehman and Prilutski were correct in their assessment of this genre as a deeply rooted and popular one among Jews. While only a few in the field could sit down and transcribe a *shpil,* almost anyone could add to the growing list of towns and cities and their attributes. One of the best correspondents was the folklorist Yehude Elzet, who sent in legends, word plays, and proverbs in connection with the collection.

Prilutski's final collection in this volume consisted of thirty-nine jokes and tales of the town of Chelm that were sent in as a result of his interest in geographical folklore. This was the first scholarly collection of Chelm tales in Yiddish, and the only prose narrative collection that Prilutski ever published. To judge by the correspondents' contributions, Prilutski's demand for exact transcription had had some influence, for many of the texts that were sent in went far beyond a literary transcription.

After the publication of this volume, in 1917, Prilutski devoted more of his time and energy to linguistics. In terms of ethnographic detail and folklife, one work worth mentioning is Prilutski's *Dos gevet* (The wager).[99] This was written in the form of a dialogue between two young men, Sender and Kalmen. The two converse on the etymologies of Yiddish words, and much folklore is brought in for discussion. For example, while discussing the word *koyletsh,* a loaf of khale bread, the two also discuss customs surrounding the *koyletsh.*[100] The dialogue form was no doubt an attempt to make the linguistic material more readable for the average reader. However, Prilutski's stubborn use of his own orthography worked against this attempt.

Some found Prilutski's scholarship and, more important, his style of writing, amusing. This reflected more upon the intelligentsia, who were not used to the relatively new Yiddish scholarship in Yiddish. The parodists found an easy target in Prilutski. *Der Tunkeler,* the best-known satiric writer in Poland, parodied Prilutski in his "Folklore and Philology: A Lecture by Noyekh Prilutski." The "dialects" that the linguist analyzed were the mute dialect, the stuttering dialect, and the nasal twang dialect. Interestingly, the parody, though including folklore in the title, parodies only the linguistic side of Prilutksi and his stubborn use of his own spelling and rare Yiddish forms.

In A. Almi's parody of Prilutski's scholarship, "Oyder-boyder-goyder: Filologishe shmuesn" (Oyder-Boyder-Goyder: Philological discussions), the author exaggerated the number of footnotes that Prilutski cited from his huge library and the overly precise transcription of texts.[101] Like *Der Tunkeler,* Almi mocked the inaccessibility of Prilutski's writings.

Prilutski did not publish any more folklore texts in the 1920s and 1930s. He did use folk texts to illustrate linguistic points, and therefore all of his writings are worth reading for the folklorist today. Prilutski's Yiddishism placed folklore and literature at the service of the Yiddish language. Folklore thus was his archive from which to retrieve materials for his study of the Yiddish language. How did this study of Yiddish language enmesh with Yiddish folklore?

In a footnote to his first *Zamlbukh,* in 1912,[102] Prilutski recalled a fieldwork experience where he recorded a young Jewish soldier who knew hundreds of songs. When Prilutski asked him to sing slowly so that he could correctly record his dialect, the singer had to stop singing, because the slower rhythm "interfered with the words." The soldier had to start singing from the beginning. Though Prilutski did not mention it, the moral implied in this narrative is that there is a danger in over-transcription (in the pre–tape recorder era). Just as in the fieldwork narratives of Lehman and Graubard, Prilutski's narrative described an incomplete, failed connection with the "folk." The "folk" in this case was hindering the study of the Yiddish language by incompetent performance. The text and the language were more important than the performer, the folk.

CHAPTER 3

Hershele, Kipnis, Elzet, and Zlotnik

Hershele

In the collection *Bay undz yidn*, a large collection of draft and soldier songs, riddles, anecdotes, and folktales, entitled *Funem folksmoyl* (From the folks' mouth), was published by a first-name-only author, "Hershele." Hershele was the pseudonym for Hershl Danilevitsh, known as a "folkstimlekher" (folksy) poet. He printed his folklore collections infrequently, although the Yiddish writers' community was aware of the large amount of folklore material that he had collected.

Danilevitsh was born on September 30, 1882, in Lipne, in the region of Plotsk, but grew up in Lodz, where he was a worker and active in the revolutionary movement.[1] His first poems were published in 1904. In Lodz, the writer Yitskhok Katsenelson supported him and helped him publish his first book of poetry, *Hershele's lider.*[2] From 1908–1910, he lived in Geneva and it is unclear what he did there, except experience extreme poverty. Hershele returned to Lodz and was arrested and imprisoned for five months as a suspected revolutionary. After his release, he worked for several Lodz Yiddish newspapers and published a collection of children's poems in 1918 in Lodz entitled "Zunfeygelekh." He then moved to the town of Henrykov, outside of Warsaw, where he owned a stationery store but had very little income. He published hundreds of poems in the 1920s and 1930s.

Hershele was quite an eccentric character, according to the memoir literature of the time. His wedding actually took place in the Jewish Writers' Union building. The union provided the dowry. He fathered two daughters and ran a small shop but was never there. The family moved to Warsaw when the Germans attacked Poland in 1939. In the Warsaw Ghetto, he continued to write. He died of hunger in the ghetto in September 1941.[3] His close friend Yitskhok Katsenelson wrote a protest poem in the ghetto after his death, accusing the Jewish leaders of indifference to the death of Hershele.[4] He also published a prose protest in the underground press of the ghetto accusing the ghetto leaders of irresponsibility in Hershele's starvation.[5]

Danilevitsh was referred to in the memoir literature as a "folks-dikhter," a "folkspoet," or a "folkstimlekher" poet. Poet Yoysef Papiernikov wrote that "it would have been a valuable contribution to the treasure of Jewish folklore if one were to gather, edit and publish the thousands of poems that he had written," implying that his poems were folklore texts rather than belles lettres.[6] The poet I. H. Radoshitski called him the "Lodzher troubadour," and "*the* folk-poet of Poland."[7]

The only recollection of Hershele as a folklorist in the field is found in the memoirs of Tsipore Katsenelson-Nakhumov, the sister of Yitskhok Katsenelson. In a scene that probably occurred in 1905–6, she describes how her brother noticed a short man with a small book writing tiny letters and recording the words of the *hoyfzingers,* the singing beggars who went from courtyard to courtyard. When Katsenelson asked him who he was, he replied, "I am a folkpoet, the Jewish Koltsov! I write and collect folk songs."[8] Danilevitsh considered himself as authentic a folkpoet as the *hoyfzingers.* Aleksyey Vasilevich Koltsov (1808–42) was one of the first Russian writers to write poetry about the life of the Russian peasant and working class in their own language as an insider, and became a popular folkpoet.[9] Hershele viewed his own literary output on the Jewish folk as an insider's view. By employing the name "Hershele," he clearly associated himself with Jewish folklore, namely the famous Jewish prankster Hershele Ostropolyer. In Jewish culture only certain people—Hasidic *rebbes,* cantors, and famous criminals, for example— were called by the diminutive form (reflected in the "ele" ending of Hershele) in a public context. This was usually a sign that they were beloved by the folk.[10]

One of Hershele's most memorable characteristics was his meticulous, tiny handwriting, with which he recorded everything in a thick notebook filled with both his own poetry and what he recorded from folk performers. He even earned some money by rewriting the works of other Yiddish writers so that their work could be legible for the printer.

Hershele's first book, *Hershele's lider: ershte zamlung*[11] (Hershele's poems: first collection), revealed the influence of the Yiddish folk song on his poetry. The prosody is mainly in iambic quatrains, with the addition of a cc rhyming couplet after each verse, echoing the refrain of the folk song. At least two of his poems—*Gey af boydems, krikh in kelers*[12] (Go in attics, crawl in cellars) and *Rashke iz a moyd a voyle*[13] (Rashke is a good girl)—were widely sung as folk songs.

The thematic emphasis of the poems is on the intense poverty of the Jew in the city and in the shtetl. One series of three poems is entitled *Folksmayses* (folktales) and includes a portrait of a learned man, a wife, and a woman in childbirth. Many other poems portray the Jewish home, unhappy couples, small-town brokers, and the Jew with many talents but no food. In one of Hershele's last printed poems, "Who [Shall Die] by Water: Poem on the Life of the Cantonists,"[14] one sees that his style did not change in a thirty-year span; he continued to write in the folk song style.

Hershele's printed collection in *Bay undz yidn* is entitled, "From the Folk's Mouth: Draft and Soldier Songs, Riddles, Anecdotes."[15] In fact, there were more generic distinctions in the collection than the title indicated. *"Dire-gelt lider"* (songs about rent) followed *"rekrutn un soldatn lider,"* and *"shmuesn un mayses"* (dialogues and tales) followed *"anekdotn."* Hershele (or the editor Vanvild?) distinguished between texts and variants, but the distinction was inconsistent. Some obvious variants were not named as such and were printed as different songs.[16] The numbering of the items was also illogical.

Hershele only occasionally noted the name of the singer and in what town or city the song was recorded. The area of collection was quite large—including Lodz, Kielce, Pietrokov, Pabyanitz, Voin (near Shedletz), and Ostrov Volin. Hershele probably did not visit all of these places, but likely met the performers in Lodz or Warsaw. Considering that Hershele was not ashamed of his poor roots, and was a proud Lodz Jew, it is surprising how little of the well-known Lodz dialect was transcribed.[17] Unlike Prilutski, Hershele was more interested in the poetry of the texts than in the linguistic features.

The "Draft and Soldier Songs" describe the czarist regime from the late 1890s to the First World War. The last song in this section is a variant of *"Kum ikh arayn in shtalekhl"* (I enter the stable), a Yiddish version of the song "Our Goodman," versions of which were sung throughout Europe, in many languages.[18] In Hershele's variant, the cuckolded husband finds a soldier in bed rather than bearded or whiskered men. This was the only criterion for its inclusion among "soldier songs." It is quite different from the others and indicates that the collector probably had a large collection of similar older ballads, from which he removed this one because it mentioned a soldier.

The riddle collection was a significant contribution to the tiny number of Yiddish riddles already in print. Why so few? In his review of Bastomski's collection of Yiddish riddles, S. Ansky explained that Jews are not the only ones who have collected so few riddles. Ansky called riddles, "a kind of edelweiss among the flowers of folklore."[19] They are the rarest of folk texts. Danilevitsh, who sought out folk poetry for his own work, may have been interested in the poetic aspects of the riddles (ten of the thirty-six riddles rhyme).

The *"anekdotn"* section includes texts that pose a question of the listener, whose reply usually involves some wordplay. These are different from traditional Yiddish riddles, but one could still consider them riddles. An example is: "How can you tell the difference between a duck and a drake? You take some bread, roll it up into little balls, and throw it to them. If *he* swims over and grabs it, it's a drake; if *she* swims over and grabs it, it's a duck."[20] The confusion of names for genres is understandable, given the rarity of folkloristic publications in Yiddish. Folklorists were charting their own terminological course.

Strained generic distinctions also characterized the next section of twenty-two texts, entitled *"Shmuesn un mayses"* (Talks and tales). The term "talks" apparently referred to the short jokes in this section. The term *"mayse"* seemed too traditional for these texts. Nowhere else does the term *"shmuesn"* come up in the Yiddish folkloristic literature. Perhaps Hershele meant to indicate the texts that are in dialogue form.

In his review of *Bay undz yidn*, Max Weinreich called Hershele's contribution *"tshikave"* (curious), singling out the anecdote section: "I could not swear that all the anecdotes are indeed from oral sources (not every expression that a clever Jew utters is folklore!)."[21] Of course it cannot be determined today which texts Weinreich had in mind. According to the contemporary usage of the term "folklore," all the texts are indeed folklore. They might not be very funny, or in good taste, as Weinreich implies, but this was in keeping with many of the works in *Bay undz yidn*. Hershele's collection is vital, therefore, for it contains materials that a more "scholarly" collector, such as Weinreich, would have dismissed. Weinreich did, however, conclude his review with an appreciation for Hershele's collection: "Perhaps it's better to present as much material as possible and let the expert come later and separate the rye from the chaff."[22]

Though the quality of Hershele's folklore collection was doubted, the quantity could never be accurately measured. Other than his work in *Bay undz yidn*, Hershele published only fragments of his folklore collection. In Yitskhok Shiper's three-volume history of Yiddish drama, almost an entire *Purim-shpil* collected by Hershele appears.[23] Only the fourth and final act is fragmentary. The collector, "had heard this variant in his youth, sung by Mrs. N, who remembered the *shpil* from 1830."[24] Several other Purim rhymes collected by Hershele were printed elsewhere in Shiper's work.[25]

The large number of folk texts collected by Hershele is confirmed by the Yiddish writer Danil Leybl, who worked with Khayem Nakhmen Bialik on a collection of twelve hundred Yiddish folk songs sent by Hershele to Bialik in Odessa in 1912. Bialik then brought the collection to Palestine.[26] Only seven *kheder* boy songs were published by Leybl in the sixth volume of *Reshumot*, edited by Bialik in 1930.[27]

Hershl Danilevitsh was unique among the Yiddish folklorists in one significant way: he was a poet himself. He drew his inspiration for his own writings from the folk literature he collected, particularly the folk songs. That people viewed his poetry as folk poetry probably would have made him happy, since, throughout his life, his identification was with the "folk." Hershele's most important collecting period was in Lodz from 1905–15. None of the writers who wrote about him in Warsaw between the wars mention any fieldwork at that time since he was known as a poet and not a folklorist. He was included in the Prilutski folklore group for the publication of *Bay undz yidn*, but was an outsider. The folklore he collected validated his own literary work, for he was one of the folk; to publicize the wonders of folk poetry was to confirm the importance of his own poetry.

Menakhem Kipnis

The best-known and most popular Yiddish folklorist in Poland was Menakhem Kipnis, a performer and collector of Yiddish folk songs and folktales. Because he traveled throughout Eastern Europe performing Yiddish folk songs, his name was surely the most recognizable of all folklorists. In addition, his popular column in the Warsaw daily, *Der haynt*, also made his name known in every town in Poland.

Kipnis was born in 1878 in Ushomir in Volynia in the Ukraine.[28] His father was a learned man and a cantor. When he was eight years old, Kipnis was orphaned and went to live with his older brother, Peysye Khazn, a cantor (and the father of the Hebrew/Yiddish writer Levin Kipnis). He received a traditional *kheder* education and joined his brother in the Chernobyl synagogue choir. He was widely sought after by other cantors for his wonderful alto voice. When he lost his high voice at the age of fifteen, he traveled with another brother in a horse and wagon, buying and selling butter and eggs. After he developed his tenor voice at age eighteen, he sang in the Korshul synagogue in the city of Zhitomir. He studied music and became a soloist with several cantors. He toured with Cantor Zeydele Rovner around Poland, Ukraine, and Lithuania. Eventually he was enticed to sing in Warsaw, where he studied in a conservatory. In 1902, he won a competition to become the first tenor in the chorus of the Warsaw National Opera. He remained there for sixteen years. Also in 1902, he began to write on musical topics, first in Hebrew, for the Hebrew journal *Hamelitz*, and eventually in Yiddish in *Der shtral*, and *Di roman-tsaytung*.

His writings in *Der shtral* were typical of his two lifelong interests: cantorial music and ethnography. "Berditchever khazones" praised the old-style cantor Nisn Belzer while criticizing his replacement, the new-style cantor Meyer Fisak.[29] This series of articles on cantors established Kipnis as the *meyvin*, the expert, in Warsaw. His recommendations could make or break the career of a cantor. His ethnographic articles combined all of his fieldwork talents: photography, an ability to transcribe songs with the musical notation, and a lucid ethnographic writing style. In a two-part series, "In a Malorosishn dorf" (In a Ukrainian village), Kipnis printed six photographs and two songs with melodies.[30]

He became most well known in the Yiddish press, however, as a popular writer in the Warsaw daily, *Der haynt*. There, in addition to articles on cantors, on famous Jewish musicians, and on Jewish music, he wrote humorous, folksy articles on Jewish types, and travelogues.

In 1913, he began earnestly to collect Yiddish folk songs and folktales as he toured for opera and cantorial concerts. For all his interest in the Jewish world, Kipnis had spent much of his time up until then in making a good impression upon the Polish-speaking world. His own editor at *Der shtral* criticized the Jewish choir he had organized, for singing in many languages except Yiddish.[31] This seemed to change on the eve of the First World War. In an article on the folklorist Shmuel Lehman, he began his tribute with a reminiscence, "Thirteen years ago, when I showed S. Ansky my collections of folk songs and folklore, scattered in paper bags, transcriptions of notes and songs collected in the cities and towns of Poland, Lithuania, Kurland and in all the places where I gave concerts and wandered during the occupation years of the World War, Ansky complimented me, 'For such an effort, we should tip our hats.' "[32] He soon devoted his concerts to the presentation of Yiddish folk songs. He traveled widely throughout Eastern and Western Europe with his singing partner, later his wife, Zimre Zeligfeld, performing Yiddish folk songs. From these collected materials he published three books.[33] According to Reyzen's *Leksikon*, Kipnis was planning (in 1929) several books on Jewish folklore, including: "Jewish klezmer in Poland," "From Primitive Folksong to Jewish Symphonic Music", and a collection, "of folk songs with tales in which every song is connected with a folktale which is often better than the song."[34] He wrote about many of these in his *Haynt* column.

Kipnis's song collections and performances sold widely and greatly contributed to the popular awareness of Yiddish folk song as an art form. The composer Henoch Kohn called his accomplishments in the dissemination and collection of Yiddish folk song greater than those of the St. Petersburg Ethnographic Society.[35] When Kipnis teamed up with the younger Zeligfeld to perform Yiddish folk songs, they were among the most popular entertainment acts in Poland. In the late 1930s, Zeligfeld performed alone and created her own reputation as an interpreter of folk song.

Kipnis also excelled as a photographer, specializing in portraits of Jewish folklife, which were printed in numerous journals and newspapers in Poland, but particularly in the *Sunday Art Section* of the New York *Jewish Daily Forward* beginning in the 1920s.[36] One must consider this aspect of his artistic life as part of his devotion to Jewish folklore. Through photography, Kipnis and others believed they were capturing the "vanishing world" of Jewish folklife. Kipnis collected not only folk songs but antiques as well—canes, clocks, and photographic equipment.[37]

During the Second World War, Kipnis and Zeligfeld were in the Warsaw Ghetto. Kipnis carefully protected his folklore collection, hoping to have it published after the war. After his death from a blood clot in 1942, his wife refused to give the materials to Emanual Ringleblum's "*Oyneg shabes*" group, which buried diaries, archival materials, and writings. She died in Treblinka and the massive collection was never recovered.[38]

Menakhem Kipnis plays an important part in numerous memoirs of Polish Jewish cultural life. He was a star, adored by thousands. Though he never achieved his dream of becoming a great opera star, Kipnis turned to the Yiddish folk song with great success.[39] In each town or city in which Kipnis sang, friends, aware of his interest in collecting folk songs, advised him on where to go to collect. From Grodne, we have the following account:

> He recorded a typical folksong also in Grodne—*A khaverte*[40]—which was very popular in that area and which became part of Zeligfeld's repertory. The Grodne actor S. Garber had told Kipnis about the song. Garber worked as a medical aide in a clinic for syphilis. There, several prostitutes sang this song. Kipnis wasn't lazy and visited Garber at the clinic. Garber directed him to the singers and Kipnis recorded the text and melody of *A khaverte*.[41]

Kipnis recorded many songs from known Yiddish writers, not just from "unknown" folksingers. He collected one song from the Romanian Yiddish writer Itsik Manger, a good singer. Manger refused to sing a song for Kipnis until he had been "paid"—that is, treated to several glasses of liquor. Kipnis wanted to hear the song first, before payment. Both were already tipsy when the friendly argument began and were quite drunk by the time the disagreement was resolved amicably.[42] Kipnis also solicited the readers of *Haynt* to send him old folk songs and *ni-*

gunim, Hasidic melodies. "The calls did not go unheeded. People used to send him mountains of old songs which were sung in every part of the country—old *nigunim* of Hasidic rabbis (he expressly traveled to the Rebbes and collected them there), songs that our grandmothers and grandfathers sang. Kipnis then filed them and arranged them."[43] Being at the right place at the right time benefited Kipnis's success in the presentation of the Yiddish folk song. The interest in folk song among the intelligentsia was at its peak between the wars.[44] Kipnis inherited a rising fascination with the Yiddish folk song; however, his performances and collections were the things that truly popularized the genre. Kipnis's songbooks sold in the thousands, while those of other folklorists, such as Lehman or Prilutsky, sold very few. Every cantor had Kipnis's collections at his side for concerts. The most widely sung Yiddish songs today can still be traced back to Kipnis's performances or publications of them.

Kipnis's Folklore Collections

Today, musical groups announce their tapes and CDs for sale during their concerts, and that venue is quite often the most lucrative. During the intermission, people buy the person's or group's recordings. One might view Kipnis's *60 folkslider: fun M. Kipnis and Z. Zeligfeld's kontsert repertuar,* printed in 1918, as a similar kind of artifact. The reminder in the subtitle of Kipnis's concerts was an incentive to purchase the book. The concerts were great successes, so it was only good business sense to establish the connection between the two.

Like other Yiddish folklore collections printed in Poland between the wars, there was hardly an introduction or preface to Kipnis's work. There was a one-page brief afterword, in which Kipnis began, "This collection presents the loveliest pearls of the Yiddish folksong treasure, from the serious lyric-romantic, religious-mystic to the humorous and joking generic song, as well as the macaronic songs such as Yiddish-Ukrainian, etc." Kipnis noted that, though some of the songs had been published before, many of them had been printed with no melody. He made special reference to the songs written by Avrom Reisin, Peretz, and Zalmen Shneur. Thus, "folk song" as conceived of by Kipnis had no pretense of originating from the folk. Recently composed songs were presented together with older anonymous songs. Kipnis said that these newer compositions were "beloved and considered authentic folk songs by the folk."[45] His criterion was that the people consider a work a folk song: he included whatever the people sang. Even the Russian song "Slushay" was included as the sixty-first song, since S. Ansky's Yiddish translation was, "very popular among the masses."[46]

The work is divided into five parts: "lyric-romantic and love songs"; *folkstimlekhe lider* (folky songs); religious, Hasidic, Misnagdic, and philosophic folk songs; humorous and family-songs; and Yiddish-Ukrainian folk songs. Every song text is presented along with its melody. In this respect, *60 folkslider* was a first in Yiddish folkloristics. Ginsburg and Marek's work had included no melodies; Cahan's volumes had included the melodies for many, but not all. What compelled Kipnis do this? As mentioned earlier, he was interested in the performance of the song, the revival of the hidden treasures. His interest was not just the appreciation of the text which earlier Yiddish folklorists had exhibited. The few annotations that he provided to the songs reiterate their performance aspect. He added the following comments after *Margaritkelekh*: "Due to the length of the song, the singer can leave out the eighth and ninth verses. The singer can also sing the melody for a second time when repeating *vi kleyninke zunen* as well as in the other verses as shown in the notes."[47]

The promotion of folk song performance was clearly his goal in this volume. Unlike Prilutski's overly dialectical features in his notation of the song texts, only standard Yiddish is used in Kipnis's work, so as not to be an encumbrance upon the potential singer of the song. There is also no reason to suspect that Kipnis "popularized" the text, changing lines to rhyme where the informant provided no rhyme, or changing the length of a line to make it more singable. The song *khaverte* has the nonrhyme of *toyt* and *mir*.[48] Editing the song texts was an accepted practice, and Kipnis surely did some rearranging of the songs.

The largest section in *60 folkslider* is the first, "Lyric-romantic and love songs," which contains twenty-three selections. In the index at the end, all of these songs were listed as "from M. Kipnis collection." The second section, "*folkstimlekhe lider*" (folksy songs), contains ten songs and is the second-largest category. In the index, the author of each text is listed. If the origin of the melody was not known, then it was listed as "part of Kipnis' collection." There were numerous melodies to some of these recently composed songs, and variation to the standard melodies and words. Kipnis helped to standardize many of these songs, as well as the older folk songs in his collections.

The third section of religious songs contains eight items, three attributed to the Hasidic leader Rabbi Levi Yitskhok Barditchever. With the description "misnagdish" in the section heading, Kipnis meant anti-Hasidic, rather than originating from the Misnagdim, the historic opponents of Hasidism. Many of these types of songs originated from "Di broder zinger," or other folk bards who began to appear in the 1850s and were the forerunners of the modern Yiddish theater. These bards and actors were neither Hasidim nor Misnagdim. In Yiddish, "Misnagdish" can connote anyone opposed to the traditional way of life, influenced by the *Haskala,* the Jewish Enlightenment, which took hold in the late eighteenth century in Eastern Europe.

The one song referred to as *apikorsish* (heretical) is *Er zol lebn,*[49] which emphasizes the Hasidic love of whiskey. The Yiddish folklorists were confused by the Hasidic and Misnagdish song genres. This was a result of collecting from other fieldworkers, as in Prilutski's case, or collecting from Yiddish intellectuals who recontextualized the song, as in Kipnis's case. The same song, when performed by Hasidim, could be deemed Hasidic, yet when sung by skeptical intelligentsia could turn into an anti-Hasidic mockery.

The fourth category, humorous and family songs, contains fourteen songs. The section title implies that the songs were meant to be sung by the family together. A number of these songs, as well as several in the previous category, have come to comprise the basic cantorial repertory of Yiddish songs. This section also includes one of the few ballads in the book, the humorous *Fort dos khosidl tsu dem rebn,*[50] which has similarities to the pan-European song, "The Friar in the Well."[51] While Cahan and Prilutski sought out international ballad motifs, Kipnis chose to publish and to perform the lyric romantic love songs. Since he sang with his wife, romantic lyrical texts would have been more appropriate. However, this also revealed his identification of Yiddish with the "masses" from whom he collected the songs. Though Yiddish historical ballads about kings and queens had been recorded, and Kipnis surely collected them as well, his image of the Yiddish folk song was primarily restricted to the emotional longing found in the lyrical love songs or to the humorous, upbeat song. The older ballads did not convey his notion of the national character of the Jewish people.

61

The last category, Yiddish-Ukrainian macaronic songs that mix languages, are humorous and clever. Once again, the songs he chose to include have become the most popular macaronic songs down to our day. Kipnis was the first to assign a songbook category to this type of song, which had undergone quite a bit of discussion in the folklore literature. [52] Kipnis included only Ukrainian-mixed songs. In the second volume, Kipnis also included Russian songs, revealing perhaps more about his roots than about the actual existence or dissemination of such macaronic songs.

Kipnis's second collection, *80 Folk songs: From Zimre Zeligfeld's and M. Kipnis's Concert Repertoire, Second Part*, was influenced by the folklore literature that had been published in the seven years since his first volume. [53] In his first collection, Kipnis was content to present just the texts and melodies. He added significant information in this second volume. Each song in the index lists from whom the song was learned. In the first volume, he merely indicated, "From Kipnis Collection" after most songs. In this second volume, each song in the index lists from whom the song was learned. Also in this volume, he added important commentary after each song text and melody on the performance style of the song, the origin of the song, and, occasionally, how the song was collected. He also left out the category of "folkstimlekhe lider" and devoted this work entirely to folk songs.

After reading the names of the informants in the second volume, one could rename the work "Yiddish writers' book of Yiddish folk songs." Almost all of the songs were transcribed from the performances of identifiable Yiddish writers: Moyshe Broderzon (1890–1956), Yankev Dineson (1856–1919), Dovid Einhorn (1886–197?), Efrayim Kaganovitch (1893–1958), Yitskhok Katsenelson (1886–1944), Alter Kazycne (1885–1941), A. Litvak (1885–1941), Danil Leybl (1891–1967), Perets Markish (1895–1952), H. D. Nomberg (1876–1927), Zusman Segalovitch (1884–1949), Sholem Aleichem (1859–1916), Yisrol Shtern (1894–1942), I. Trunk (1887–1961), and I. M. Weissenberg (1881–1938). Kipnis collected from other cultural and political figures as well: Aren Albek (?–1943), writer and publisher in Bialystock; Berl Locker (1887–197?) and Borukh Tsukerman (1887–1970), leaders of the Poale Zion Party; Ayzik Samber (1889–1943) and Vladislav Godik (1893–?), Yiddish actors; and Leo Low, composer and choir director. Three of the five "street and thief" songs were learned from Shmuel Lehman.

Kipnis's collection implies that the "folk" that sings "folk songs" need not be from the lower or "hidden" classes of groups. Rather, "we" are also the folk, and what "we" sing, no matter who we are, are folk songs. According to this interpretation, the folk includes the intelligentsia as well as the uneducated Jew. This attitude was introduced in the first volume when Kipnis included *folkstimleke* songs alongside *folklider*.

Though I. L. Cahan never reviewed Kipnis's collection, his conservative opposing approach was made quite clear in numerous published articles, and especially in his posthumously published "*Folkslid un folkstimlekh lid*" (Folksong and folksy song), where he rejected Prilutski's opinion on the matter.[54] Kipnis went far beyond Prilutski in expanding the definition of the folk song, by incorporating modern secular Yiddish writers among the "folk" who sang them and among the "folk" who wrote them.

Kipnis's remarks on the songs ranged from one-line performance clarifications to elaborate contextual information. In "Sorele dushinke," the author relates how the writer/photographer Alter Kacyzne, collected the song. "Alter Kacyzne sang the song to me. He had heard a small girl of five years sing this song while playing outside. Since she could not talk, the song sounded like this: 'u-ye-ye, u-yinte, teyn a du a bum. . . .' And with difficulty, he was able to get the correct text from the bad one."[55]

Kipnis was amused by the anecdote and impressed by Kacyzne's efforts to reconstruct the song. Indeed, the child's text was so far removed from what Kipnis had published, one has to ponder what actually was the "correct" text. In any case, Kipnis the folk song collector wanted to share a "collector's narrative" with his reader to impress upon him or her the fascinating adventures of the Jewish folklorist. Metaphorically, the narrative works as a reinforcement of the notion that the folk need agency, and that the folklorist provides that agency. The folklorist is required to "translate" (literally in this case) the unintelligibility of the "folk" to the intelligentsia so that the "folk" and their literature can be appreciated.

Other comments on the performance of the songs tell the singer where and how to sing and sometimes why to sing. In "Mir zenen nikhter," his note informed the singer that the song should be sung as soon as one sits down to eat at a celebration, for it "immediately creates a happy mood."[56] Other comments discussed the creation of the song. "Mir zogn der baleboste" states that *yeshivenikes* who used to "eat days"—that is, eat meals at different homes each day—would sing this song.[57] After "Baleboste zisinke" Kipnis noted: "For this folksong, Sholem Aleichem sang many folksy, double meaning flattery and praise words for the hostess. Unfortunately, I did not record everything, and it is possible that Sholem Aleichem also didn't write them down."[58]

The only older-style ballad in the second volume, "Zits ikh mir in tatns gortn," is found in the section entitled, "Songs from Life."[59] Kipnis recorded this song from a Christian girl in Radom. This dialogue between a girl in the garden and an old man "death" (called "*zeyde*," grandfather, in the song) was traced back to German sources by Prilutski.[60] The intriguing idea that perhaps older Yiddish ballads could have been recorded from Christian singers was never mentioned in the Yiddish folklore literature.

Having had success with folk songs, Kipnis published a collection of folktales as his last major work. *Chelm Tales,* which depicted the Jewish town of fools, was published in Warsaw in 1930.[61] Kipnis had published a series of these tales in the Warsaw *Haynt* through the 1920s which was very widely read throughout Poland. Eventually, the story goes, the editor of *Haynt* told Kipnis that the column had to stop. Letters were pouring in from mothers who lived in the real city of Chelm who were begging for pity: they could not marry off their daughters, for when possible bridegrooms heard the brides were from Chelm they could not stop laughing.[62] The title page states, "collected and reworked by M. Kipnis. In this reworked collection which I bring to the public, I attempted, as far as possible, to present a selection of Chelm tales which have a stamp of folkiness, and folk manner and specificity which characterize all authentic Chelm tales."[63] Kipnis "reworked" the Yiddish folktales only slightly stylistically. He had no intention of offering "literary" adaptations of the tales.[64] There is no way to tell how much Kipnis left verbatim from storytellers, and how much was written by him. He provided no footnotes, no comparative apparatus, again marking this collection as a popular one, not intended to be thought of as a scholarly contribution. When compared to Prilutski's collection of thirty-nine Chelm tales, directly recorded from oral tradition, Kipnis's tales are longer and have occasionally incorporated several of Prilutski's variants into one longer tale.[65] Though the Chelm tale genre was perhaps the most widely known Yiddish folktale genre, only Kipnis, Prilutski, and Bastomski among the Yiddish folklorists printed these tales.[66]

Though *Chelm Tales* was not a best-seller like Kipnis's song collections, his *Haynt* column was extremely popular and the Chelm tales were a popular feature in it. Kipnis wrote in a folksy style in all his fiction in the *Haynt*. In his only published work of short fiction, *Nisim veniflues: kuriozn un bilder* (Wonder of wonders: Curiosities and portraits), a small, twenty-nine-page booklet, the narrator speaks directly to his reader in a style reminiscent of Sholem Aleichem's monologues.[67] Kipnis humorously portrayed shtetl life and the simple Jew in this work. In the *Haynt yoyvl-bukh (1908–1938)*, Kipnis contributed a "folksy story" entitled "Reb Khayem Sholem the Dead Is Going To Die."[68] The story revolves around the folk custom of giving a dying person, in this case the town rabbi, one's own months or years of life to extend the dying person's life. The story may have been based on a tale told about the Rabbi of Lubomir, Poland. Unfortunately, Kipnis never published a larger work of his journalistic writings, which contained much folklore and many ethnographic details.

Through his journalism, his printed folklore collections, and his performances, Kipnis attained a place in the pantheon of Yiddish cultural figures in Poland between the wars. Though few of Kipnis's collected materials were ever published, one must turn to his two small volumes of songs and his performances across Poland as an important factor in the revival of folk song performance at home and in the theater. In 1934, the journal *Khazonim velt* published a brief article praising Kipnis's twenty-fifth year of "literary-musical" activity.[69] Though the author of the article stressed Kipnis's achievements on behalf of cantors, he confessed,

> The greatest achievement of our celebrity, however, is his collecting, popularizing and interpreting the almost forgotten Yiddish folk songs which he used to help build the wonderful structure of Yiddish folklore. The songs which he, together with his wife, the talented lyrical, dramatic singer Zimre Zeligfeld, sang at concerts in various lands and in every city in Poland, penetrated every level of our Jewish population; even into the damp basement of the poor Jewish artisan and the servant girl, where they sweetened their worried and darkened lives, connecting them back with the future of the Jewish people and its eternal hopefulness.[70]

No other folklorist was so beloved by the "folk," or had such an effect upon them. Kipnis sought to sweeten Jewish lives, to raise a consciousness of Jewish nationalism with Yiddish folklore. All the Yiddish folklorists attempted to do this in their own way; no other was as successful as Menakhem Kipnis.

Yehude Elzet and Yeshaye Zlotnik: Orthodox Yiddish Folklorists

YEHUDE ELZET

Though he did not live in Warsaw, Yehude Elzet, a pseudonym for Yehude Avide, was an active folklorist in Poland in the years between 1910 and 1920, and interacted with and contributed to the Warsaw group before leaving for Canada in 1920. All of his folkloristic works in Yiddish and Hebrew appeared under the pen name. He was born in 1887 in Plotsk, Poland. He became rabbi in Gombin in 1911 but briefly moved to Warsaw in 1919 after he helped found the Polish Mizrachi Party (the religious Zionist party), where he eventually led the liberal faction.[71] He settled in Montreal to direct the Mizrachi Party in that country, then lived in South Africa from 1938 to 1949 before settling in Israel. He died in Israel in 1962.

Under the influence of Prilutski's activities, he took an interest in folklore and began to send Prilutski materials and comments, beginning in 1910.[72] In the second volume of Prilutski's *Zamlbikher*, his contributions figured prominently.[73] He published his first larger folklore work, on Jewish customs, in the first volume of the Hebrew journal *Reshumot* in 1918.[74]

Elzet became a significant participant in the Yiddish folklore movement with the publication of his series of four books, *Der vunder-oytser fun der yidisher shprakh* (The wonderful treasure of the Yiddish language), published from 1918 to 1920.[75] Though a religious Zionist, Elzet gathered hundreds of folk sayings and idioms from the works of the "fathers" of modern secular Yiddish literature, S. Abramovitch (Mendele Moykher-Sforim), S. Rabinovitsh (Sholem Aleichem), and I. L. Peretz, thereby by placing them at the center of Yiddish folklore.[76] As he examined German collections of verbal lore, Elzet was struck at how much poorer the Yiddish language was. He soon realized that this was untrue: "How shocked I was, though, when I began to listen closer to the refreshingly direct Sforim, Sholem Aleichem, and Peretz, who understood not to switch the rich blossoming folksy language for a freshly baked, dried out, supposed literary style."[77] The three writers were a revelation for Elzet, who proceeded to give them the closest reading, noting all of the verbal folklore encompassed in them. He considered himself a folklorist, remarking that other nations had entire societies devoted to the collection of verbal folklore, while the Jews had barely begun such work. He called upon people to collect folklore; for he that did saved it from being lost forever.[78] His devotion to this task is symbolized on the cover page of the first volume in his series which shows a templelike structure with two eagles on top and two menorahs below. The implications are obvious: the treasure of the Yiddish language is a holy endeavor.

The four volumes of Elzet's work were divided thematically into "Prayer," "Jewish Food," "Trades and Tradespeople," and "The Human Body." Though almost all the quotations are from the works of Sholem Aleichem, Mendele, and Peretz, other sources are the Ignaz Bernstein collection of proverbs and the works of Mordkhe Specktor (1858–1925), A. M. Dik (1814–93), I. I. Linetski (1839–1915), I. Aksenfeld (1787–1866), Yankev Dinezon (1852–1919), and S. Etinger (1801–56). These authors wrote their major works from the mid- to late nineteenth century. Elzet thus drew the core of this lore from the *maskilic* period of Yiddish literature, a time when the Yiddish writings were antithetical to traditional Jewish ways. Elzet correctly understood, though, that the proverbs and idioms that these writers employed were accurate representations of Yiddish folk speech, though the overuse of them in the literature could have been a result of the satiric view of the "backward" *shtetl* Jew that these *maskilic* Yiddish writers shared. Elzet did not allow the ideological context of these writers to disrupt his appreciation of their language.

In addition to the citations of written sources, Elzet included many examples of verbal lore that he collected from oral sources. Frequently, Elzet used the phrase, "From oral source I heard the following . . ." or, "they say the following . . ." citing no author. These oral sources are interwoven with the written ones, implying a parity in quality and value.

Elzet was eager to find the source or the reason for the sayings and to explain their etymologies. He also provided alternate usages and meanings for proverbs found in Bernstein's collection. Thanks to his great knowledge of traditional Jewish literature and folkways, Elzet's comments were usually informative and insightful.

Why Elzet would print a first volume on prayer is readily understood because of his religious views; however, why a second volume on

"Trades and Tradespeople"? According to his introduction, Elzet wanted to explain the poor image of the tradesperson, the *bal-melokhe*, since the verbal lore portrayed such a degenerate type. The author surmised that only poverty could be blamed for this state.[79] As a Zionist, it would have been ideologically compatible to accent the economic hardships inherent in the Jewish existence in Eastern Europe. Elzet, though, never framed his topic in any political context. The only emotion evoked in his introduction is one of pity for the worker; no Zionist agenda is hinted at.

This second part was divided according to trade. Elzet's own fieldwork is here attested to as he records his own collected klezmer terminology, which he gathered from two *badkhonim* (wedding entertainers) and one band of klezmer (Jewish wedding) musicians.[80] The last two volumes, on *The Human Body* and *Jewish Food*, were the largest, at 116 and 122 pages.[81] In *Jewish Foods*, Elzet attempted a cultural atlas of sorts: which Jews ate what foods where, as well as an analysis of the economic life of Jews through their foodways.[82] His methodology for this grandiose attempt was disorganized and arbitrary, for it depended on his limited literary sources and own fieldwork. Nevertheless, any future attempt at such an atlas will be greatly in Elzet's debt for the huge amount of ethnographic information on foodways. Elzet had planned at least one more volume, on plants, but it was never published.[83] He claimed to have accumulated enough material for forty such volumes.[84]

His next major folklore work was in the collection *Among Us Jews* in 1923, though probably submitted to the editor in 1918.[85] Here he clearly aligned himself with the major Warsaw Yiddish folklorists—Graubard, Lehman, and Prilutski. His article, "Idiomatic Expressions: Materials for a Phraseology of the Yiddish Language," was placed in the philology section rather than the folklore section of the book.[86] The editor, Vanvild, admitted the difficulty in defining the boundaries between the two fields and the arbitrariness of the decision to place an article in one section and not the other.[87] Elzet's work consisted of sayings, proverbs, and idioms, and the material is similar to that found in his *Wonderful Treasure* series. He sought materials "which in the sense and form as they are found in Yiddish, are not extant in other languages, or which are sometimes impossible to express in another language."[88]

He began this collection with an attempt to analyze the ways in which the idioms were put together formally, rather than thematically. The first few subgroupings of texts examined idiomatic expressions with dyadic elements such as "In leydn un freydn" (in sufferings and in joys) and "kider-vider" (intense dislike). This structural approach, after the first few pages, quickly yielded to random themes: folk speech that used people's names, animals in folklore, the Jewish alphabet in folk sayings, idioms with biblical and *gemore* terms. The materials were almost all from Yiddish literature; few were from his own fieldwork. His comments, which often discussed the meaning and the Talmudic sources for the Yiddish proverbs, were new in the Yiddish folklore literature, which usually provided no comments at all.

Elzet had already left Warsaw when this article came out. His next and last major work on Yiddish folklore work was printed in Montreal in 1927. The work examined a Yiddish *brivnshteler*, a book on how to write letters, that had been published in the late eighteenth century in Poland.[89] Though the work dealt primarily with folklife, rather than oral genres, he still used the Yiddish writers as his main source of comparison.

Elzet went on, over the next thirty years, to contribute to Jewish folklore in English and especially in Hebrew. His years of involvement in the Yiddish folklore field in Poland, from 1910–1920, the focus of this study, formed only a small part of his oeuvre. His work introduced a new perspective of a Yiddishist Orthodox Zionist. Elzet's Yiddishism, as reflected in his *Wonderful Treasure,* exceeded in some respects that of his secular colleagues. The cover pages to the four volumes of the *Wonderful Treasure* depict the entrance to a temple of Yiddish verbal lore. Yiddish language and folklore was to be worshipped for its genius and creativity. No Yiddish folklorist spelled this notion out as explicitly as did Elzet.

YESHAYE ZLOTNIK

Yehude's younger relative Yeshaye Zlotnik also was active in the Mizrachi Party and became a rabbi and folklorist. He was born in 1892 near Warsaw and was killed by the Nazis in 1943 in Radom, Poland. Yeshaye Zlotnik began to collect materials on Jewish humor in the 1920s and wrote numerous articles based on his materials.[90]

In 1930, he published his first folklore work, *Leksikon fun yidishe khokhmes: gute verter fun kluge yidn* (Lexicon of Jewish witticisms: Bon mots of learned Jews). According to the title page, the texts had never before been published. They were collected from oral sources and were "stylized."[91] The work includes anecdotes attributed to fourteen rabbis. His next work, *Yomim-toyvim folklor* (Holiday-folklore), a compendium of jokes, proverbs, and anecdotes, proudly announced on the cover page that the texts "were mainly collected from oral sources!"[92] By adding this detail, he made sure that his readership knew the volume was something new, and not rehashed materials. Unlike his relative Yehude, who used Elzet as a pseudonym and did not want his community to know that he wrote books on folklore, Yeshaye proudly put his name and rabbinic title on the works, and employed the word "folklore" to define his field.

The introduction hinted at the beginning of a religious Jewish folkloristic approach, which one would have expected from Elzet. He criticized the idea that Jewish humor was a product of the diaspora and cited an example of the same kind of sarcastic humor as existed in the diaspora from the Book of Prophets. He referred to the misconceptions of "our folklore-scholars," and particularly to Alter Druyanov's conclusion that Jewish humor, unlike the humor of other nations, was not based upon wordplay, but was more profound and based upon a conceptual twist which Druyanov expounded upon in his work, "The Jewish Folk Joke."[93] Zlotnik did not offer his own countertheory. He seemed intent upon derailing the secular "folklorists' " conception of Jewish humor. He claimed his one example from the Bible "entirely shatters the scholarly conclusion of Mr. Druyanov for we see that the typical (I believe the oldest Jewish joke must also be the most original, folkiest) folksy Jewish joke is based upon a double entendre."[94] It was true that for most of Zlotnik's body of jokes, wordplay provided the punch lines. Most of the humor centered upon Talmudic and biblical passages.

He also disagreed with the historic understanding of Jewish humor as discussed by secular folklorists who saw its self-mocking qualities as a result of the social position of the Jew in the diaspora. Zlotnik believed that the sarcasm of modern Jewish humor and the bitterness in biblical humor were one and the same: "The contempt and lighthearted approach of the folk to all its difficult problems is much older than the whole Jewish Diaspora."[95]

In this introduction, Zlotnik called for a widespread collection of jokes in Eastern Europe, for the Jewish diaspora had become "problematic." Since life in the "old-new" land, Israel, was becoming closer and closer to a reality, Zlotnik felt that one should collect all the treasures of the Jewish people that had been created under "other conditions," and

then "mummify" that treasure for eternity. Not only were the older traditions ending; Zlotnik felt that the entire life in the diaspora was coming to an end.[96] Zlotnik maintained that holiday folklore was the most
"authentic" and profound form of Jewish folklore. On the Sabbath and
holidays, the Jew was able to relax, to feel more spiritual, and to create
humor that "would be winged with true Jewish folks-genius."[97]

Finally, in 1938–39, Zlotnik produced a series of three volumes
of *Khumesh folklor* (Pentateuch folklore) arranged according to biblical
passage.[98] He was "giving the people back its own work as a gift."[99] These
volumes concluded the folklore work of one of the few religious Yiddish
folklorists in Poland between the wars. His approach to folklore had
popular support, as is attested to by the multiple editions of his first two
works. He had only begun to formulate a Zionist-religious folkloristics
in Yiddish folklore. His sources of folklore, unlike those of his relative
Yehude-Elzet, were the great rabbis rather than the great Yiddish writers.

PART II

An Ethnographic Vision Emerges

CHAPTER 4

S. Ansky Vilne Jewish Historical-Ethnographic Society

Nationalist Yiddish sentiments rose sharply in Lithuania during the First World War with some help from the occupying German forces. In Vilne in 1915, the Germans forbade the Russian language and ordered the national minorities to establish schools that taught in their own languages.[1] All segments of the Jewish population united to organize Yiddish-language schools and social work organizations.

The world war also introduced what Moyshe Shalit termed "the new historiography of Vilne," which reflected the tumultuous times and was free of religious constraints. Instead of focusing on the "deeds and virtues of individuals," this new approach examined "the life and misfortunes of the whole community." There was a crucial ethnographic component in this historiography. Because of the almost daily upheavals during the war, there was a need to record daily life. An important place in the ethnographic description was the collection of folklore.

The scholarly institution that arose from this nationalist awakening was the Jewish Historical-Ethnographic Society of Lithuania and White Russia. Amidst great political turmoil, S. Anksy founded the society on February 20, 1919. The writer and folklorist had moved to Vilne at the end of 1918, having been active in the Jewish Historical-Ethnographic Society in St. Petersburg since its founding in 1908.[2] As the First World

War ended, the city of Vilne changed hands seven times between the Germans, Russian Bolsheviks, Lithuanians, and Poles. The founding took place just two months before the bloody April pogrom in Vilne executed by the Poles.[3]

When Ansky died on November 8, 1920, the name of the organization was changed to the S. Ansky Vilne Jewish Historical-Ethnographic Society (AVJHES).[4] Before his death, Ansky had attempted unsuccessfully to create the same kind of organization in Warsaw.[5] At Ansky's urging the organization was apolitical, and the board included Jews of all political persuasions. The first director was Dr. Avrom Virshubski; the first secretary, Khaykl Lunski. Ansky's request for nonpartisanship was understandable, since the Jewish Historical-Ethnographic Society's museum in St. Petersburg, which housed most of his collection, was closed down by the Bolsheviks in 1917.

There had been earlier attempts at scholarly ethnographic societies in Vilne. The "Vilne Society of Lovers of Jewish Antiquities" established a museum on March 14, 1913.[6] The impetus for this organization was also apparently the influence of S. Ansky.[7] The call to support this earlier museum also had folklore in mind,

> Not only in holy letters, on parchment and paper, have hundreds of generations eternalized their souls, recorded their testament. In each unique edifice, in each carved and chiseled "living" stone, in every carved Holy Ark, embroidered Ark curtains, in every painting, drawing and portrait, in every spice box and Khanike lamp. To sum up, in everything that throws light upon our past life and creation, on our sufferings and joys, laws and customs there is, as there is in every book and manuscript, as there is in every folksong and folktale, a spark of our spirit, a brilliant drop from the holy cup of tears, a recollection and a comfort.[8]

The museum sought particularly objects that related to "religious life," written documents and records such as organizational and town chronicles and protocols, and materials of "Jewish ethnography and Jewish folklore," including "texts and melodies of folksongs, folktales, proverbs, riddles, exorcisms [opshprekhenishn], etc."[9]

The "call" pointed out that all other nations, young and old, looked out for the "survivals of the past," including "our brothers" in Western Europe, thus stressing the museum as an important symbol of nationhood. The AVJHES inherited the conviction to save "the past" from the earlier Vilna Society of Lovers of Jewish Antiquities.

They also inherited a popular approach to historic and ethnographic collection from the earlier society. At the time of the "afruf" (the appeal to found the museum), the Yiddishist intelligentsia was impressed that the "cultured" bourgeoisie, the organizers of the plan, who were usually disdainful of Yiddish, sought to include the Yiddish-speaking folk into their plans for a museum.[10]

The first director of the museum, Ben-Zion Rubshteyn, collected close to two hundred items on an expedition into smaller Lithuanian towns.[11] The world war saw the dispersal and loss of most of the collection. Writer A. M. Goldshmidt took over as director in 1914–15. The society then dissolved in 1915, and was reopened under the supervision of the AVJHES in 1919. Many of the board members of the earlier society became board members of the newly transformed one.

The statutes of the AVJHES state that the objectives of the society were "to recognize and to collect the artifacts of Jewish archeology, ethnography, history and art."[12] In 1922, the AVJHES was divided into the following sections: music, folklore, history, art and museum, Ansky section, catalogue section, literary, and *pinkes* section (community record books). It had developed a museum, a library, and an archive. The music section, headed by the Cantor A. M. Bernstein, concentrated on the collection of folk music, particularly religious *nigunim*, prayers, dance tunes, and wedding music. The section published a selection from its collection in 1927.

The folklore section was directed by teacher and folklorist Shloyme Bastomski, and had by 1922 collected 65 children's songs, donated by Bastomski, as well as 284 folklore texts, donated by the *Mefitse Haskole Children's Club*. Other leading collectors were Khaykl Lunski and Yitskhok Broydes, who had contributed much wedding folklore. The section met numerous times to help edit and "complete" Bastomski's proverb collection, *Baym kval*, which it also subsidized.[13]

The material culture side of folklore was represented in the museum collections, which included "old house utensils, copper tea pots that people used to prepare tea, *tsholent* pots, [and] dippers with two ears," as well as religious artifacts.[14]

The first three years of the AVJHES were characterized as years of "fears and suffering," but the period ended with the publication of *Pinkes: For the History of Vilne During the Years of War and Occupation*, which included folklore and ethnography.[15]

After the founding of YIVO in 1925, the combination of the two organizations seemed logical and inevitable. Yet, for unknown reasons, only parts of the AVJHES were incorporated into YIVO in 1928. A personality clash between Max Weinreich of YIVO and Moyshe Shalit probably was partly responsible. Both organizations thus maintained their autonomy. The library and archive of the AVJHES were transferred to YIVO, while all museum artifacts of YIVO were given to the AVJHES. [16]

Under the leadership of Moyshe Shalit, the society acquired new energy and concentrated on its museum. In 1929, almost ten years after Ansky bequeathed the Vilna society half of his folkloric collection, the legacy finally arrived from Russia. The material that Ansky collected on his ethnographic expedition in 1912 included every genre of folklore. [17] In 1932, the Vilne Jewish community gave the AVJHES several rooms in the community building for its museum, now called the "Anski Museum."

The final major project of the AVJHES was the publication of a journal, *Fun noentn over* (From the recent past) from 1937 to 1939. The ethnographic/folklife component termed the "new historiography" by Shalit was well represented in the journal. One of the best examples was the series on the occupations of village Jews in Lithuania by Hirsh Abramovitsh. [18] Three active board members of the AVJHES were folklorists: Khaykl Lunski, A. M. Bernstein, and Shloyme Bastomski. The first two were Orthodox Jews, while the third was a socialist who led the struggle for a modern secular Yiddish culture and was one of the leading Yiddish folklorists of the era. The fact that all three were active in the same cultural organization reflects the broad appeal that Yiddish folklore possessed in Vilne at this time.

Khaykl Lunski

Lunski, the secretary of the AVJHES, was known by all as the librarian of the Strashun Library. He was also among the most beloved characters in interbellum Vilne. "There were many libraries in Poland, but the Strashun Library and its warmth and folkiness, and the friendly smile and charm of its librarian, Khaykl Lunski, made it unparalleled." [19] He was also a rare breed: an old-fashioned religious Jew who worked together with the Yiddishist circles. "There is not one Yiddish intellectual [in Vilne] who does not appreciate this Jew from the Synagogue courtyard."[20]

He was born in Slonim, Lithuania, in 1881, and received a traditional education but had to work as a *shames,* a beadle, in the old synagogue in Vilne at the age of thirteen. In 1895 he became the librarian of the Strashun Library in Vilna, and in 1919 he became the secretary of the AVJHES at its founding. He was killed by the Nazis in 1942 in Vilne.[21]

Lunski had a very poor and tragic life. He lost his parents, wife, sisters, and brothers at early ages. The Strashun Library had chronic financial difficulties and he was paid very little.[22] He lived in the Orthodox community, and began to collect oral folklore, historic documents, and old *sforim.* His first book as a result of this collecting was *Toldes r'Mordkhe Ayzl Kharif,* in Hebrew.[23] His depressed outlook on life was expressed in the short book *Fun vilner geto,* written in chronicle form during the First World War, when many were dying of hunger and disease.[24]

As a traditional Jew, Lunski was an interesting figure among folklore circles. Having lived in the *shulhoyf* (courtyard of the synagogue), which was surrounded by many smaller prayer houses (*kloyzn*), he was able to gather legendary materials on rabbis through oral tradition. When he presented this material in printed form, he mixed legends from oral sources with those from printed sources (frequently from old and rare chapbooks) to present as full a picture of the rabbis as possible. As an observant Jew, Lunksi's concept of history was a combination of oral and written history. Perhaps this view is what drew him to the dual nature inherent in a "historic-ethnographic" society and allowed him to work comfortably in such a place. The "historic" element was usually written history. The "ethnographic" half represented oral history or folklore. Orally collected tales were history, no less than printed ones.

In 1920, just as the AVJHES was getting under way, Lunski published "Vilner kloyzn, the Jewish neighborhood and the Synagogue courtyard."[25] He had written the work in 1917, during the worst period of the war. The work is a house-by-house, synagogue-by-synagogue tour of the old Jewish section of Vilne. Lunski told the reader what had been in each location before the war, and what had happened since. The matter-of-fact style of the narration in juxtaposition with the physical destruction brought on by the war powerfully heightened the effect of his description. For example, poor people had come to the *kloyzn* to die, and, as a result, signs hung on the entrances warning *kohanim* (Jews of the priestly class) not to enter, for *kohanim* are not permitted to be in the presence of a corpse. Lunski's reputation as the chronicler of Vilne's traditional life was sealed with this work. In his case, the need to record "vanishing ways of life" did not spring from a modern folkloric impulse, but from a traditional responsibility. The folkloric ethnographic field, however, allowed him to chronicle and to publish in a new context, with secular scholarly approval. When Lunski's collection of legends on the great rabbi, the Vilner Gaon (1720–97) was published in 1924 as part of Shloyme Bastomski's "Library for Young People" series, the author's subtitle stated that the legends were collected "from people and from religious books."[26] One reviewer aptly said, "Just the subtitle gives you an idea about the author. It is such a clumsy expression at first glance: 'collected from people and religious books,' but how much simplicity, humility and holiness are found in this clumsy expression. Lunski is positive that books do not lie, nor people, especially when they speak about the Vilner Gaon, the guiding light of the Diaspora."[27]

Lunski combined numerous legends around each phase of the rabbi's life: "His Parents, Birth and Childhood"; "The Rabbi Suffers Exile"; "The Rabbi Settles in Vilne"; "Hasidim and the Goan"; "The Writings of the Goan"; "How He Taught, His Influence and His Virtues, His Last Years." There is no commentary. Since the work was published for older schoolchildren, several Hebrew-Aramaic words are translated at the bottom of each page. Many of these words would be considered basic vocabulary for any religious or learned Jew. This creates a striking impression of incongruity: a new collection of legends written in a traditional style but geared toward a readership who might not understand the religious underpinnings or moral values that the legends reflect. One cannot imagine that it was Lunski who translated the words; more likely it was the editor and publisher, Shloyme Bastomski. Yet, the vocabulary lists show that Lunksi was indeed caught between two worlds.

As secretary for the AVJHES, Lunski announced the meetings and kept the minutes. He also collected historical documents, particularly relating to the Orthodox Jewish life in Vilne. With the founding of YIVO and the growing interest in Yiddish philology, Lunski also collected examples of old Yiddish as found in the older books of the rabbis.[28]

One of the greatest results of the "new historiography in Vilne" was the massive volume (almost six hundred pages) *On the Ruins of Wars and Turmoil: Pinkes,* published in 1931 by the social welfare organization YEKOPO and edited by Moyshe Shalit.[29] In addition to articles that survey the cultural and social affairs in Vilne between 1919 and 1930, several contributions deal with the folkloric and ethnographic aspects of Vilne's Jewish life. Lunski contributed a short description of a Lithuanian town, "Olkenik: A town of legends."[30] In his tour-guide style, Lunski discussed the synagogue, the rabbis, and past town personalities and the legends surrounding them. The second half of the article examined sociologically the town population and occupations. Lunski wrote that the "town had her own folklore." Specifically, he meant the nicknames that referred, for reasons unknown today, to the town's people ("Olkeniker retshke bandes"—gangs of buckwheat). Preceding Lunski's article was a short compilation of Zhetler folklore by Yoysef Vinyetski.[31] The collection included nicknames, proverbs, sayings, local idioms, a curse, and some customs. They are not annotated.

In 1931, Lunksi published another short collection of legends and tales, *Great Rabbis and Sages of the Recent Past: Tales and Legends on Their Life and Work.*[32] Lunski began those legends that were collected from oral sources with the phrase, "*me dertseylt,*" "it is told," while for those legends gleaned from written sources, the textual sources were mentioned. Again, the critics praised his interweaving of oral and written sources: "Maybe because of this [interweaving], he succeeds in encompassing in a consistent frame the wholeness of a personality and in rendering him alive, plastic and interesting for the reader."[33]

In the 1930s, Lunski devoted more and more time to bibliographic work in the Strashun Library and less to the society. His dual support for Orthodoxy and for secular Yiddish culture was a rare chemistry which adds weight to the popular notion that, "Say what you will, but such a sage as the Vilner [Goen] and such a writer and librarian as Lunski . . . could only come out of the most Jewish of all the cities in the world— Vilne."[34]

Avrom-Moyshe Bernshteyn

A. M. Bernshteyn was the musicologist in the AVJHES. Like Lunski, he was a unique combination perhaps possible only in Vilne: an Orthodox cantor who collected songs, melodies, and prayers for the society. Whereas Lunski was part of an older style of Orthodoxy, Bernshteyn was more representative of a modern Orthodoxy.

All cantors, by the nature of their work, are performers who are judged by the congregation or audience that comes to hear them. From the mid–nineteenth century until today, they have been drawn to opera, theater, and secular art songs as well.[35] In Bernshteyn's case, he was a leading composer, and the first to compose for the modern Jewish poets, in Hebrew and in Yiddish.[36] As the editors of *Di khazonim velt* characterized him, "He always took the 'the middle path' between classical and modern, but simultaneously he was religiously folksy. He possessed a great Jewish joyous soul."[37]

Bernshteyn was born in Shatsk, near Minsk, in 1865 and was an apprentice cantor and choir director in numerous towns and cities in Lithuania and White Russia before becoming the cantor at the Vilne synagogue, "Taharas-hakoydesh." He served that congregation for thirty years, from 1893 to 1923. He was then fired, an action that was viewed as scandalous by the cantorial world, which viewed the firing as a symbolic event marking the end of the appreciative older generation and the coming of the ignorant younger one.[38] He died in Vilne in 1932.

As a composer and organizer, Bernshteyn was an important figure in the modern history of cantorial music. In 1907, he helped to organize a union of cantors in Russia that was soon illegalized. His compositions of modern Jewish poetry totaled in the hundreds.[39] In 1914, he published two volumes of cantorial compositions by himself and others, *Avoydes haboyre* (In the service of the Lord).

The collection of tunes and songs is not a strange conception for a cantor; every cantor is a collector to a certain extent. If he hears a compelling melody from a fellow cantor or any Jew, he will surely remember it for future use in his synagogue. There is, however, a major difference between random and occasional collection and the careful annotation and publication of folk melodies by a cantor. Bernshteyn was perhaps the only cantor to have published a collection of folk songs and melodies. Menakhem Kipnis had done this as well and had been a cantor, but for him this was only one vocation among many—opera singer, journalist, popular singer. Bernshteyn was a professional cantor his whole life, albeit an unemployed one late in his career.

After he left his job of thirty years in 1923, Bernshteyn spent most of his time teaching music in the Hebrew and Yiddish schools in Vilne, composing, and collecting musical pieces for the AVJHES. Bernshteyn was the driving force behind its musical section from the society's inception. In fact, only two people were active in the section at all: Bernshteyn and Lunski. Lunski, "brought live singers from whom A. M. Bernshteyn elicited the melodies and immediately transcribed them."[40] Several evenings were organized to present the collected songs, and an active effort was made to collect. After eight years, the section published *Musikalishe pinkes* (Musical record) in 1927. This was the only folklore that Bernshteyn ever printed and the only folklore volume that the society ever published under its auspices.

The work includes 243 pieces divided into ten sections, all related to religious folk music. The planned second volume, which never was published, would have included folk songs, cantorial pieces of the previous century, and old melodies for prayers. Though it was not mentioned in the introduction, most of the melodies were collected in Vilne, and almost all in Lithuania and White Russia. A number were recorded from fellow scholars, such as Lunski and Mordkhe Kosover.

In Bernshteyn's lengthy introduction, he explained why he chose what he did, discussed the nature of collecting, and provided a brief, general introduction to cantorial music. Half the collection are *zmires,* hymns or songs sung during and after the Sabbath meals and at the Passover seder. Bernshteyn wrote that the *zmires* were a source of joy for the Jew who had worked hard all week. He sang them to rise above his downtrodden feelings, to honor the holy Sabbath. The section of *lomdisher nigunim* comprised melodies that Yeshiva students created and sang while learning. These were not related to the *gemore-nign,* sung to accompany the study of the *gemore,* but were independent creations. Bernshteyn pointed out that despite the negative attitude that "our spiritual aristocrats" had toward music, the youth, the Yeshiva students, sang their own melodies based on passages from the Bible and Psalms. Bernshteyn was the only Yiddish folklorist to divide the religious sector in this class- and age-conscious manner. While folklorists such as I. L. Cahan categorized all educated religious Jews as *lomdish,* which for Cahan was a negative connotation, Bernshteyn was sensitive to differences in outlook and creative processes among the various kinds of religious Jews in

Poland. Some learned religious were not part of the folk and folklore, but others were, he implied.

The third section of the *Pinkes* included melodies that accompanied the priestly chant, the *birkhas kohanim*. The editor believed that some of these might have been very old, since the ritual itself was ancient, and therefore included them. The Hasidic *nigunim*, melodies without words, he believed were authentically Jewish, not comparable to other nations' folk traditions.[41] Though Bernshteyn was a Litvak, and the northern Litvaks were frequently antipathetic to the southern "emotional" Hasidim, he did not hesitate to embrace the Hasidim's musical genres as the epitome of Jewish folk creation. Bernshteyn also made an interesting comparison among Hasidic traditions, referring to the Voliner *nigunim* as "solid, profound and mystical," the Polish as "temperamental," and the Litvish as "melancholy."

The second half of the introduction discussed general issues in Jewish folklore. Were these melodies and songs worth printing? "Everything that the folk has created in the cultural field, whether it be better or not so good, should be recorded and given over to future generations."[42] Bernshteyn differed from other Yiddish folklorists, who, inspired by Herder's notion of *Volkspoesie*, sought out only the lyrics of songs. Bernshteyn took an opposite position: without the melodies, the songs "do not have enough soul." Every folk melody, "is a seed of art," he said, "and a great composer can find the theme for a large concert work planted in it."[43] The use of the term "soul" parallels Herder's "Geist." Herder was thinking of poetry and Bernshteyn of music. In either case, the musical or the textual, folk creations are sources for greater works.

The author was very eager for "great artists" to use the folk melodies for concert pieces, and clearly placed folk music on a lower plane, but was very proud of the Jewish folk music as he found them, "though in relation to artistic music our folk music is backward and we are at the letter Alef [the very beginning], in relation to folk creation, our folk music is wealthier than all other peoples."[44] From his text, it is apparent that by "wealthier" he meant the richness of the various genres of Jewish music: dance, *nigunim*, religious, secular, and prayer modes. Yet no one, he bemoaned, was collecting this folk music. "With every dying old man, it is possible that we are losing treasures of historical memoirs, folkloric, folksy and musical creations which are then irretrievable."[45]

84

The genre of religious folk music was "more in danger of being forgotten" than other genres. As someone who had been replaced by a younger cantor, he must, no doubt, have been particularly sensitive to the difference between the religious worlds of the old and the new. While collecting folklore, Bernshteyn encountered the usual reactions from informants at that time: "What do you need it for? How could it be of any value? What, me sing?" Since he collected religious musical folklore, he heard one reaction that other folklorists did not—the melodies were holy and, as with the oral Torah, his informants told him, it would be blasphemy to record the notes and to print them.[46] Unfortunately, the folklorist does not say how he countered such an argument.

In Bernshteyn's discussion of the difficulty of recording the tunes, numerous critcisms of the "folk" arise. Some informants were off-key, others hadn't "the slightest notion of rhythm."[47] Still others "improved" the text on their own. Like many of the Warsaw Yiddish folklorists, Bernshteyn appreciated the treasure, but not its keepers. He did not comment positively upon one aspect of his informants. The folk creations were lovely, but the folk were clumsy and incompetent. Regardless of this view, Bernshteyn did retain the "mistakes" in the Hebrew that he heard from the singers. His transcription was accurate and did not "prettify" the melodies. He had envisioned the work as a handbook in the schools and so kept the work as simple as possible. It seems that every project with which the AVJHES was associated attempted to tie into the Yiddish schools in Vilne in some way.

When fellow composer Yisroel Gladshteyn reviewed the volume, he noted the pioneering nature of the collection: Bernshteyn was among the first folklorists to collect this religious material. The reviewer characterized the material as "Hasidic-religious folk creations."[48] Vilne and Lithuania were historically the last Jewish communities to accept Hasidic Judaism, which developed in the mid–eighteenth century. Vilne was considered a center for the opponents of Hasidim, *misnagdim,* and while Gladshteyn overstated the Hasidic origin of the melodies, he sensed the oddness of printing in Vilne a collection of Jewish folk music that was full of Hasidic works. Bernshteyn was clearly taken with the spirit of Hasidic tunes, and the goal of the *Muzikalisher Pinkes* was to revive that spirit, or at least not to let that "old-time religion" be forgotten. Like other folklorists of his generation, he was also caught up in the spirit of Jewish nationalism and therefore composed for secular writers, became involved in the AVJHES, and related his work to the Yiddish secular schools in Vilne. His *Muzikalisher pinkes* reflected these two spirits and his simultaneous longing for the past and desire to create something new and better than the folk creations of the past.

Shloyme Bastomski

The leading folklorist in the AVJHES was Shloyme Bastomski. Though he was a close associate of the YIVO Ethnographic/Folklore Commission from its founding in 1925 until the war, his loyalty remained with the older society and his own projects. In the YIVO folklore volume, *Yidisher folklor,* which included texts contributed from hundreds of collectors, Bastomski did not contribute one item.

He was born in 1891 in Vilne to a poor family, attended *Talmud-toyre* (traditional elementary school for the poor), and was orphaned at an early age. He graduated from the Vilne Teacher's Institute in 1912 and taught in nearby towns until 1914, when he returned to Vilne to teach in the newly formed *folkshul* for boys of the *Khevre Mefitse Haskole* (Society to Promote the Enlightenment). This was the first nontraditional boys' school in Vilne in which Yiddish was the language of instruction. He taught there through the 1930s. Politically, Bastomski was a member of the Socialist-Zionists and later became an active territorialist.

Bastomski became known internationally among Yiddish culture circles for his publishing house, "Di naye yidishe folkshul," which produced numerous reading texts and anthologies, arithmetic texts, songbooks, and children's journals for the newly developed Yiddish secular school system. His coeditor, Malke Khaymson, became his wife. They are considered among the central builders of the modern Yiddish school. They both died in Vilne during the war; Bastomski before the Nazis arrived in 1941, Khaymson in the ghetto a short time later.

According to Reyzen, Bastomski began secretly to collect folklore while teaching at a government school in 1912. In his introduction to his collection of proverbs of 1920, Bastomski stated that he had been collecting materials for twelve years, or since 1908. Other statements by Bastomski indicate that his collection of folklore was tied to his teaching career, which would corroborate the 1912 date.[49]

In 1913, he sent a collection of proverbs to writer Shmuel Niger for publication in his historic volume, *Der pinkes*. In a letter to Niger in 1913, Bastomski asked for his collection back so that he could classify his materials and look them over again. "Now I look upon folklore quite differently; every proverb has its place [here Bastomski was quoting a well-known proverb—*yedes vertl hot zikh zayn ertl*]. I see in Yiddish folklore the Jewish spirit and the Jewish diaspora."[50] How this new attitude affected his editorial program was not specified; however, Bastomski had given the nature of folklore considerable thought, and this would be reflected in his later works. He did not publish this collection of proverbs until seven years later.

His first published collection was of riddles, entitled *Yidishe folksretenishn* and published in 1917. A second edition was published in 1919, and reprinted in 1920.[51] The first edition predated the establishment of the AVJHES. It is the first published collection of Yiddish riddles in Yiddish. Bastomski's introductory, "Instead of an Introduction," lamented the pitiful amount of Jewish folklore that had been published, particularly in comparison with other nations.

> Until today, no one has produced the golden book which would give us the opportunity to examine our rich folk treasure. The book would be of great use for our Jewish people. It would also be invaluable for the Yiddish reader, for the new school, for the new textbooks. In the new paradise of the Yiddish folkshul, the teacher, especially the Yiddish language teacher, will be standing at the well and water the young green trees with living water from the eternal well of Yiddish folk creativity. The teacher must be well acquainted with the Yiddish folk creation. He must be a *folksmentsh*, otherwise he will not be able to get close to the Jewish child.[52]

Bastomski inextricably linked Yiddish folklore, Yiddish language, and the new secular Yiddish schools. Folklore, in his vision, would nurture the child. The youth should be guided by its folk treasures in the folk tongue. Ansky, in his review of the collection, picked up on the pedagogical implications of Bastomski's work and praised the author as one of the first to use folklore for the new Yiddish secular school.[53] Ansky framed his praise in the context of how the new pedagogy could learn from the "*alte folks-pedagogye*." Bastomski envisioned the new schools in much more revolutionary terms, as something completely new. Though he made a very tight connection with the "old ways of life" and the new folklore, Bastomski probably would have preferred that Ansky not use the term "alte folks-pedagogye" for his vision. The term stirred up visions of the old *kheder* school, and it was the revision of this "alte folks-pedagogye" that was one of the central themes of *maskilic* politics and literature in the nineteenth century.

Ansky was correct in stressing the author's concern for education through folklore, for this was at the heart of Bastomski's work, and set him apart from the other Yiddish folklorists throughout his life. Though active as a folklorist in the AVJHES and in the YIVO, his first priority lay with the Yiddish schools in Vilne. The "golden book" of folklore would be the ultimate textbook for the new schoolchildren. Bastomski found a "lively interest" and "an indescribable joy" when he told the children tales and asked them riddles. "Woe to the teacher who is so far from that which the children hold so close and dear." [54]

The warning that Bastomski sounded for teachers was directed at those Jewish teachers and schools who taught in languages other than Yiddish—Hebrew, Russian, and soon Polish. Without Yiddish language and folklore in the school curriculum, he preached, the teachers and students would be speaking two different languages, linguistically and spiritually. Jewish children, he said, inherited "the love of riddles" from their parents. "Talmudic education, innate cleverness, and the merchant's life experience had formed in the Jew, and especially the Litvish Jew, a life that is full of various logical, clever, mathematical tricks, riddles, and puns." [55]

Children continued the tradition of their grandfathers and great grandfathers, who would test each other during the winter evenings between the *minkhe* and *mayriv* prayers. In this analysis, Bastomski believed that the play of children copied the play of the older generation. Because the older generation was dying, most of this play-folklore was being lost. To prevent this loss, he felt, the Yiddish teacher should collect. As a teacher himself, he had collected the riddle material, and the published collection was a gift to the children. In this manner, he had provided a model for the other teachers of the new synthesis of the old Yiddish folklore and the new Yiddish pedagogy.

The riddles, 222 in number, are printed in large type, with the answers given at the end. [56] They are printed in standard Yiddish and neither the names of the informants nor the place of recording are provided. No annotation or cross-references are provided. This was not designed to be a scholarly folklore collection; it was to be a collection for the child of the Yiddish school.

In Ansky's review he leveled three criticisms at the texts: the lack of systemization of the riddle texts; the failure to transcribe the riddles phonetically; and the lack of information on where the text was recorded. In his next printed collection, Bastomski took Ansky's advice and corrected the first two criticisms. However, he would continue to print his texts in standard Yiddish, since the schoolchild was his intended reader. A dialect transcription would only confuse the young reader.

In his next folklore publication, Bastomski again had only the Yiddish student in mind. *Yidishe shprikhverter far shul un heym* (Yiddish proverbs for school and home) is a short booklet arranged according to topic (e.g., "work," "father," "laziness").[57] The proverbs were taken from his own collections and other folklore collections. He wrote that the other proverb collections "had a total folkloric character and could not be used in the school as they stand now. A good deal of the material, and the system by which they are arranged, are not suitable for children."[58]

Again he discussed the importance of the teacher familiarizing him- or herself with folklore; not just the Yiddish teacher, but the teachers of all subjects. If they did not, the classes, "will not be folksy, not alive, not Jewish."[59] He dedicated this book to the children of the *Khevre mefitse haskole* school, where the first attempt was made to create "an authentic, secular, folksy, Yiddish school."[60] Folklore was a basic component of this new movement, thanks to his efforts.

His next publication, in 1920, was entitled *Baym kval: Yidishe shprikhverter, vertlekn, glaykhvertlekh, rednsartn, farglay khenishn, brokhes, vintshenishn, Kloles, kharomes, simonim, sgules, zababones* (At the source: Yiddish proverbs, sayings, aphorisms, expressions, similes, blessings, wishes, curses, vehement curses, omens, folk remedies, folk beliefs).[61] The AVJHES had been founded one year earlier, in 1919, and its helpfulness was acknowledged. Bastomski was the collector and annotator. Zalmen Reyzen was the editor, together with the folklore section of the society. Bastomski published the work in his own publishing house, Di naye yidishe folkshul (The new Yiddish folk school).

The title, *Baym kval* (At the source), is a slight alteration of the expression *funem kval* ("from the source"). In the introduction Bastomski stated that he had stood for years, "at the source." The title is self-referential but also refers to a more experiential approach to folklore. Bastomski hoped that when one read this folklore, one would experience the folk source, just as he did, and not divorce the texts "from the source."

Bastomski's introduction showed the influence of the formation of the AVJHES and the striving for scholarship in folklore. He reviewed the short history of Yiddish folkloristics and placed his work in that context. He reiterated ideas on Yiddish folklore that I. L. Cahan and S. Ansky had expressed: the creative process of folklore as a collective or communal one, and the importance of folklore for the historian examining the past life of the folk.

Bastomski then provided a brief (yet, the most analytic up to that time) description of Yiddish of proverbs, based on the idea that every proverb had a premise (*hanokhe*) and a conclusion or deduction (*oysfir*)—an "if" and a "then" component.[62] Aphorisms, on the other hand, were used to express something, "in a hidden manner, allegorically, by way of example, . . . ironically, by giving hints or pokes."[63] He did not define "sayings" (*vertlekh*); he merely pointed out how numerous they were, as were the Yiddish similes (*farglaykhenishn*).

In the introduction, Bastomski enumerated a genealogy of Yiddish folklorists. The first folklorists were the three classic Yiddish writers: Mendele, Sholem-Aleichem, and Peretz. "They, the *klasiker*, the classic writers, gathered together the dispersed folk treasure and through these collected language treasures, they created the foundation of the national culture. The writers did not specifically collect material for Yiddish folklore. That work was carried out by folklorists who have set a specific goal—to register and to systemize all the proverbs and sayings that exist in the Yiddish language."[64]

By the 1920s, this *yikhes*, or ancestry, for Yiddish folklorists had become commonplace. The *klasiker* had created the field of Yiddish folklore by consciously using oral folklore forms in their work, thus raising the consciousness of Yiddish folklore among the East European masses. Modern secular Yiddish culture began with these writers because they appreciated the value of Yiddish folklore. They are the heros whose portraits will hang in every secular Yiddish schoolroom. Bastomski singled out Elzet's contribution as especially important for the use of literary sources.[65] Bastomski then immediately added that though folklorists take their material partially from "folk writers," most of it comes directly from the "folk mouth."

His short history of Yiddish proverb scholarship in Yiddish criticized Ignaz Bernstein's opus of Yiddish proverbs as faulty for its incompleteness: "he did not work in the center of Jewish folk creativity, in Lithuania." A *Litvish*-chauvinism ran through Bastomski's work, a chauvinism that is not noticeable with other Yiddish folklorists from other regions. This pride in his own territory may also have been a reason for Bastomski's strict adherence to standard Yiddish when transcribing his texts. Phonetically, standard Yiddish is closest to the Lithuanian dialect.

Bastomski assured the reader that the material had never been published anywhere else. For the past twelve years he had been collecting the material, "from the folk mouth in the authentic folk environment among the folk masses and also during talks with old people, artisans, wives, and others at home, in the market in the street."[66] The persons and places to which the folklorist ascribed "folkiness" followed the lead of the *klasiker*, who in their works created an "authentic" folkish environment in the shtetl. Bastomski ignored contemporary Yiddish folklore collectors such as Shmuel Lehman in Warsaw, who were including social groups previously deemed off-limits to folklorists. Bastomski's contribution was not in redefinitions of folk and folklore, but in the practical application of the material.

The proverb section in *Baym kval* was systematized in the manner set down by Bernstein: the key words in the proverb rather than the general meaning served as the marker in the systemization. Bastomski went one step beyond Bernstein by dividing the various genres. He claimed the section on "curses, wishes, blessings, oaths" was the first such collection in Yiddish folklore, though he reprinted some omens from the previous collection of A. Bukhbinder. Since the earlier collection had no system and was hard to find, he justified its inclusion.

Bastomski concluded his introduction with a call for the collection of all proverbs and sayings, for the number was so large that, "one needs a pail to draw them, in the words of Noyekh Prilutski."[67] The folklore would be for the new "*folks-inteligent*, led by the new teacher. . . . What belongs to the folk, we will return to the folk and we will do it in the same way all other peoples do it—through the young, yet already developed and powerful, modern Yiddish school."[68]

Though the work is more scholarly than the earlier ones by Bastomski, annotation is infrequent, and many texts are not understandable. References to parallels in Ignaz Bernstein's work are given, and an occasional anecdote to illustrate the proverb. The proverb section is not numbered and occupies the first twelve pages. The sayings, expressions, and idioms occupy half the book, seventy-six pages of the work. The ten pages of similes that follow are also cross-referenced with Bernstein. The third section, "Wishes, Blessings, and Oaths," the fourth section, "Curses," and the fifth section, "Folk Omens, Beliefs, Folk Remedies," conclude the work. This last section is a wonderful contribution to a genre that was overlooked almost completely by the Warsaw folklorists and would be later pursued by the YIVO Ethnographic Commission, in the second half of the decade. It was the only section in Bastomski's book that was not oral folklore. Its inclusion implies that Bastomski ideologically viewed omens and remedies in the same manner as he did proverbs. Did the folklorist believe that schoolchildren should be taught the old omens and remedies? Whether Bastomski would have included them in a school curriculum is never described. Bastomski published smaller works of tales and jokes, but never school texts of beliefs, omens, or remedies.

After *Baym kval*, Bastomski continued his application of folklore to school pedagogy in his small booklet, *Der kundes* (The prankster).[69] The small-format collection contains 121 riddles not previously published. Bastomski was earnest about his goal to have folk literature become part of the new school curriculum. The booklet was just the beginning of dozens of such books containing folk material for "the new school."

In 1922, Bastomski published his first collection of Yiddish folk songs, as a supplement to the first publication of the AVJHES, *Pinkes: To the History of Vilne during the Years of War and Occupation*.[70] This entire collection and its introduction were reprinted and enlarged for publication as a book a year later. *Baym kval: materialn tsum yidishn folklor—yidishe folkslider* (At the source: Materials for Yiddish folklore—Yiddish folk songs) appeared in 1923.[71] Bastomski's twenty-three-page introduction dealt entirely with the nature of the Yiddish folk song and concluded with the "Guidelines to record works of folk creations," which S. Ansky had put together for the AVJHES.

Cover of Tunkeler's *Yidishistn* satirizing the "discovery" of folklore among older Jews.

Shmuel Lehman listening to an informant of Yiddish folklore and transcribing her text, Warsaw, 1931. Surrounding him are admiring folklore students. (*YIVO Institute for Jewish Research, New York.*)

Pinkhes Graubard. (*YIVO Institute for Jewish Research, New York.*)

Hershele, on the left, in Lodz, 1909. The Yiddish writer I. H. Radoshitski is on the right.(*YIVO Institute for Jewish Research, New York.*)

Menakhem Kipnis, center. (*YIVO Institute for Jewish Research, New York.*)

Yiddish folklore as temple: cover of Yehude Elzet's work, *Der vunder-oytser fun der yidisher shprakh* [The Wonderful Treasure of the Yiddish Language].

Photo of Shloyme Bastomski and Gershon Pludermakher, fellow Yiddish
pedagogue in Vilne, at Pludermakher's summer home, 1938. (*YIVO Institute
for Jewish Research, New York.*)

Group photo taken on the occasion of I. L. Cahan's folklore seminar in YIVO
in Vilne, 1930. Cahan sits in the middle; to the right is Nekhame Epshteyn;
next to her is Shloyme Bastomski; and far right is Shmuel Zaynvil Pipe; seated
far left is Aron Engeltsin; next to him is Khaye Feyn-Engeltsin. (*YIVO Institute
for Jewish Research, New York.*)

Khaykl Lunski in Strashun Library. (*YIVO Institute for Jewish Research, New York.*)

Shmuel Zaynvil Pipe and Nekhame Epshteyn taking inventory of Judaica in YIVO archives, Vilne, in the 1930s. (*YIVO Institute for Jewish Research, New York.*)

YIVO *zamler* Khayim Sheskin in his Brooklyn apartment with his wife, Brayne, an informant for the *zamler* Berl Verblunski, 1991. (*Photo Itzik Gottesman*)

YIVO *zamler* Moyshe Tolpin, Ostrow, Poland, in the 1930s. (*Courtesy Martha Tolpin.*)

Noyekh Prilutski. (*YIVO Institute for Jewish Research, New York.*)

Bastomski articulated the reasons why Yiddish folk songs were important. He had written that proverbs were vital because they were part of our folklife, and fast disappearing with the older generation. But he did not explain why the proverb genre specifically was vital to collect. Folk songs, Bastomski wrote, reflected the memoirs of a people. Borrowing an image from I. L. Cahan, he added that folk songs direct one to the "most hidden corners of the folk's soul."[72] The entire introduction draws directly from Cahan's introduction to his two-volume collection of folk songs, in terms of ideas and style—the latter exemplified by long citations of songs to illustrate a point. Like Cahan, Bastomski believed that the author of the folk songs, "is the folk itself." The folk song poet, he felt, reflected the folk directly: "His ideas are directly drawn from life around him, from the folk mouth and from his own soul."

This was a slightly more individualistic conception of the folk song writer than that of Cahan, who had deemphasized the individual's role. Perhaps this was a result of Prilutski's writings, which gave a larger role to the individual in the folk song creation process. Bastomski quoted Prilutski a page later on the "quivering of the soul" as the spark of folk song creation.

For Bastomski, folk songs were also valuable in the study of the ethnography and the history of the Jews; a "mirror of the one time patriarchal Jewish life." Historically, the songs pointed out the suffering of the poorer masses during pogroms, recruitment, and the First World War. He mentioned S. Lehman's songs on the Russian revolution to underline the emergence of a new workers' movement with its own songs. Since the introduction first appeared in a *Pinkes*, or book of records, about occupied Vilne, much of the discussion was centered upon recent events and the songs that had evolved as a result. Bastomski's introduction revealed the influence of Cahan's and Ansky's romanticism (the idea that the folk song must be old and composed by the folk, the importance of the melody), Prilutski's expanded definition of the folk composer, and Lehman's broad view of what was a folk song. Bastomski believed that the Yiddish folk song, alone among the genres, was appreciated by the Jewish intelligentsia. He attributed this to the melodies that "find a reaction in everyone's heart."

In the introduction, Bastomski reviewed the Yiddish folk song literature and assured the reader that none of the songs he printed had been printed before. He published variants, since each variant had its own unique characteristics. The author had collected most of the songs over the previous ten years. Other songs were from material collected by the AVJHES, particularly Khaykl Lunski. Other collectors for the AVJHES were from the Literary Section of the First Yiddish Children's Club, led by Emindov Margolin and Yitskhok Broydes.[73] Only at the end of the introduction does it become clear that the collection in the volume was a collaborative effort, in part organized by the AVJHES. Bastomski's title page referred to himself as the one who "collected, annotated, classified, reviewed, and edited" the texts. The work should be considered a partial manifestation of the work of the society, particulary the children's songs section, one-third of which is made up by contributions of the Jewish Children's Club.

Bastomski acknowledged that the transcription in literary or standard Yiddish was an error. He also regretted the lack of musical notation. In earlier works, this transcription would have made sense, since the Yiddish schoolchild was the top priority. This work makes no mention of the new Yiddish school student. It was to be a strictly scholarly edition. The "folksinteligent" (folk intelligentsia) replaced the "yidishe shul kind" (Jewish schoolchild) as the intended reader for this volume. Bastomski still referred to the teachers as the heads of these "folksinteligentn." However, Bastomski called upon his readers to collect, rather than to teach. They were to lead the way in the field of folklore.

To add to this scholarly apparatus, Bastomski added "Guidelines for Recording Items of Folk Creation," prepared by S. Ansky for the AVJHES.[74] These guidelines offer some technical advice (e.g., one text per page; record name, age, occupation, where born, date; transcribe exactly as spoken) and emphasize the oral nature of the folklore: the folklorist should not let the informant write the text, and should ensure that the text was not learned from a written source. One point raised the issue of obscenity, which the Yiddish folklorist had not dealt with in the open: "One should not refrain from recording the most obscene, cynical words and expression. In ethnography there is no cynicism or obscenity."[75]

How would the Yiddish folklorist reconcile the wonderful vision of the masses with obscene folklore? Such a reconciliation never occurred, for no obscene folklore was published, though it was collected. Only Ignaz Bernstein published a collection of Yiddish erotica, a volume that was never mentioned or cross-referenced by other Yiddish folklor-ists.[76] Both Graubard and Lehman collected from lower-class elements, yet even their texts, while shocking for some readers, contain few ob-scenities.

Many of Ansky's points were not followed in the collection that fol-lowed. The names and places of informants were rarely printed. The di-alect was not transcribed at all. Bastomski occasionally cross-referenced previously printed works, but he did not do a thorough job.[77] The texts are printed in small type and it is sometimes impossible to tell where one stanza ends and another begins.

While technically flawed, the collection is particularly good for its children's games and songs, of which few previously had been published in Yiddish. Together with Lehman's collection in *Bay undz yidn,* also published in 1923, the genre of children's folklore had taken a central position in Yiddish folklore studies. Given Bastomski's work as a teacher, the amount of children's folklore is not surprising.

In a section entitled "Religious-National and Chasidic Songs," Bas-tomski included three variants of the woman's prayer, "Got fun avrom." Ansky and Cahan had protested vigorously against this inclusion when Prilutski had printed them in 1911. This revealed a certain independence on Bastomski's part. He learned from many folklorists but did not prefer one's outlook over another. He was clearly influenced by Ansky, but did not share all his opinions. The section of historical songs, which included songs describing events only a few years earlier, also contrasted with the "old songs" notion of Cahan. Bastomski reaffirmed Lehman's and Pri-lutski's ideas of what constituted a folksong, but only to a point: Bastom-ski said one song should not have been incorporated into his collection, since the author, *maskilic* writer Mikhl Gordon, was known. Prilutksi and Lehman also did not include the *maskilic* writers in their collections, but theoretically they could have, for they printed songs whose authors were identified.

Half of the section entitled "Parodyes un folks-humoreskes" is made up of humorous folktales. The reason for their inclusion in a vol-ume of folk songs is unclear. There are other errors that a good editor would have caught. A famous song by Mark Varshavski, "Di yontifdike teg," is included and is unidentified. Two additional supplements at the end of the volume add to the impression that Bastomski worked and edited quickly. In summary, this key work was the sloppiest edition of all the Yiddish folklore collections: barely legible, poorly annotated, and inconsistently categorized.

Several years later, in 1929, when Bastomski reviewed Lehman's *Ganovim-lider*, he criticized the author for not transcribing phonetically or adequately classifying.[78] He also questioned whether the included songs were "authentic" folk songs. What qualified their authenticity? Their distribution, and that factor had yet to be researched. Bastomski analyzed Lehman's work psychologically, examining the emotions of the Jewish thief as revealed in the songs. Bastomski had constricted his definitions of "authentic" and "folk song" since his earlier work. Ironically, Bastomski wrote of Lehman's collection, that the use of a literary transcription in an attempt to popularize the work was "a great minus." This was written at a time when Bastomski published only folk texts edited for children. The contradiction revealed his dual loyalty to folklore— one to the scholarship, the other to the popularization of folklore in the new Yiddish secular school.

On the inside back cover, Bastomski concluded his collection with a call, "To all friends of the Yiddish language and of the Yiddish folk creation." He called on all those who consider "the development of the Yiddish language, of Yiddish literature valuable" to assist. The teacher would have a special role in this endeavor: "A special obligation to take on this work lays with the Yiddish folk-teacher, who is found in the towns. There in the province, where there are still survivals of the old-time patriarchal Jewish life, one can accomplish a great deal for this effort."[79]

There were therefore two reasons to involve the teachers: not only could they inculcate the new secular folkloric Yiddishist values to the children, but they could also collect folklore as a result of their geographic distribution. The YIVO Institute for Jewish Research continued this strategy and also, upon its founding in 1925, immediately called upon the teachers for help. When Prilutski and Graubard made their call on the eve of the First World War, the teachers had not yet become a sizable force. By 1923, the teachers of secular schools had grown to be a group worthy of attention.

Bastomski asked the collectors to send him the material, and did not mention the AVJHES. Since Ansky's "guidelines" at the beginning of the volume instructed collectors to send materials to the AVJHES, the

potential *zamler* ("collector") would have been confused. The influence
of Bastomski's call to collect had some effect. Khayim Sheskin, a future
collector for YIVO's Ethnographic/Folklore Commission, began to collect Yiddish folksongs after having read Bastomski's call in 1923.[80] Before
the YIVO was organized, he had collected and sent materials to Bastomski. When YIVO was established in 1925, he received a letter from Zalmen Reyzen asking him to now send the materials to YIVO, a sign that
Bastomski was no longer seeking outside collections. He had given that
activity over to the YIVO.

The folk song collection, *Baym kval,* was Bastomski's last truly
scholarly folklore work. His future projects, while keeping scholarship
in mind, were geared for the schools. In 1925, he edited a collection of
legends on the founder of the Hasidic movement, Yisrol Baal Shem Tov.[81]
This was the first of a projected series of "Jewish Folktales and Legends."
In the introduction, the author decried the lost treasures that "modern
Jewish culture" had neglected. The blame lay with the intelligentsia,
who "hated the vernacular and despised the folk's creations." Bastomski
thought that the folklore genre that suffered the most from this neglect
was the folktale. Proverbs and sayings are transferred with the language.
Songs are remembered thanks to the melodies. Fortunately, a "miracle"
occurred to help the folktale: many of the folktales were saved in the
numerous ethical holy books and tale collections published for women.
Other nations had expeditions and organized efforts to collect such tales;

> In our case, the simple preachers did the work, or miracle workers, or book
> peddlers who could not write a sentence correctly. Of course, the work was
> not done appropriately; but it is no wonder. In addition to the fact that
> they were not educated, their attitude toward this work was very different.
> Their goal was to instill traditional belief in God. They did not care so much
> about the tale, as about the moral, without which there would be no tale.
> We are interested in the tale itself—the directness of creation, the purity and
> substantiveness of the folk tongue.[82]

In the next paragraph, Bastomski quoted Ansky on how folklore provides us with an understanding of national character and worldview. Yet
from the above citation, it is clear that Bastomski attempted to examine national character by excluding the morality of Jewish folktales, a
morality that comprises the heart of that worldview. Bastomski tried to
reconcile the paradox of using texts of the small-town "patriarchal" Jewish society and recontextualizing them for a new generation of Yiddish

schoolchildren removed from the original context by emphasizing the stylistic and aesthetic dimensions of the texts.

Bastomski called this work the first Yiddish folktale collection. If he meant as a separate volume, in Yiddish, and with a scholarly apparatus, he was correct. Earlier, Lehman and Prilutski had each published collections in larger anthologies. In a letter to Shmuel Niger, Bastomski referred to it as "the first modern publication of Yiddish folktales."[83] Bastomski told Niger that the work was only a beginning and that he planned to read the old chapbooks and cull tales from them for future volumes. In another letter to Niger, he mentioned his editing of old chapbooks: "There is much [old folktale material], but the gold in them has been dumped with garbage and to clean them one needs much time and money. I am not stingy with time; with money, it's this way—when I earn something from the textbooks, I sink it into folklore. No publisher will publish these things."[84]

Only a few tales in the volume were collected orally. Almost all of the tales were from previously published collections; mostly from earlier Hasidic collections, since, "those legends were for the most part communicated almost untouched—in their primitive folk tone with all their folk expressions."[85] However, he did edit, "clarifying the mistakes, extracting the story, comparing with variants." Some were taken from more modern works, such as Ansky's *Khurbn galitsye* (Destruction of Galicia), where the tales were not "artistically reworked" but written as heard.[86] The introduction concluded with a call for artists to turn the "raw primitive folktales into folksy stories." "Folksy stories," or "*folkstimlkhe geshikhtn*," was a reference to the book of reworked folktales by I. L. Peretz and a turning point in the interest in folklore by the Yiddish intelligentsia. This was the first time that Bastomski looked to belles lettres as a model for the readaptation of folk materials.

Bastomski's selection of Hasidic tales distinguished him from the other Yiddish folktale collectors. I. L. Cahan had sought folktales with international parallels, and S. Lehman published texts of the lower classes, cante fables, and tales of Elijah the Prophet. Though Bastomski was the most closely aligned with the modern secular Yiddishist movement of all the folklorists, he chose the traditional tales of Hasidim. Since he claimed that he was not interested in the ethical implications of the texts, Bastomski saw no contradiction in presenting Hasidic tales. I. L. Peretz, after all, the spiritual godfather of the Yiddishist movement, saw Hasidic literature as the beginning of modern Yiddish literature. The cover to the volume reveals the opening of a scroll, inside which one will find old, bearded religious Jews—living people, looking at the reader. This suggested that by reading these tales, the twentieth-century reader would encounter and connect to these Jews of the nineteenth century. Bastomski's publishing house trademark, a scroll with "Di naye yidishe folkshul" printed inside, is a symbolic secularization of a religious artifact: what is done iconographically on the cover is done textually inside the covers. Religious materials are recontextualized for a secular world.

The following year, 1926, Bastomski published his only collected *purim-shpiln*. The booklet contains two *shpiln* taken from old printed versions and represents an attempt on Bastomski's part to ease, "the work of researching or restoring the *purim-shpiln* to the stage."[87] His attempt was inspired by Max Weinreich's modern production of an old *purim-shpil* with the students of the Vilne Teacher's Seminary a few years earlier. This production traveled around Vilne and to Warsaw and was quite successful. After his 1926 book on *purim-shpiln*, Bastomski did not write any more folkloristic introductions; he would publish only the texts of the tales and legends, edited for students. All together, he published thirty-two such booklets.

Bastomski was usually occupied with the editing of two popular journals, *Der khaver* and *Grininke beymelekh*, the former a periodical for older children, founded in 1929, the latter a journal for smaller children, founded in 1925. Both journals contained jokes and tales from Bastomski's collections, often collected orally. The folklore material in these journals was not unanimously greeted; as one reviewer phrased it, "Why lug out-of-date tales from the archives, which do not contain one ounce of artistic color, and which, except for the moral and religious examples that are enveloped in gray rhetoric, never existed in them?"[88]

Yet Bastomski was dedicated to the use of folklore and his critics did not deter him. In 1931, Bastomski published a small collection of Yiddish jokes collected by him which was also geared for the schoolchild.[89] There is no indication how the texts were collected. During the 1930s, he concentrated his folklore efforts on jokes and witty tales. Even under Soviet occupation in 1940, he continued to publish such works.[90] He was an indefatigable collector, editor, publisher, and pedagogue and one of the leading spokespeople for Yiddishism in Vilne, which was the center of the new ideology. As would be expected, he particularly concentrated his efforts on the school front.[91] In 1937, he called for a united front on behalf of the Yiddish schools internationally.

His contribution to Yiddish folkloristics, because it was so entrenched in the new Yiddishist nationalist ideology, was full of contradictions. He, more than any other Yiddish folklorist, introduced ideology into the discussion of why collecting and teaching folklore was important. Ultimately, he felt impelled to "save" as much as he could for his schoolchildren, whether the materials were appropriate or not. In this respect, caught between the traditional world and the new modern Yiddish world, he is a symbol of Vilne at that time, a city that was simultaneously the "Jerusalem of Lithuania" and the theoretical center of Yiddish secularism. Bastomski brought the two together through Yiddish folklore.

PART III

The Culmination:
YIVO Ethnographic Commission

CHAPTER 5

The 1920s

$\cdot\!\!\cdot\!\!\S\!\!\cdot\!\!\S\!\!\cdot$

Yiddishist Scholarship before the YIVO Institute

The establishment of a "Yiddish University" was realized with the founding of *Der yidisher visnshaftlekher institut* (YIVO) in Vilne in 1925. This was the culmination of a dream that Yiddish intellectuals had discussed ever since the Chernovitz Language Conference in 1908. At that conference, Matisyohu Miese's talk on the history of Yiddish was an eye-opener for the participants, who had never heard a scholarly paper in Yiddish, much less such a talk as Miese's, which aggressively defended the status of the language against its detractors.[1] At Chernovitz the need to organize disparate cultural activities became apparent, and this eventually led to the discussion of a Yiddish academy.

The sorry state of the collection of folklore and the need for a structuring of the discipline was also part of this discussion.[2] In an essay in *Der pinkes* entitled "The Goals of Yiddish Philology," Marxist-Zionist leader Ber Borokhov called for the institutionalization of Yiddish philology, yet did not use the term "university" but instead spoke of "a degree-granting" national organization for philological goals.[3] In another, lesser-known, article in that same year, he called for "a stable academy or society for philological purposes in general."[4]

Borokhov could have been called the initiator of YIVO, but that credit was given to Nokhem Shtif, whose "Memorandum" led to YIVO's creation twelve years after Borokhov's essay. In the years before the First World War, when the first serious debate on a central Yiddish institute emerged, Shtif reviewed *Der pinkes* and thought Borokhov had overstated the importance of philology in the national revival of the oppressed nations. What about "history," asked Shtif?[5] Borokhov compared the nationalism of other nations, such as the Bulgarians, to that of the Jews, and Shtif found this inappropriate. The Yiddish-speaking Jews were in a much worse situation, Shtif maintained, for they had, from without and from within, enemies who denied the very uniqueness of their language. Shtif preferred to be compared, if at all, to the German-language reformists or the Russians, who were linguistically closer to Yiddish.

In 1914, there was more discussion in the Yiddish press of a Jewish university in Eastern Europe.[6] That campaign, however, was a result of the exclusion of Jews from non-Jewish institutions, rather than a quest for an original Yiddish scholarly institute. Yiddishists also rejected the idea of a Jewish university in Jerusalem, for they viewed the result of such a project as a tool of the Zionist Party and not of "klal yisrol," the entire Jewish people.

The impulse to evolve a scholarly apparatus in Yiddish found expression in the idea to publish a Yiddish encyclopedia. Jewish scholars had by the 1930s published encyclopedias in Russian, English, German, and Hebrew. Like the university, the encyclopedia symbolized an entry into the international world of scholarship. The first effort for a Yiddish encyclopedia was made in 1905, but many ideas floated around Yiddishist circles and an attempt to publish such a reference work was done every few years.[7] These projects stressed the connection with the "masses" that such an encyclopedia sought to educate.[8] The idea of an encyclopedia also fit into the positivist foundation of the emerging Yiddishist ideology, since the amassing of knowledge was considered the first step in scholarship.

In addition to the desire for an encyclopedia, Yiddishists also promoted the "folk universities" as another means to disseminate Yiddishism among the populace. According to one of its greatest proponents, frequent lecturer Avrom Gliksman, the "folk university" phenomenon took off throughout Europe after the First World War. Well-known professors preferred teaching the workers who attended the "folk universities."[9] Warsaw had three such Jewish institutions in 1925. If Gliksman were typical of the activists in the "folk universities," then it seems that by the 1920s, the idea of such institutions had evolved into the alternative to the higher "elitist" institutions of learning represented by YIVO. Gliksman rejected the notion that the Yiddish classicists wrote the finest works in Yiddish literature; he felt that they only widened the distance between the intelligentsia and the folk. They did not write for *all* of the people. The sciences, he maintained, were a more urgent field of study than literature. [10]

YIVO could have taken the direction of or partially incorporated the "folk university," but instead rejected it. [11] In the Soviet Union, Yiddish scholarship had a more populist approach and had begun its institutional development before the founding of YIVO. In 1923, the Yiddish section at the Chair for Scholarly Linguistic Research in Kharkov published its first journal, *Yiddish*, "the first fruit of Soviet-sponsored Jewish scholarship in Russia." [12]

In Warsaw, the idea of a philologically oriented academic institution was kept alive by Noyekh Prilutski, who envisioned his *Zamlbikher* of 1912 and 1917 as a beginning in that direction. These volumes were, however, one-man operations, and did not include the wide network of contributors one found in Niger's *Pinkes*.

The first coming together of the Warsaw and Vilne Yiddishist scholars was in the journal *Yidishe filologye*, which first appeared in early 1924. [13] This was a "A Journal for the Investigation of the Yiddish Language, Literature, and Ethnography"—the three pillars of philology. The editorial group included two philologists from Vilne, Dr. Max Weinreich and Zalmen Reyzen (thirty and thirty-seven years old, respectively), and one from Warsaw, Prilutski, who was forty-two years old. Weinreich and Reyzen had published an open letter to all interested in Yiddish philology a year earlier, in 1923, which appealed for the organization and establishment of an "institute for Yiddish linguistics and literary research whose first goal will be the creation of a permanent philological journal." [14] The journal was born before the institute, and *Yidishe filologye* was the first Jewish philological journal. One can surmise that it was Prilutski who added the ethnographic component in the title, since Reyzen and Weinreich did not include this third "pillar" in their plan.

Yidishe filologye was a forerunner to YIVO's Yiddishist approach and the institute's attempt to define Yiddish secular culture. The first essay in the journal was Nokhem Shtif's analysis of Yiddish literature of

the Middle Ages. As other Yiddishists before and after him, Shtif sought
to establish a genealogy of Yiddish secularism. In his account, Yiddish
literature was from its inception not only a religious literature. In fact,
the most popular literature was secular Yiddish folk songs adapted from
German sources, and Jewish reworkings of world literature. Shtif concluded, however, that while the secular Yiddish literature was well received in Germany and Western Europe, it did not have a great impact
on Polish Jews until the nineteenth century.[15] The location of this essay
as the introduction to the journal implied a vague program in which the
editors agreed with Shtif's genealogy. In fact, they would expand upon
this Yiddishist literary genealogy in years to come.

The first issue of *Yiddishe filologye* included bits of folklore and
ethnography scattered among the articles by N. Prilutski, Alfred Landau,
F. Alfabet, and Moyshe Lerer.[16] These articles, which were concerned
with the etymology and explanation of words, also included occasional
discussions of local Jewish customs. For example, Lerer, who collected
material in his hometown of Chelm, explained the term *gele matses* (yellow matzohs) as the egg matzohs eaten on the Sabbath after Passover. He
suggested that the term was a folk etymology of *geules-matse,* redemp-
tion from the matzoh.

Such ethnographic details also surfaced in the penultimate section of "Miscellaneous notes," most notably in Prilutski's contribution,
"Grins af shvuos" (Greenery for Shavuoth), where he listed the terms for
reeds that were strewn on the floor during the holiday of Shavuoth.[17] The
editors also took the opportunity to print some of the folklore material
sent to them by a growing number of collectors. "Two Contemporary
Folksongs" about the rise of the value of the dollar were submitted by
Khane Perlshteyn and Borukh Kats from the town of Vashlikova.[18]

In the next issue, much more folklore was included. Alfred Landau's review of Prilutski's first volume of folk songs was a serious contribution to the discussion of what makes a Jewish folk song Jewish.[19] Most
other folklorists probably did not agree with Landau's inclination toward
finding German origins for almost all the songs. The article should have
engendered a lively debate on the issue, but since Landau was considered
the "Dean" of Yiddish philology, his viewpoints on language or folklore
were never challenged in print.

The first serious article in Yiddish on Jewish folk medicine by
Elye Sosnovik, with supplemental annotation by Max Weinreich, fol-

lowed Landau's review.[20] Weinreich's notes were the innovative part of this work, for he compared the Jewish customs with German, Polish, Ukrainian, Lithuanian, White Russian, and Russian customs and determined that Sosnovik's material was Jewish folklore and not entirely borrowed from other peoples, as Max Grunwald, among others, had written in German-Jewish periodicals.[21]

The next and last issue began with a translation of an article on the evil eye by Regina Lilienthal, one of the leading Jewish folklorists who worked in the Polish language.[22] Lilienthal, unlike the philologists, was not interested in the comparative approach to the material. She began her analysis of the evil eye in Jewish tradition with the Bible and ignored coterritorial evil eye customs. For other folklorists writing in Yiddish, this was an example of how to combine analysis with texts, something that the Yiddish folklorists were then only attempting to do.

The publication of analytic essays and not just collections was also a sign that the discipline was maturing with some self-confidence. This would become evident in YIVO's *Filologishe shriftn* and *YIVO-bleter,* in which folk text collections would predominate the literature, but occasional articles on the meaning of the texts would also be published. *Yididshe filologye* was published for just one year, as the editors moved on to the founding of the Yiddish academic institute they had sought to erect, the YIVO. All that was needed was some organizational prompting. Nokhem Shtif provided that motivation.

The Founding of YIVO

Nokhem Shtif (1879–1933) was one of the leading Yiddish philologists, specializing in the field of linguistics and cultural history. It was Shtif's memorandum, *Vegn a yidishn akademishn institut* (On a Yiddish academic institute), which he sent out in February 1925 to various Yiddish scholars in Berlin, Poland, and the United States, that led to the founding of YIVO.[23] According to Shtif, Yiddish scholarship in Yiddish, or Yiddishist scholarship, began with Niger's *Pinkes.* For Shtif, Yiddishist scholarship denoted an academy whose goal would be to make the folk aware of its scholars and whose scholarly work would benefit the folk. Shtif's words were also part of the nationalist discourse of the Jews in interwar Poland. The Jews were a people with national rights and were determined to study themselves on their own terms. Shtif wrote, "We should begin to research the Yiddish language for itself, as an organic development, not as an aid to *Germanistik.*[24] The time was ripe for an organized Yiddishist scholarship.

In his layout of the various disciplines that would be researched in such an academy, Shtif stressed philology as "the most natural for the Yiddish linguist who grew up in a Jewish atmosphere."[25] His review of Yiddish folkloristics within his broader delineation of the history of Yiddish philology included a discussion of folk song, proverbs, folk drama, and jokes. He singled out Prilutski for praise for his accurate transcription of folk texts. Shtif pointed out that no matter how wonderful the collections were, the methodology was more important. The non-Yiddish journals that printed the folklore often "ruined" the Yiddish. In a Yiddish journal, Shtif implied, the texts would finally get the respect they deserved. His use of the term "methodology" referred only to the publication of the texts, not to the analysis of them. The *Memorandum* followed the Grimms' tradition, placing folklore at the service of language study. This would later also be the approach of the YIVO Ethnographic Commission.

Shtif proposed to divide up Yiddish scholarship into four sections: one for Yiddish philology; one for Jewish history; one to deal with social and economic issues; and a pedagogical section. Within the philology section, he proposed a department for folklore which would "collect, research, systematize, and publish critical editions of our '*folkshafung.*'"[26]

After the release of the *Memorandum,* the Central Educational Committee (TsBi.Ko) in Vilne soon assembled the leading Yiddish teachers and scholars, including Max Weinreich and Zalmen Reyzen, and composed a reply to Shtif's memo. This response, entitled "Vilner tezisn vegn yidishn visnshaftlekhn institut" (Vilne theses on the Yiddish scientific institute), was soon published together with Shtif's essay.[27] The Vilne circle suggested replacing the "philological section" with a "linguistic-literary research section," which would be divided into language and literature. The collection of folklore would belong to the language subsection. The Vilne document also included the notion that fieldwork "instructions will be sent to teachers and other collectors," which the Ethnographic Commission (EC) did indeed do soon thereafter.[28] As in Shtif's work, the "Theses" stressed the collection process and did not concern themselves with methodology.

Shtif had considered Berlin the natural center for a Yiddish academic institute, since the city was a gateway to both Eastern and Western Europe, but Shtif was insecure about the future of Jewish intellectual life in Berlin. Though he agreed that Berlin would be more attractive to the international scholarly community, he campaigned for Vilne, Lithuania, to become the home of the institute. He felt that mass support could be found only in a city like Vilne, where there would be a "lively atmosphere." The Vilne activists thought their town was already overburdened with too many organizations. A compromise left the official center in Berlin, but the East European division in Vilne.[29] In fact, other than Shtif's canvassing for YIVO in Berlin and a few meetings, all of the institute's work was conducted in Vilne by the fall of 1925. Shtif left Europe to head the "Chair for Jewish Culture" at the Ukrainian Academy of Sciences in Kiev in 1926 and YIVO established itself in Vilne as they became more organized.

Writing ten years after the founding, Max Weinreich stated that the Lithuanian city was appropriate, for Vilne incorporated both Jewish tradition and Jewish modernity. The city had had its share of pogroms and "Only in the houses and in the stones where there remained a remembrance of those horrible times, could secular Jews build institutes which could be secular and still Jewish."[30] This notion that anti-Semitism kept the Jews together is interesting in light of Weinreich's later characterization of Yiddish as "the language of the *derekh ha-shas*," the way of the Talmud (Has-shas refers to the six books of the Talmud).[31] *Derekh ha-shas* explained the interdependence of East European Jewish life and the Yiddish language and begged the question of how one maintained the Yiddish language if one left one's religious roots, as Yiddishist intellectuals had done. What would nourish their culture if not the religion? Weinreich never answered this question directly, but in his statement on why Vilne could foster secular Yiddishism, he offered an indirect reply; a view that is based on territory and historical, collective memory.

The YIVO Ethnographic Commission: 1925–27

In the first issue of YIVO's bulletin, "Yedies fun yidishn visnshaftlekhn institut," which was published in the Warsaw *Literarishe bleter* of October 9, 1925, no mention was made of folklore, though questionnaires were discussed for other disciplines.[32] In the next issue, printed two weeks later, notice was given that "Di folkloristishe komisye" had begun work and a work plan was in the process of being devised. In the third issue of the bulletin, on November 6, 1925, the Folklore Commission, part of the Philological Section, announced that its first meeting had been held on October 27. At that meeting contacts with other countries were discussed. It was decided that instructions would be sent out to collectors (*zamlers*). Questionnaires for specific genres would be "systematically distributed." Max Weinreich directed the commission at this earliest stage and would head it for its entire fourteen-year history. He was the driving force and intellectual organizer of its activities.

The next issue of the YIVO bulletin (November 20, 1925) revealed how quickly the commission had developed. The title of the group now read "Ethnographic (Folklore) Commission" and the commission printed its "Rules for Collectors of Ethnographic Material" and the first questionnaire sent to collectors on Jewish legends.[33]

The "Rules" listed ten points, most of them technical advice. The first point warned not to decline to write something down "because it is already known." This was to prevent the sort of experiences that other collectors had had when the informant laughed at the very idea that someone would be interested in what he or she had to say or sing. Since folklore collection was a new phenomenon, the commission worried that folklore would be seen as insignificant by collector and informant. The Rules, therefore, explained the notion of "variants" to highlight the individual contribution that each collector could make. "It could be that it has already been transcribed, but in a slightly different version. And even so, for science it is important to determine how wide the territory of an ethnographic development has spread."[34]

Other points discussed the importance of exact transcription in regional dialect of the unedited text. The *zamler* was told not to shy away from obscene folklore, for "Ethnography does not measure aesthetics and records everything that exists in the folklife." Other technical points advised the collector to use a pad and pencil, to leave a margin, and to use one piece of paper per item. This was asked because the "Commission had much material to look at." Apparently, in just a few months' time, people in the field had been sending in texts even before the first questionnaire was printed.

During these first months, the commission apparently expected that the correspondents themselves would be the informants. Point nine asked collectors, "if the item is recorded from someone else," to please write down the informant's name, the date, and the collector's name. The phenomenon of folks-intelligentsia actually going among fellow townspeople to record folklore might have taken the commission by surprise when it began on a large scale soon after the organization of the EC. The "rules" were clearly concerned with the texts, and required minimal information on the performers. The commission did not ask collectors to include any other extensive background information on the informant or the collector (such as age, job, or family background). The purpose of this project was to collect texts only. The "Rules" became an important document for collectors in the field when they were published separately and distributed some time in 1926.[35] Correspondence with *zamlers* over the next five years showed a close reliance on this field-work guide.

Whom did the commission target as its first collectors? The representatives of the Yiddishist movement had always been the teachers of the Yiddish schools, and they were to form the first pool of collectors. For Bastomski's collections, teachers had sent him materials from Vilne schools. Shtif, in praising the new Yiddish school movement, was well aware of the importance of the teacher as intermediary between folk and scholar.

In a letter dated October 26, 1925, Weinreich wrote to the board of the Jewish high school in Wilkomir, Latvia, about the activities of the new, "Ethnographic-Folklore Commission." One should remember that the boards of Yiddish schools, the *farvaltung*, at that time were composed of the teachers themselves and other Yiddishist intellectuals in the town. Weinreich appealed to them to participate, so that "great treasures" would not be lost.[36] In January 1926, a similar letter in the form of an appeal was sent, "to all friends and lovers of the Jewish folk creation, especially to all teachers of all Yiddish schools; to the youth, no difference what political leanings."[37] The appeal also singled out those who could transcribe music to work with collectors in recording dances, tunes, and *purim-shpiln*. The instructions, "Rules," and a questionnaire would be sent to those who replied.

In late November the commission, now officially referred to as the Ethnographic Commission, met with various schools in Vilne to discuss its work. The commission hoped that teachers would interest their students in collecting as well.[38]

The EC and the AVJHES combined forces for a couple of years, beginning in early 1926, and the official name of the commission became the EC of the AVJHES and of the YIVO Institute. This must have elevated S. Bastomksi to one of the leaders of the EC, for he was the most experienced folklorist in Vilne and was also a member of the AVJHES.

The first questionnaire, sent out in November 1925, was on Jewish legends, and introduced the genre in the following way: "The Jewish people have among them a certain type of 'tale' which describes great personalities: kings who persecuted Jews or helped them; wealthy Jews, clever ones or close to the heads of state. Today, these stories are all far from reality, but the folk hides in them their longing for better times or fear of the horrible past."[39]

As sample questions for collectors, the EC mentioned legends about the biblical patriarchs, the prophet Elijah, kings or other rulers who oppressed or helped Jews, Napoleon, wealthy philanthropists such as Rothschild, or Moses Montifiore. It is unknown why this was chosen as the first questionnaire. The psychological motivation that the EC gave for the telling of such legends among Jews considered the legends a reflection of the tension among Jews in Poland at that time. Perhaps the EC believed this type of folklore was the most relevant to the current condition of the Jews and would inspire extensive participation.

The next questionnaire, published a month later, in December 1925, was numbered "1a" and dealt with local Jewish legends.[40] In Vilne they sought legends about the Vilne Goan, for example;[41] in the Ukraine, legends on the "Ludmirer moyd," a nineteenth-century woman in Ludmir who was a Hasidic leader; in Congress Poland, tales about the Polish uprising;[42] and in Eastern Galicia, legends about Karmelin and Dobosh.[43] While many local legends about old synagogues were printed in the EC's volume of 1938, *Yidisher folklor,* few legends about local people were printed. This genre apparently did not receive as large a response as the commission had hoped.

Below this second questionnaire, the EC printed its first list of folklore collectors. The list included a wide geographic area, though primarily collectors from Vilne and a number of Yiddish writers or future writers, such as Menashe Unger (Tel Aviv), F. Halperin (Vilne), and Moyshe Petrushke (Warsaw). Unger later wrote several volumes on

Hasidism and had his own folkore column, "Funem altn kval" (From the old well/source), in the New York Yiddish daily *Tog-morgn zhurnal* in the 1950s, no doubt inspired by his earlier days as a *zamler* and his Hasidic upbringing.

In early January 1926, *zamlers* wrote to the central office in Vilne asking for official authorization to collect folklore. They felt this would make their job easier. The commission agreed, and sent out official letters of authorization. At this time, the first groups of collectors in the same town or city organized themselves into "ethnographic circles." This was done on their own initiative and not at the request of the commission in Vilne. The first circle to organize was in Makov, near Warsaw. The commission, of course, endorsed this idea. They also again pleaded for help in transcribing musical notes.[44]

During the first few months of the commission's existence, it was clear that it could not decide what to call itself. First, it called itself the *"folkloristisher komisye,"* then *"folkloristish-etnografishe komisye,"* and finally *"etnografishe komisye,"* which it would keep until 1930, when it changed its name to *"folklor komisye."* Why "ethnographic" and not "folklore"? There had been a Jewish tradition in organizational nomenclature to use the term "ethnographic."[45] "Folklore" became the term used only for the texts, the material. "Ethnography" defined the academic discipline that studied these materials.

In his article of January 1926, "The Tasks of Jewish Ethnography," Khayim Khayes, a member of the EC in Vilne, ended the confusing status of the terms "ethnography" and "folklore" in the discourse of the EC.[46] "Folklore" was not mentioned once in the article. "Ethnography" was the science that analysed the people. While sociology did the same on an economic basis, ethnography studied the "spiritual essence of the *folksmentsh*" and his way of life. Khayes enumerated six genres that comprised the "folk creation": proverbs, riddles, and jokes; folk songs; folktales and legends; folk drama; folk medicine; and folk art. The last genre, he pointed out, had been excluded in other Jewish ethnographic endeavors, though this was not entirely accurate. The association of folklore with purely oral genres prejudiced the EC against its usage, for the YIVO EC envisioned a field of study that encompassed much more than oral genres. In fact, however, the EC did concentrate almost entirely on oral genres, and this was surely a result of the Yiddishist ideology behind the YIVO Institute. They were aware of the full scope of folklore and ethnography, but prioritized those texts connected to language. Khayes concluded his article with a call to organize collectors for ethnographic fieldwork. The article was mainly a public relations piece for the EC, and the author proposed that the Ethnographic Commission be the central archive for this work. As Weinreich and others had done, he directed his comments specifically to teachers and students.

In January 1926, the third questionnaire, numbered "2," was published, this one dealing with the approaching festival of Purim.[47] This questionnaire was much more comprehensive than earlier ones, since it dealt with a festival genre and thus included questions on oral texts (curses of Haman, folk songs, Purim-kiddush), folk drama (*purim-shpil*), material culture (*gragers*, holiday food), custom (methods of drowning out Hamen's name, purim-rabbi), and folk art (*megiles* with illustrations). The emphasis was obviously on the collection of *purim-shpiln*. Of the twenty-one points, six were devoted to the *shpil*. The recent publication of the first volume of Yitskhok Shiper's history of Yiddish drama may have influenced this emphasis.[48] Weinreich had himself a couple of years earlier adapted and published an old *purim-shpil*, hoping to revive the old tradition.[49] The antiquity of many of the texts fascinated linguists, literary critics, and historians alike.

Sometimes the EC would ask for a very specific regional tradition, usually one that the EC felt was near extinction. Question fourteen asks, "Have you heard of a 'Purim bear?' If not, ask around." This would become a common method of inquiry in many of the questionnaires that followed.

The Purim questionnaire was the first of the holiday questionnaires, which would eventually be collected into a brochure. The departure from a genre approach indicated a desire on the part of the EC to increase support and fieldworkers. By tying in the request for folklore with the Jewish calendar, the EC allowed greater variety in the kinds of materials one could send in, and it also implied a specific date and time for fieldwork. The correspondence with the *zamlers* revealed a need for greater structuring of the fieldwork effort. Though the "Rules" were helpful, the fieldworker still needed guidance. The EC also appealed to the nostalgia of the collector. The introductory paragraph reminded the reader that Purim that year would be joyous, "but the old folks say that it is not what it used to be."

In addition to monthly questionnaires, the YIVO also printed general news of the institute, which included information on the EC. These reports were printed in the *Literarishe bleter* more frequently than the monthly or bimonthly questionnaires. Occasionally, some instructions were delivered to collectors through these columns as well. In February 1926, after the Purim questionnaire, the news of the EC included several inquiries on folklore. The importance of recording *purim-shpiln* was reiterated, for they were "disappearing before our very eyes."[50] One question asked about certain customs of the traditional burial societies, the *Khevre kadishe*. Two other questions asked about Jewish customs on Christmas.

The list of contributors to the EC had grown to forty names by February 1926. The contributors were from Poland, Latvia, Lithuania, Rumania, France, and Berlin. *Zamlers* contributed songs, folk remedies, proverbs, tales, jokes, and curses. In a list of contributions published on March 12, 1926, only a couple of *purim-shpiln* and some legends had been collected. It seems that the questionnaires had little effect in determining what collectors sent in.

Others, outside of the EC, were inspired by the questionnaire method of collecting, and submitted their own ideas for projects to the EC. These proposals were also published in the *Literarishe bleter*. Noted ethnographer S. Weissenberg sent in a request to investigate the "blond type among Jews," and Menashe Unger in Tel Aviv composed a questionnaire on the folklore of West Galicia.[51] Some of these projects would be acted upon in years to come.

The next questionnaire was on the Passover holiday and was an extensive twenty-eight-question document from which one could learn much about the holiday itself.[52] In this regard, S. Ansky's questionnaire on the life cycle, with its fine detail and specificity, was, in all likelihood, used as a model.[53] Like that questionnaire, the order of questions in this document was basically chronological, beginning with the preparations for Passover and concluding with the end of the festival. Then various general questions on tales, songs, and games were posed. The questionnaire appealed to the *zamler* to consider the ethnographic and historical significance of the materials collected on this holiday: "The Jewish holidays, as holidays among all peoples, are treasures of folk culture, monuments which speak to us in the language of ancient times, and are immeasurably important, not only for the ethnographer but for the historian as well."[54]

In this opening statement, the historic connection to the pre-Yiddish era in Eastern Europe was made not in the context of Jewish history, but in the context of world history. To have referred to Passover in biblical terms would have undercut the Yiddishist notion that modern Jewish culture should be based on the East European experience. The Yiddishist folklorists gravitated toward international parallels, for this allowed them to avoid the distant Jewish past. In the above passage, the ancient past is de-Judaized: Passover is like all holidays among all nations. If the folklore of the Yiddish folk could be paralleled to other nations, then a "Yiddish nation" would have a legitimate culture to which to turn.

The collection endeavors of the EC were a stupendous success. By April 1926, only a few months after the EC had organized, numerous ethnographic circles had formed and the EC counted 150 correspondents, primarily, "workers, teachers, appointees, students—in general, *folksmentshn*."[55] *Zamlers* were sending in materials from all over the world. The EC was the most successful and popular project of the YIVO. News of the EC dominated the monthly reports. Many people had answered the Purim questionnaire and sent in important material; so much, in fact, that the EC announced the publication of a volume on Purim folklore to contain collected materials and scholarly articles on Purim. Unfortunately, no such volume ever appeared. Almost all the Purim materials were lost during the Holocaust.

The fourth and fifth questionnaires were printed together; one on the festivals Lag B'Omer and Shavuoth, the other on tall tales and lies.[56] The Lag B'Omer questionnaire contained four questions and sought information on the association of the holiday with the Jewish child. The collectors were encouraged "to ask the old people" to record how the festival was celebrated long ago, as on the Purim questionnaire. In addition to descriptions of how the holiday was celebrated, the EC asked that examples of the games children played (such as bows and arrows) be sent in. The Shavuoth questionnaire (seven questions) concentrated on the paper cut tradition, called *reyzelekh* or *shvueslekh* in Yiddish.[57] As can be seen from the questionnaires, the EC did not ignore material culture. *Gragers, reyzelekh*, bows and arrows, food, photographs, books—

the conception of material folklore was broad, and everything was acceptable if it figured into the life of the East European Jew.

The short questionnaire on tall tales and lies was a break from the holiday-oriented inquiries. It asked correspondents to collect exaggerations and lies, and to find the *ligners* (liars) and *barimers* and *baleyguzmes* (boasters) of the towns. The questionnaire gave the tales of the size of the *Og melekh haboshon* (a biblical giant) and of the wealth of Rothschild as examples: a biblical reference and a modern one.[58] To emphasize the importance of these apparently trivial stories, the questionnaire appeals to the nationalism of the collector, "but that which distinguishes one folk from another, is reflected as well in its tales."[59]

The topic of the sixth questionnaire, published in June 1926, was "Children's Creativity."[60] This two-page questionnaire was the most extensive yet, with eighteen main divisions and questions on every kind of play: indoor and outdoor, solitary and in groups, in *kheder* and at home, Sabbath and holiday, counting out rhymes, tales, animal sounds, and nicknames. The questionnaire was partially based on A. Landau's pioneering article of 1899.[61] A supplemental questionnaire (number 6a) on children's play was printed in the next *Yedies* which concentrated on the mischievous side of children's play.[62]

For the first time, the EC connected the collection work with the development of a modern Yiddish culture: the collected material would be used for the Yiddish schools. They specifically appealed to the teachers and older students to help collect. YIVO recommended the collection of folklore as a summer homework assignment. Much children's material was sent in as a result of this campaign—enough to furnish YIVO researcher S. Z. Pipe with months of work in the 1930s (as will be discussed further in chapter 6).

More than sixty years later, the Yiddish poet Mates Olitski recalled that he was a schoolchild in Poland at this time, when his town was gripped with "collection fever" as a result of YIVO's appeal to the schools. Parents, teachers, and library patrons began to bring in old books, posters, and letters. Actors sent in costumes. People brought photographs of weddings and organizational field trips. The teachers had assigned as homework the collection of songs, sayings, proverbs, and other forms of folklore. The children walked out the entire town in order to draw an accurate map. Olitski's school sent two packed large boxes to the YIVO Institute.[63] Judging by the large and growing numbers of contributors, "collection fever" had spread through much of Poland among the Yiddish intelligentsia.

With the approach of the High Holidays in the fall of 1926, the EC returned to the holiday theme for its questionnaire; the seventh questionnaire included sixty questions on all aspects of the holidays.[64] As a result of some interesting customs sent in for the High Holiday questionnaire, a supplemental questionnaire was printed a few weeks later.[65] The numbers of *zamlers* was now more than two hundred, and masses of materials poured in. As a result of the mounds of material culture that had arrived at YIVO, the institute established a "Museum of the Ethnographic Commission," where photographs and children's toys, among other objects, were displayed.

In December 1926, the EC next asked the *zamlers* to look at a folk group, rather than a genre or a holiday. The Warsaw group, Lehman and Graubard in particular, but also Elzet, centered most of their work on social groups. Perhaps the EC wanted to attempt something new in order to receive different kinds of materials. The *khevre kadishe*, the burial society, was thus the focus of the eighth questionnaire. The EC characterized the society as a "closed organization," whose old customs were disappearing and were being forgotten. As an example, the *khevre kadishe* custom of drinking in the cemetery on the fifteenth of Kislev and then feasting afterward is described. The EC informed the reader that the custom had parallels with traditions among other peoples and was very old. Any information sent in would, therefore, benefit not only Jewish ethnography, but the entire discipline[66] In every questionnaire, the importance of the task was spelled out in terms of age, importance, threatened "disappearance" of the folklore, or all three, as in this case. The EC also gave some fieldwork advice: gain the trust of the members of the organization; they should not feel you want to learn their "secrets."

The *Yedies* also printed a letter from a *zamler*, I. Lindnberg from Warsaw, who suggested that addresses of family and friends of other *zamlers* who lived in small towns be made available to the EC, for it was in those areas that "the real source" was found, and the youth "was dying of boredom. They would thank God if they were given something to do."[67] Let them collect folklore! Of course, the EC agreed. Folklore fieldwork would conceivably become a respectable way to keep the Jewish youth out of trouble.

The ninth questionnaire returned to Jewish holidays as its topic; this time Hanukkah was the focus.[68] The acknowledgment column of materials received had become so large that it was presented chronologically by day. The monthly lists revealed that while "collection fever" had indeed set in, replies to the questionnaires comprised only a tenth of the materials received. Collectors sent in much more material that had no connection to the questionnaires than material that did.

As the EC was swamped with materials, the questionnaires became less frequent. The next questionnaire topic, in April 1927, was the "war years" of the First World War, an area that had been covered in part by S. Bastomski and S. Lehman.[69] The eleventh questionnaire, on "tales" (*mayses*), in July was a return to a genre approach, but with a more sophisticated questionnaire this time. The "Tales" are divided into three main subgenres: wonder tales ("vunder-mayses"), legends ("legendes"), and Hasidic tales ("rabonishe mayeses"—tales of the Hasidic rabbis). Distinct in the questionnaire is the EC's attempt to describe the typical storyteller for the collector. In this way the EC sought to inspire the collector with the idea that he was surrounded by tales; he just had to know how to find them. Who told them? First and foremost, the merchants who traveled and met various people; village tradesmen who went from village to village; musicans and *badkhonim* who traveled from wedding to wedding; matchmakers—no reason given; poor people, blind musicians, singers, and the Hasidim, who traveled to the Rebbe and heard various tales and legends. The EC promoted these tales as a sign of spiritual creativity in an era of darkness: "Let the coming generations see what a wealthy and beautiful storyland our grandfathers built in the tortured, fearful Jewish quarter!" The YIVO would create a "valuable memorial for the unknown poets and tellers," and revive the Yiddish story for the Yiddish school.[70] The collector would be doing him- or herself a service, as well as providing a service to the entire modern Yiddish culture.

The old folklore would have a new context that would be free of the past negative associations. The Yiddishists believed they had entered a new phase of Jewish experience which would take the best of the diaspora past and leave the worst behind. The twelfth questionnaire on the custom of "Opsherenish," the cutting of the boy's hair for the first time at three years of age, was the first extensive questionnaire (twelve questions) on a custom associated with the life cycle.[71] After two years of questionnaires, the EC had chosen folklore based on calendrical customs, genre, and life cycle. In this case, as in others, it seems the EC felt the custom was waning at the time and needed immediate documentation. Given the widespread practice of this custom today, particularly among Hasidim, one wonders whether the EC, by its location in non-Hasidic Vilne, accurately gauged the dissemination of customs across Poland. The questionnaire implied the practice of the custom was known in only a few areas. It is more likely, however, that the custom was known everywhere except in *"di Lite"* (Lithuania, White Russia, Estonia, and Latvia). One cannot dismiss the possibility that the YIVO researchers in Vilne were geographically biased in what they chose to collect and in how they perceived the important materials of Jewish folklore. What they may have viewed as rare in Vilne might have been quite popular in the rest of Poland.

By September 20, 1927, the EC had inventoried 15,500 items. Half of them were proverbs and sayings; folk remedies and songs were a distant second and third. Thirty-seven genres were enumerated. The EC estimated that another 15,000 items were yet to be accessioned! Why were proverbs the most widely collected? The EC later assigned the blame for this preference on previous Yiddish folklore scholarship. A more logical conclusion is that they represent the easiest oral genre to collect. Sayings and proverbs also reflected positively on the wisdom of the (Jewish) folk, and the wonders of the (Yiddish) language. Other genres, such as folk medicine, presented a more ambiguous picture of folk knowledge: "yes, our ancestors did these things, but of course we do not believe in them anymore." Proverbs, on the other hand, have multiple meanings according to the context of their performance.[72]

In 1927, YIVO published a brochure summing up the first two years of activity. The section on the Ethnographic Commission surpassed all of the other sections in terms of participation and collection activity.[73] The report complained that the collectors were enthusiastic in their work but did not follow the questionnaires. They had collected songs and proverbs, ignoring the requests of the EC. The report attributed this to the "precedent" established by the previous twenty years of folklore collection by a few individuals who had concentrated on those genres. Why the EC believed this was not stated. Realistically, few of YIVO's *zamlers* were familiar with the earlier collections of Bernshteyn, Bastomski, Prilutski, or Lehman. Those works were not best-sellers by any means, and were hard to obtain. The only apparent reason for the EC making this claim was to underline the difference between the "old way" of collecting Yiddish folklore and the "new, YIVO way" in Yiddish folkloristics. It implied that the "YIVO way" would be a more systematic, holistic approach, encompassing all genres. The report concluded that the collectors needed training in order to answer the given questions.

Sometime late in 1927, the EC established a museum, which had accessioned five hundred items, principally pictures, photographs, and "portraits of Jewish life." The collection also included thirteen Purim *gragers*, flags, buttons, and children's toys. The EC report referred to the museum as "poor," and made it clear that money was needed.[74]

Folklore in the *Filologishe shriftn*

During the first four years of its existence, YIVO published three large-format collections of essays and materials entitled *Filologishe shriftn* (Studies in philology).[75] While the accomplishments of the EC demonstrated the popularity of collecting folklore among the folk, the high percentage of folklore writings in this series evidenced the attractiveness of the folklore field for scholars as well and the central role that folklore played in Yiddish scholarship in interwar Poland.

The first volume, entitled the *Landoy-bukh* in Yiddish (English title reads *Jubilee Volume for Dr. Alfred Landau*), was assembled in honor of Alfred Landau (1850–1935), a philologist who had been one of the early Yiddish folklorists, though he published in German. His life's work was a Yiddish dictionary which remained incomplete and unpublished. He was the first to point out that Yiddish did not stem from modern German, but from Middle High German dialects. As a result of his great erudition, Landau was admired by all of the younger Yiddish philologists.[76] The work, in format and in spirit, followed in the tradition of Shmuel Niger's *Pinkes*, and was meant to be an impressive display of the capabilities of Yiddish scholarship. A particularly inspiring contribution for *zamlers* in the field was the collection of similes recorded by the students of the Vilne Teacher's Seminary.[77] The EC *zamler* now saw for the first time that his or her collection could be published. This was a sincere and preponderant concern for the collector.

Several of the works published became instant classics in the field. Landau's own article, a review of Bastomski's folklore collections, exhibited his mastery of the German, Polish, and other coterritorial folklore literatures and the importance of knowing these materials for the history of Yiddish language and culture. By comparing German versions of a Yiddish children's rhyme, he concluded that the Yiddish variants had emerged from an Alsatian one, and documented the migration of Alsatian Jews eastward to Poland.[78]

I. L.Cahan, living in New York, reviewed S. Lehman's *Labor and Freedom* and dissected the revolutionary song texts to arrive at a judgment on what was and was not a folk song.[79] Rather than looking for origins as Landau had done, Cahan saw a need to lay out the terminology of the new Yiddish folklore field. He felt that collectors were not sensitive to the differences between folk songs and pseudo- or non-folk songs.[80] His article established him as the final arbiter of authenticity in the Yiddish folklore field, and YIVO would look to him to direct the next phase of its folklore work.

Max Weinreich's etymological work on the mischievous spirit, *Lantukh*,[81] led him to the commentary of Rashi[82] and the Romance component of Yiddish. Landau employed philological analysis to substantiate aspects of East European Jewish history; Weinreich used linguistic analysis to corroborate ethnographic observations. Weinreich's article, together with his article on folk medicine, proved that a philologically based approach to folklore need not be restricted to the usual oral genres, such as folk song and proverb. The EC sought to expand the genres that collectors were sending in, and Weinreich was leading by example. As with his view on folk medicine, Weinreich avoided any ideological dilemmas inherent for the Yiddishist in the subject of demonology by strictly adhering to a linguistic breakdown of the term *Lantukh*.

Several leading Jewish folklorists of the older generation, including Bernard Wachstein and Dr. Shmuel Weissenberg, who had never before printed materials in a Yiddish publication, did so for the first time in the *Landau Book*.[83] This gave significant prestige to the Yiddishist scholarly movement. Weissenberg's collection of nicknames opened up a new genre in Yiddish folkloristics and his brief categorization should have directed future research on the topic, but his work in this area has remained the only one so far in Yiddish studies.

In addition to folk song and proverb collections submitted by Shmuel Lehman and Shmuel Rubinshteyn (1885–?), the first volume of *Filologishe shriftn* includes "discoveries" of old documents and texts of great interest to the Jewish ethnographer and folklorist.[84] Isaac Rivkind (1895–1968) printed an old Yiddish song on artisans;[85] Elye Sosnovik (dates unknown) published a betrothal contract in Hebrew and Aramaic that a young man drew up between God and the Jewish people so that he could escape prison; Dr. Arthur Goldmann found an early-fifteenth-century description of *vakhnakht,* the evening before the circumcision, in the national Library of Vienna.[86]

Three major articles on folklore were included in the second volume of *Filologishe shriftn,* which appeared in 1927. Coeditor Max Weinreich pointed out in the introduction that materials from the YIVO's archives were used for a number of the contributions. Khayim Khayes, who was the secretary of the Ethnographic Commission, assembled a large collection on death beliefs and customs, "Beliefs and Customs Related to Death."[87] The collection includes hundreds of beliefs, customs, and oral texts, such as laments, curses, and wishes, that had not been published before. Khayes noted, in his brief introduction, that the behaviors of primitive man and the *folksmentsh* were different, but that "the means with which he [the *folksmentsh*] reacts and protects himself [from death] have developed from that distant primitive time." Whereas the more philologically oriented scholars such as Weinreich skirted the issue of ethnographic origins and emphasized word etymology, there were other folklorists, such as Khayes, who foregrounded the behavioral origins of customs and beliefs and were fascinated with the connection to earlier stages of civilization.

Khayes took some of his materials from the work on beliefs of Regina Lilienthal, published in Polish folklore periodicals.[88] The author collected most of the texts with questionnaires in the Jewish Teacher's Seminary in Vilne in June 1925, before the founding of YIVO. Only a small portion of the material was taken from the YIVO archives. The entire structure of the work was based upon a recent Polish collection on the same theme.[89] Khayes was struck by the negligible Jewish component in the Polish work and set out to partially fill the lacuna.[90] He did this to an admirable degree, considering how few Yiddish folklorists had published on custom and belief, since this genre touched upon the very nature of Jewish identity.

Tsvi Shpirn's article, "The Role of Names in Our Mother Tongue," looked at the folkloric dimension of Yiddish onomastics, continuing Weissenberg's earlier work in a different direction.[91] Shpirn's collection of proverbs, sayings, and similes (e.g., "drunk as Lot") concluded with a request from the editors that the reader accept the article as a questionnaire and send in other materials to the Ethnographic Commission. Khayes's article implied that the work should be construed as an *ankete* for the YIVO *zamler*. The reaction of the *zamlers* to the first volume of *Filologishe shriftn* can be gauged by the addenda in the second volume, especially to M. Weinreich's article on *Lantukh*. Dozens of readers contributed new information, allowing the author to round out his study.[92]

YIVO was also able to draw respected folklorist Walter Anderson, professor of Estonian and comparative folklore, into their ranks with an analysis of the Yiddish First World War song, "Dos lid fun der mobilizatsye" (The song of the mobilization).[93] This was the first monographic approach to folklore in Yiddish of the historic-geographic or Finnish method.[94] The author sought to reconstruct the "normal text" from the variants that he had recorded from Minsk schoolchildren. Anderson's work with Yiddish-speaking schoolchildren was his first endeavor in this type of school fieldwork, which he later applied to Baltic-German folklore, Estonian folklore, and lastly to Italian folklore.[95] The work should have been impressive, particularly to the YIVO collector in the field who had difficulty understanding the importance of recording so many variants of one text. Anderson, in his concluding remark, stated: we will "possess a more exact and more complete reconstruction of the normal form only when we will have many more variants of our song. I appeal with an urgent request to all readers who have heard or will hear the song of the mobilization (particularly outside the borders of the previous Minsk and Vilne provinces) to transcribe exactly and completely and send it to me."[96]

Scholarly discourse on Yiddish folklore had evolved into a true dialogue at the YIVO Institute between field collectors who gathered the folk texts and academic scholars who analyzed those texts. The dialogue, of course, extended only to those fieldworkers who received the *Studies in Philology*—many could not afford it.[97]

In his review of the volume, the historian I. Shiper sharply criticized Khayes's work as that of a "total dilettante." The review accused the author of a complete lack of preparation for the subject and suggested several works (all German) he should read if he wanted to continue his research.[98] Shiper reviewed the other folklore articles much more positively, though he expressed the opinion that the subjects themselves were trivial and a waste of time. So from both sides, from the uneducated and from the well educated, the study of Yiddish folklore was attacked as inconsequential. This, needless to say, was exactly the message the YIVO did *not* want the potential collectors to hear. While the EC was proclaiming the idea that *all* folklore was important and would be lost if not recorded, here was a well-known Yiddishist historian claiming otherwise. Fortunately, Shiper's attack was a rare one, for it rocked the underpinnings of the field in a most vulnerable spot. With revolution, upheavals, and economic disaster on the horizon, was a study of a Jewish hobgoblin or of one Yiddish song in Minsk so crucial? As the 1930s went by and the political situation worsened for the Jews in Poland, the "apolitical" scholarly approach of the YIVO came increasingly under fire. Shiper's criticism was framed with a research agenda, but his implied question about the priorities of Yiddish scholarship would arise again in a new political context a few years later.[99]

When the third and final volume of *Filologishe shriftn* appeared at the end of 1928, the concern with the communication between scholars and folklore field collectors continued.[100] The editors, Weinreich and Reyzen, reprinted one section of the questionnaire-book "The Jewish Ethnographic Program. Part One: The Person" by S. Ansky and many collaborators, and edited by Lev Shternberg, an eminent Russian anthropologist.[101] The editors chose the section on death to couple it with Khayes's earlier work on the same subject and to motivate collectors to respond on the subject to the Ethnographic Commission.[102] The selection included 219 questions and was much more detailed than the EC's questionnaires.

The article on Lilith, by I. Zoller of Trieste, examined the origin of Lilith and the belief in the demon among Italian Jews.[103] It also included a discussion of many Jewish birth customs and served in the volume as a counterpart to Ansky's article on death.

One of the leading YIVO *zamlers* in Warsaw, M. Gromb, published an original collection of Yiddish street calls heard in the yards and streets of Warsaw.[104] This folklore genre attracted Gromb because of its creativity and folkiness. He divided the collection according to the product sold and left the price announced, "so as not to disrupt the completeness of the calls." A couple of examples of street cries for bagels are:

*Oylem, oylem ests bikhinem, ests bikhinem—fir beygl a tsenerl, fir a
tsenerl! fir a tsenerl!*
beygl on lekher, groys vi di bekher—dray a tsenerl! dray a tsenerl!

(People, people eat for free, eat for free—four bagels for a dime!
Four for a dime! Four for a dime!
Bagels without holes, as big as goblets—three for a dime! Three
for a dime!) [105]

Gromb's footnotes on who sold what and other folklore of the sellers
present a lively picture of urban life among the poor, reminiscent of
Henry Mayhew's *London Labour and the London Poor*.[106] Linguistically,
there was little of interest in the texts themselves; however, the collection
impresses the reader with the vitality of Jewish life in Eastern Europe
and the basic role that the Yiddish language played in that energetic existence. Gromb's collection also exhibited how a *zamler* became interested
in something far removed from the EC questionnaires, and how his personal ethnographic impulse led him to something new and innovative.

The other folklore article of note in this third volume was a study
by Naftuli Vaynig of a Polish folk song about Jews, "The Polish folk song,
'The Jewish War.'"[107] This was a popular song, first printed in 1606,
which humorously described the manner in which the Jews prepared for
war. Vaynig believed that part of the Jewish ethnographer's role was to
investigate the social and psychological relations between the Jews and
their coterritorial inhabitants. He presented an in-depth motif analysis and arrived at the most detailed study of one song by any Jewish
folklorist—ironically, however, the study was of a Polish song. In the
introduction to the volume, the editors pointed out Vaynig's work as an
example of a possible direction future YIVO publications would take: to
include materials not necessarily on Yiddish themes. In terms of folklore, Vaynig was the only Yiddish scholar dedicated to the study of Pol-
ish/Jewish images of each other. (Vaynig will be discussed in more detail
later in this book.)

The third volume of *Filologishe shriftn* marked the end of the first
period of YIVO, characterized by the editors as, "a period of prepar-
ing and assembling supporters and organizing them around YIVO."[108]
Weinreich and Reyzen were self-conscious of the "non-systematic"
nature of the three volumes and looked ahead to a YIVO periodical

dedicated to longer, more profound analyses. The American YIVO section, which had already begun to publish its own series, titled *Pinkes*, continued the *Filologishe shriftn* approach of printing texts, shorter essays, and comments.[109] The YIVO in Vilne would soon publish a new series, *YIVO-bleter*, which would fulfill the desire for a more concentrated, scholarly effort. It would include fewer collections and texts, and more monographic studies. The field of Yiddish folklore would be a component of that series, but less visible than in the publications of YIVO's first few years. Folklorists capable of writing learned essays were only then beginning to be trained.

The Ethnographic Commission 1928–30

After two years, the main problems that the Ethnographic Commission still faced, in its estimation, were its inability to persuade the collectors to follow the questionnaire instructions, and the lack of collectors who could transcribe the music as well as the lyrics.[110] By 1928, Yiddish schoolteachers had organized *zamler-krayzn,* or collectors' circles, with their students in many Polish cities and towns. Though the teachers were the target *zamlers* of the EC, after three years of work, most *zamlers* were *folksmentshn,* minimally educated working-class people. According to a poll probably conducted in 1928, of 136 *zamlers* who replied, 43 were "physical workers" (31.6 percent), 27 were white-collar employees (20 percent), 18 were students (13.2 percent), 15 were teachers (11 percent), 8 were merchants (5.9 percent), 7 were journalists (5.1 percent), two were Yeshiva students (1.5 percent), and two were at home (1.5 percent).[111] Why did these *folksmentshn* collect? The EC speculated that, "For most of them, the *folkshafung* (folk creation) was for a long time the only spiritual nourishment; before they exchanged it for modern literature and theater."[112]

One such *folksmensh* was one of the leading *zamlers* in the field: Berl Verblunski, from Grodne.[113] In one YIVO Bulletin, the EC proudly described how he befriended wandering beggars, who willingly told their tales once convinced that he was not mocking them. "Many then asked whether there were others in other towns in his group," implying that the performers told their tales for the sheer joy of telling.[114] What the EC did not mention, and probably did not know, is that Verblunski paid the beggars; naturally they wanted to meet others who would do the same.[115]

By June 1928, the EC had inventoried 34,000 items. Proverbs, sayings, curses, and expressions again accounted for half—five times more than the other genres of folk remedies, folk omens, and folk interpretations of dreams. Songs without tunes was the next largest category, with 2,692. *Purim-shpiln* were the least collected, with 57 texts. The EC further classified tales, songs, jokes, and legends by motifs. The tale collection was further divided as follows: "gnomes, sunken churches, ghosts and spirits, debates between Jews and priests, dybbuks, emperors, Russian emperors, libels, a rabbi and his wife, from old chronicles, hidden treasures, twelve midnight in the synagogue, a letter to God, Gentile lords and Jews, three brothers: two clever and one foolish, two brothers: one rich the other poor, hidden saints, robbers and thieves, tales of ox merchants, war years, evil stepmother, the groom—a horse, a snake, three mute brothers, witches, tales of Israel, and so on."[116]

The questionnaires and the YIVO Bulletin did not appear for months at a time in 1928. In the meantime, the EC had announced work on a "Folklore Volume" consisting of material sent in by *zamlers*.[117] This volume, immediately given over to I. L. Cahan to edit in New York, would not be published for another ten years.[118] The EC also conducted a contest for the best folklore collections submitted from December 1928 to May 1929. Contests replaced or were used in conjunction with questionnaires. YIVO used this method for other branches as well, to gather material. The winners of the first folklore contest were Berl Verblunski and the Ansky Collector's Circle in Warsaw. A second competition on the theme of "war folklore" was announced in early 1930.[119]

The first YIVO Conference was held from October 23–27, 1929, in Vilne and was a major celebration for supporters of Yiddish culture from around the world. At that conference, several leading collectors from the field and Vilne folklorists came together to discuss the work of the Ethnographic Commission. Among the *zamlers* were Berl Verblunski from Grodne, Shmuel Zaynvil Pipe from Sanok, and Khaye Feyn-Engeltsin from Prodbrodz. The Vilne and YIVO folklorists were represented by Shloyme Bastomski, Naftuli Vaynig, and Khayim Khayes from Vilne. Fifty thousand items had been accessioned by this time.

Vaynig, in the name of the Ethnographic Commission, discussed the future plans of the EC: to distribute questionnaires on beliefs and folk medicine; to catalogue the folktales in the archives according to tale type; to put together a bibliography of Jewish ethnography; to organize expeditions to eastern Galicia, Volynia, and the Carpathian region, "where the pure primitive Jewish life still survives";[120] to develop the ethnographic library holdings at YIVO; to form a federation of all Jewish ethnographers and make YIVO's EC a central office for all Jewish ethnographic researchers; to establish courses to train collectors in the field; to publish a folklore volume based on the YIVO's collections; and to print a thesaurus of Yiddish proverbs. Vaynig concluded with a personal request to reorganize the Ethnographic Commission into its own section. Of these many plans, only the questionnaires on beliefs and folk medicine were realized. From the protocols of the 1929 YIVO conference, it became clear that Vaynig, Khayes, and Weinreich had become the policy makers at the EC.

The Ethnographic Handbooks

The Ethnographic Commission published two eagerly awaited handbooks for the *zamlers* in 1928 and 1929. The first was a compilation of all of the questionnaires on the Jewish holidays. They were printed together with slight reworkings, as one booklet, *Etnografishe anketes—heft eynts: Yon-toyvim* (Ethnographic questionnaires—Volume one: Holidays).[121] The booklet began with the YIVO "Call" to gather folklore, originally issued in 1926. The text had not been changed, so that "teachers in the Yiddish schools" were still singled out as the prime audience. In an introductory note, dated the end of May 1928, the author(s) described how the vast materials contributed by *zamlers* had uncovered unknown customs or customs long believed "dead." Therefore, the booklet advised, the *zamler* should, "record everything, record precisely, for everything has a value for the researcher!"[122] The EC made a sharp distinction between *zamlers* and researchers. The collector did not help Yiddish culture directly; he or she labored for the "researcher," who, in turn, advanced the cause of Yiddish folklore.

The questionnaires were slightly supplemented or altered to reflect the material that had arrived into the archive. Five short new questionnaires were added. They were on: Shabes-shire (a special Sabbath), submitted by the Makov *zamler* circle; Tishe-B'ov, (the mourning day on the Jewish calendar); Khamishe oser b'shavat; the fifteenth day of Kislev; and Jewish behavior on Christmas.[123]

The authors noted that though each questionnaire asked about holiday foods, there were few who responded to those questions. At fault, they believed, was the assumption by the *zamler* that his or her food was nothing special; many collectors thought to themselves, "They must think over there [in Vilne] that we truly have wonderful baked goods. What shall I send them, a challah?" Just like any custom, the EC countered, "each holiday has its baked good whose form has been sanctified by tradition." With a good collection of foods, one forms a valuable contribution to the cultural history of the Jews in that area. "Even a regular challah can contribute something." The authors asked the *zamlers* to take a special interest in foodways in the future.[124]

Now that the questionnaires were in booklet form, the YIVO hoped that more and more collectors would join the ranks of the EC. The widespread miscomprehension of what exactly comprised folklore and ethnography and what the *zamlers* were suppposed to collect was not solved by this booklet. To do that, the EC next published a basic handbook that would serve as an introduction for the collector.

The Yiddish Folklorist's Guide: What is Jewish Ethnography?

In early 1929, YIVO published *Vos iz azoyns yidishe etnografye? Hantbikhl farn zamler* (What is Jewish ethnography? Handbook for fieldworkers).[125] Two members of the EC, Khayim Khayes and Naftuli Vaynig, wrote this thirty-two-page booklet which became the "Bible" of the YIVO folklore *zamlers*, who desperately needed guidance. It was the first handbook on the subject for Jews that was not just a compilation of questions for the fieldworker, as was Ansky's book or the *Ethnographic Questionnaires*.[126] *What Is Jewish Ethnography?* explained the fundamental terms of the fields of folklore and ethnography for the "lay" fieldworker, though the term "folklore" is carefully avoided. Almost all bibliographic references were to works in Yiddish; the authors did not expect the *zamlers* to analyze their materials comparatively with other folklore traditions. Nor did the handbook foresee any need to deal with the period after the collection process, including arranging and maintaining the materials. The EC would take care of those aspects after they had received the texts—thus further demarcating the boundaries between the collector and the researcher. The YIVO guide was also not a handbook to instruct one in method and technique, as was the contemporary

German-language *Folklore Methodology,* published in 1926 by the Nor-
wegian Kaarle Krohn. [127]

As the interrogative title implied, *What Is Jewish Ethnography?* was
designed to illuminate the puzzled *zamler* on the nature of the fieldwork
enterprise. From the opening lines of the work, the tone was an aggres-
sive one, expressing the voice of the underdog.

> Usually, the case is that we underestimate or completely overlook objects
> whose sense or worth is unknown to us. Most of our intelligentsia still does
> not understand today the importance of collecting and protecting our Jewish
> folk creativity and looks with disdain upon this task. The ordinary person
> [*folksmentsh*] expresses this as suspicion or distrust. . . . But why write these
> things down? Are there not better things to do? It must be that they want to
> mock him and make a fool of him for the world. Many a time the fieldworker
> stops and does not know what to reply, if one were to ask him: why do you
> need all this foolishness? [128]

It is remarkable how similar the discourse to justify Yiddish folklore is to
the many defenses of Yiddish language and culture in general. Folklore,
the field most closely associated with the Yiddish-speaking folk in Yiddish scholarship, was a metonym for the entire Yiddish cultural movement. As with the Yiddish language, the educated and cultured stratum
of Jewish society looked down upon its folklore; the lower stratum neglected or took its "treasure" for granted. The introduction to the handbook also highlighted the awareness of the intelligentsia/folk division
among non-Jews; for example, "The silk kaftan [*zhupitse*] that the Polish intellectual derides, is merely an old Polish garment which Jews took
over and wear until today." Class difference was a key component in the
rhetoric of the Yiddish folklorist. The same class rhetoric also accompanied the Yiddishist debunking of the Hebraist camp for being elitist and
out of touch with the people. [129] The Yiddish ethnographer and folklorist
safeguarded the interests of the people against the snobbish intelligentsia
and even against the people themselves, since they could not appreciate
their own creativity.

The booklet introduced the subject with an ideological, polemical
tone before settling down in the second paragraph to the explication of
"ethnography." The text described ethnography as the study of the Jew
apart from modern life; "separated and isolated" in the small town or
village. Instead of modern medicine, this Jew had folk medicine; instead

of books, he had songs and tales; instead of theater, he had folk drama. What had kept the generations together was a tradition that barely transformed itself, so that the modern folklore, "clearly transmits the moods of ancient epochs."[130] One could therefore research the past history of the Jews, using these materials. Before modernity destroyed the little that was left, one needed to collect it.

The handbook is divided into three larger sections, "Der shtof fun der yidisher etnografye" (The material of Jewish ethnography), "Di gebitn fun der yidisher etnografye" (The subjects of Jewish ethnography), and "Kurtse etnografishe terminologye" (Short ethnographic terminology). The "Stuff of Jewish Ethnography" discussed the "ethnographic" and "social" groupings that comprised Jewish ethnography. The authors did not include the Sephardic and "exotic" Jews as subjects of the handbook, for that would have made their undertaking unwieldy. The Yiddish speakers had enough differences among them to concern the *zamler*. Each region of the Yiddish-speaking territory (Galicia, Lithuania, and the Ukraine, for example) had major ethnographic differences. These regional groups could be further divided into social groups: professional groups (by occupation), children, actors, Yeshiva students, lumpen proletariat, the underworld, *klezmer* (Jewish folk musicians). "In general, every collective which leads a separate way of life," is an object of ethnographic study.[131] The marginal social classes received particular attention. The Yiddish folklorists had a special affinity for peripheral social groups, since they themselves felt marginalized by Jewish society.[132]

The handbook divided the field into three areas: material culture, social culture, and spiritual culture. The "international community" had separated the discipline this way and so it was felt that the Jews should accept the division; however, the proportion of importance would be different: "For us, the proportion of the three realms will be different, because issues that relate to material culture occupy a minor place for us. It is a fact that is a result of historic conditions in which we live. We could never develop our own style of building settlements, and in terms of architecture our accomplishments are also not great because of limitations."[133] On the other hand, Jewish folk art did often display an original style, which one found in Jewish ritual objects, old *sforim* (holy books), synagogues, gravestones, and home decorations. Food and clothes also represented Jewish individuality, and collectors were encouraged to send in samples to the YIVO Ethnographic Museum.

In the section on "Spiritual and Social Culture," the authors included all oral genres but discussed folk remedies (*zababones*) at greater length even than folktales. These *zababones* were remnants of past times, they wrote. Some of these beliefs and customs were from eras when, "people lived as they do today in Africa and Australia."[134] Primitive man viewed the world as full of good and evil spirits who wanted to help or injure him. Amulets and charms were a result of these beliefs, as were omens, dybbuks, blessings, and oaths. A Jew answered a sneeze with, "To your health, to your life," and the origin could be found among primitive peoples who asked the spirit for life and not death when they sneezed. The modern Jew did not take these things seriously; but, for the Africans, it was not just a saying.

This comparative analysis did not previously exist in Yiddish and was an indication that the Yiddish folklorists had read the international folklore literature of the day, especially that taken from England. Yiddish folklorists had read J. G. Frazer's *The Golden Bough* (1911–15) and E. B. Tylor's *Primitive Culture* (1871), and their influence upon *What Is Jewish Ethnography?* is clear.[135] Tylor's diachronic comparative method, with no regard for context or function, led him to a comparison of "savage" customs with contemporary way of life, and to find striking similarities. The notion of "survivals" from a time when Western cultures were primitive was popularized by Tylor, and he is credited with coining the term "survivals" in an evolutionist context.[136] Tylor desired to eradicate these survivals, which had no place in modern "civilization"; the authors of the EC text basked in the glory of these survivals. The exalting of customs and beliefs in the context of primitive culture was surely problematic for most Jews. Traditional Judaism is not evolutionist; Jews revered their past generations. Were their ancestors, their grandparents or even parents part of primitive society? Until this time, the *zamlers* were told to collect, for their history was being lost before their eyes. They reacted immediately to this urgent call, for they greatly valued this past. As traditional Jewish society broke down, they witnessed the erosion of this way of life. Were they to be inspired to collect after comparisons to African societies? The handbook avoided Hebraist leanings by not mentioning ancient Jewish life; the work, however, also skirted Yiddish nationalism by not reaffirming Jewish roots in Eastern Europe.

Not all Yiddish folklorists agreed with the view espoused in the handbook by Khayes and Vaynig. In a letter to Khayim Khayes, I. L.

Cahan chided him for an unpublished article Khayes had written that had been sent to Cahan for review. Cahan was also aware of a series of talks that Khayes had held at the Vilne Teacher's Seminary to respond to the question, "Does this material have any value?" posed by many *zamlers*. Khayes gave the impression that science knew the origin of all the customs and beliefs. Why give that impression, wrote Cahan—no one will collect if we know all the answers. The fieldworkers will argue that their collections are not needed. He continued, "What should we tell the poor *zamlers* if they ask about it? I have no idea." Cahan had no answer, and suggested that Khayes write on the issue.[137] The fact that Cahan, the patriarch of the Yiddish folklore movement, could not express the motivation behind the collection of Yiddish folklore betrays a profound absence of purpose in the developing Yiddishist ideology.

Cahan, however, was sensitive enough to the Yiddishist agenda and to sensible scholarship to criticize Khayes for relating current Jewish folklore to primitive peoples, skipping over an analysis of the folklore of coterritorial peoples and old Jewish/Yiddish literature: "I can imagine what an interesting work this could be [Khayes's unpublished article] if you were to find among the Poles, the Lithuanians, Germans and so on, similar customs and beliefs as are found among Reb Ber and Reb Motele Chernobler.[138] This would truly be a scholarly discovery. It would open the people's eyes, and state on its own: here, look how distinguished we are! See what we are proud of? And from the other side: how are they better? Those who look down upon us?"[139] Cahan returned the locus of the comparative method to Yiddishland and provided an ideological aim in doing so. The Hasidic rabbis and old Yiddish literature were the beginning of Yiddish "history"; one needed look no further. The Jews' non-Jewish neighbors believed the Jews were not their equals. Through folklore one could prove this was not so.

The concept of survivals and primitive cultures was mentioned only in passing after the entry on folk beliefs. The entry on the folktale and the folk song emphasized the creativity of the tale-teller as a possible co-creator. The tale-teller was portrayed as one who dreams, "the dream of a people who live in poor dark houses and in great poverty. He quiets the thirst of the masses for a bit of sun, a little shimmer, a speck of good fortune."[140] The folk singer was not viewed as a co-creator on an individual level, but as part of a communal creation. This was the accepted view among Jewish folklorists and was taken from I. L. Cahan's introduction to his two-volume folk song collection.[141] The authors also stated the importance of transcribing the melodies as well as recording the non-Jewish songs that Jews sang, to indicate the repertory of the singer and his taste. This latter task was never taken up by prewar folklorists, and its appearance in the handbook showed a prescient understanding of the worldview of the folk singer.

In the section on jokes, the authors stated that all were aware of the superiority of the Jewish/Yiddish joke.[142] Jews produced more jokes during stressful times, such as war and revolution. Other genres discussed were proverbs, names and nicknames, regional words, riddles, folk drama,[143] *sforim* (religious books),[144] Jews in the folklore of others,[145] and customs. The term "social folklore" was finally defined under the genre of customs: "When certain customs, songs, etc. are carried out as an expression of a collective activity, we call this a social cultural phenomenon."[146] Therefore all of the holiday folklore festivals were included in the category of "social folklore."

A short ethnographic terminology followed as the next section in the handbook. Many of the genres and subgenres of folklore not included in the larger entries such as folk medicine, folk meteorology, or children's creativity were listed and defined. A number of these short definitions were taken from the EC questionnaires. For a number of the entries, the handbook's definitions are the only extant definitions in the Yiddish folklore literature, and are therefore significant.

The term "anecdotes" was defined as "short humorous joke-tales [*shpas-dertseylungen*]." In the examples given, the jokes were all associated with a certain character (Hershl Ostropolyer, Motke Khabad), which would more closely align the definition with the English understanding of the genre as of a biographical nature. Jokes were defined as "short, witty anecdotes, usually in a dialogue form"—a definition similar to that held by contemporary folklorists.[147] The *shprikhvort*, or proverb, was a folksy opinion in a self-contained sentence. *Glaykhvort* was a humorous proverb. A *vertl* was an aphorism attributable to a known historic figure. The prime distinction of a *rednsart* or idiom expression was its form, which, unlike the proverb, could not stand as a complete sentence. A *zogvort* was a saying that was once part of a tale or anecdote. *Tsushprokh* was a psycho-ostensive expression.[148] The terminology section was the most helpful section in the handbook for the collector. It assured that the EC and the *zamlers* would speak the same language: the new language of ethnography and folklore. In publicity brochures, YIVO emphasized the significance of the terminology as an aid to its constituency.[149]

Vos iz azoyns yidishe etnografye was warmly received by the field-workers. Its practical utilization went into effect immediately upon publication. As a theoretical statement of Yiddish folkloristics, it represented an attempt to partake in both international folkloristic discourse (survivals, terminology) and a developing indigenous version of the folklore field (bibliography, specifically Jewish traits). Though scholarly in character, the authors could not refrain from framing their field of study with a touch of Yiddishist ideology.

CHAPTER 6

The 1930s

⋅⦙⦙⋅

The steady stream of folklore materials that had flooded the YIVO archives had slowed down considerably by 1929. This was mainly due to the overworked resources of the EC in Vilne, who then had enough materials to catalogue for several years. They thus decided to process the materials before actively seeking any more. Khayim Khayes directed the sorting process, which went slowly until 1935, when advanced research students (*aspirantn*) worked in the archive. Khayes was also occupied with the massive daily correspondence to *zamlers,* encouraging them to continue and reassuring them that their materials were indeed valuable.[1] He wrote to I. L. Cahan that he was determined to print some of the folklore materials, "to push a new effort in collecting which has almost stopped during the past four years."[2] When Cahan heard in 1930 that the EC was stagnating, he decided to visit the YIVO to view the archives himself. At his request, he taught a two-day seminar for the most active collectors, and paid for their expenses to travel to Vilne. This was an event that brought together older and younger folklorists and inspired them to more intense work.[3] The group included the experienced folklorist Shloyme Bastomski, YIVO staff workers Khayem Khayes and Nekhame Epshteyn, and avid fieldworkers S. Z. Pipe, Khaye Feyn-Engeltsin, and Aron Engeltsin.[4] Thirty-two participants from six cities and towns attended the course, which took place on October 31 and November 1, 1930. Most of the discussion revolved around the "authenticity" of the materials, which had been a preoccupation of Cahan's.[5] If Cahan's influence on one of the attendants, S. Z. Pipe, was any indication, his seminar was immensely important in revitalizing Yiddish folklore activity at YIVO. Cahan was respected as the highest authority on Yiddish folklore, and when he suggested that the Ethnographic Commission should change its name to "Folklore Commission," the YIVO did so, on November 2, 1930. Cahan was well informed about the international folklore world, and the shift in nomenclature signified a break with the Dubnovian "historic-ethnographic" tradition and a step toward becoming a member in the scholarly folklore community. Even after this official name change, the press and YIVO occasionally still referred to the commission as the Ethnographic Commission.[6]

The *Aspirantur:* The Training of Yiddish Folklore Scholars

After Cahan's visit in 1930, the emphasis of the YIVO Folklore Commission gradually changed from the collection of materials to the training of younger scholars. To this end, the YIVO established the Tsemakh Shabad Research Program, or, as it was known in Yiddish, *Aspirantur.*[7] The YIVO had listed the training of scholars as one of its goals from the beginning of the institution, and this was also stated in the *Vilner Theses* of 1925. Now, after almost ten years, they finally embarked upon the program. YIVO staff Max Weinreich, Zalmen Reyzen, and Zelig Kalmanovitsh were to train the students. In addition to their training, these *aspirantn* would simultaneously work with the YIVO materials related to their field—either folklore, history, or pedagogy. The program would involve a one-year course and would seek applicants from Vilne and all over Poland between the ages of seventeen and thirty with a high school education or equivalent. Students would receive a scholarship of fifty Polish guilden over the course of ten months. In August 1935, the first students began to work. By the time the *Aspirantur* began, the EC had collected nearly one hundred thousand items. In the second year of the *Aspirantur,* two students were given folklore assignments: S. Z. Pipe and Nekhame Epshteyn.

Shmuel Zaynvil Pipe

We know more about the young scholar S. Z. Pipe than about almost any other YIVO personality, thanks to his published letters and to biographical information from his two surviving brothers.[8] Pipe was born in 1907 in the Galician town of Sonik (in Polish: Sanok), the son of the head of a tailoring workshop. He and his three brothers had little education, since they were needed at home to help out in the family trade. At the workshop, workers and family sang songs to accompany the work, and it was here that Pipe first learned to appreciate folklore.[9] In the mid-1920s, he became active in the leftist Zionist youth organization, *Hashomir Hatsair* (Young Guard) and soon took a leading role.[10] Soon after the founding of YIVO in 1925, he read one of the "Calls to Collect Folklore" and became one of the EC's leading *zamlers*. In 1928, he eagerly answered the YIVO questionnaires and urged his younger brother Oyzer to do so as well.[11] Pipe was overjoyed that Jewish scholarship was growing and that they could contribute to this development. His 1928 letters urged his brothers to nag their informants to contribute texts or old books to the YIVO. He and his brother hoped to win the contest for the best folklore collections, but had to settle for the second prize. When, in one letter, Oyzer asked whether he had collected any "trifles" (*narishkeytn*), Pipe replied sternly, "First off, I must tell you that I have the greatest respect for Jewish folklore. If you used the term 'trifle,' it must have surely been in jest."[12] The passion expressed in the following passage probably reflected the emotions of many YIVO fieldworkers: "To tell you the truth, if I don't collect, I feel as if something is missing. . . . In short, I'm a passionate collector. I feel impelled to record. Why should a Yiddish word, or song or a game be lost when it can be saved? Everything that Jews have ever or today created, I find valuable. Religious objects, art objects, even the tiniest thing is holy and valuable to me."[13]

Pipe's method of collecting was also typical of most YIVO *zamlers*. When he received the *opsherenish* (traditional haircutting ritual) questionnaire, he went to pray in the synagogue, chatted with the old folks at the oven that provided the only warmth, and recorded their descriptions of the custom, though they initially hesitated and thought the rite stupid and fanatical.[14] After laboring so hard in his fieldwork, Pipe wanted reassurance from YIVO and his brother that their collections were worthwhile and were appreciated. The positive replies from YIVO were crucial in keeping Pipe and other *zamlers* motivated. Surrounded by friends and informants who doubted the purpose of the whole folkloric endeavor, the *zamlers* looked to YIVO, an enlightened institution, for support and direction. Pipe idolized YIVO, though his Zionist affiliation placed him in an awkward position in relation to the Yiddishists in Vilne. He read the Hebrew press, which criticized YIVO for anti-Hebrew sentiments, and noted these attacks to his brother but did not comment.[15]

Pipe knew his hometown well, and while in the army, he sent Oyzer instructions about the best informants for each genre.[16] As one of the EC's best collectors, Pipe was rewarded when I. L. Cahan came to YIVO in 1930 and paid Pipe's way to the seminar. Cahan was very impressed with Pipe, and in 1932 the two began to correspond. This correspondence continued until the elder folklorist's death in 1938. Pipe looked up to Cahan as a mentor, and Cahan viewed Pipe as his protégé.

By 1932, Oyzer, the brother who was Shmuel Zaynvil's collaborator on folklore field trips, was living on a kibbutz in Poland to prepare for eventual settlement in Israel. Pipe's letters to him exuded the same enthusiasm as in 1928: "Collecting is going quite well. I have hit upon the sources of Jewish folklore."[17] In Sonik, Pipe and a younger brother, Gershon, arranged the song collection, and sought variants of the songs in other collections. By August 1932, the three brothers had collected four hundred songs. When no variants were found, they were especially pleased. They were desperate for folklore literature but could not afford it. Pipe sent his brother Oyzer several samples of songs, to teach him to recognize the distinctions between genres. He also warned his brother to ensure that the materials were authentic, and that the informant was not simply inventing things in order to get rid of him. Cahan had instilled this fear and Pipe admitted that this had happened to him. Cahan told him that even a German professor had made such an error.[18] Pipe sought out the folklore types that the YIVO questionnaires recommended, though he was aware that all Jews could contribute something. He recorded a song text from the wife of a well-known poet but the husband panicked and asked Pipe not to use her name. Pipe commented sarcastically, "We saved his honor," clearly annoyed at the embarrassment certain sectors of Jewish society felt about what he was doing.[19]

In September 1932, Pipe had sent a collection of his children's songs to YIVO for publication in the *YIVO-bleter*, which had just begun publication. He wrote his brother Oyzer that their dream to be published would soon be realized.[20] A part of their collection, though not the children's songs, would eventually be published, but not until 1937. As a result of this frustration, Pipe wrote Oyzer that they should hold off sending materials to YIVO immediately and instead establish their own archive. Pipe was also typical of many of the *zamlers* in his strong desire to publish his materials. Ultimately, Pipe believed that it was not enough to send the folk texts to the YIVO archive and have them lay there. He felt that the *zamlarbet,* the work of collecting, would be complete only when the collections were printed. At one point, when Shmuel Zaynvil discussed marriage with Oyzer, he wrote jokingly that with the dowry he would publish two volumes of folk songs.[21] Publication was the dream of the collector. YIVO knew this from the many letters from fieldworkers who had hoped to be published, and therefore promised a folklore volume, which eventually was published in 1938.

In December 1934 he applied for the *Aspirantur.* In the two-page "life description" (*lebns-bashraybung*) that he submitted, Pipe recalled his love for collecting from a very young age. At first he collected buttons and seeds; then bottles, which he sorted and kept in the attic; then stamps. After YIVO was founded, he collected folklore. Folk texts were the continuation of his interest in buttons, seeds, and stamps! Pipe attributed his interest in scholarship and literature to his group leader during *hakhshara* (Zionist training to prepare for settlement in Palestine). In his autobiography, he described his tireless collecting from rich and poor for the EC and how he also inspired his brothers and friends to collect. He described how they would chase after people for weeks until they relented and told them what they wanted to hear. When people saw them coming, he said, they would say, "Oh no, the YIVO is coming, prepare a song or a tale."[22] Pipe and his brother Oyzer felt responsible for the recording of all Galician folklore, since it was considered an undercollected area. He described his joy at collecting a text and finding variants for it in the literature, "as if we had discovered a treasure." His reason for joining the *Aspirantur* program was to complete his studies in the field of folklore. He intended to print two books of Yiddish folk songs from Galicia.

Pipe was accepted into the *Aspirantur* and in August 1935 he arrived in Vilne. The EC placed him in charge of organizing the EC archive, which had fallen into disarray due to Khayes's departure a short time earlier. Pipe was asked to work on children's folklore, a topic he admitted he knew little about.[23] The month he arrived, YIVO celebrated its ten-year anniversary with an international conference. At this conference, he experienced firsthand the ideological struggles within the Yiddishist camp that YIVO had to face. The socialist Bundists protested that the YIVO should have protested the attacks on Yiddish in Israel and should become closer to the masses. The scholars argued that this was not their role; they were for all of the Jewish people. Pipe sided with this latter position, though he rarely expressed his political opinions.[24]

Pipe collated the children's folklore material and used K. Wehrhan's *Kinderlied und Kinderspiel* as a guide for classification.[25] By September he had finished the systemization. All *aspirantn* were required to present progress reports to the other *aspirantn* and the staff. At his first report, at the end of September 1935, the issue emerged of exactly what qualified as children's folklore; was it what children created, what adults created for children, or what children did to adult material? Pipe's inclusive approach met with little argument. Pipe was aware of the "survivals" and *Gesunkenes Kulturguts*[26] approaches in Wehrhan's work, but was interested in the book mainly as a guide to categorization of the genre of children's folklore, and took little note of the theoretical implications.[27]

Pipe settled into an academic environment, and his brother Oyzer in Israel became the prime fieldworker in the family. All at YIVO respected Shmuel Zaynvil for his knowledge of folklore and his skill at work. His good humor also made him the most popular *aspirant*.[28]

Pipe had prepared a classification for children's games for his second report on children's folklore. He told the group that he had rejected other classifications and had established his own based on the materials before him. Cahan had recommended he do this.[29] The report revealed Pipe's mastery, in a brief time, of the materials and literature on the subject.[30] In addition to classification, Pipe also showed interest in the psychological aspect of the texts and what they revealed about the life of the Jewish child. Since his time in the program was running out, he suggested working only with children's games, classifying and looking for variants.

Pipe was granted another year in the *Aspirantur*, but told Weinreich that he could not live in Vilne with the subsidy he had been receiving.[31] His completed classification of children's games with comments comprised 496 pages and included 805 items. Weinreich wanted to publish it as a volume, but this never materialized.[32] Pipe's introduction to a collection of children's games appeared in the *YIVO-bleter* at the beginning of 1936.[33] This was Pipe's first printed article. In writing it, he had before him the largest collection of Jewish children's games ever assembled. He compared them with the coterritorial variants, and confidently refuted earlier statements on Jewish children's games, namely Regina Lilienthal's assertion that the Jewish child had few original games and that the games reflected the sadness of the Jewish child.[34] He also believed that a close examination of Yiddish children's games would destroy the stereotype that Jews had little connection with nature. Pipe found possible "remnants" of older Jewish customs in some children's games—a notion that paralleled I. L. Cahan's idea that some of the older Yiddish songs had survived in children's songs.[35] After only one year at YIVO, Pipe showed a firm grasp of the Yiddish folklore material and established himself as an able writer as well.

During his first year at the *Aspirantur*, Pipe also worked on publishing a collection of Yiddish folk songs that he and his brother had recorded. Zalmen Reyzen sent Cahan 146 of Pipe's Yiddish folk songs from Galicia, asking for his evaluation.[36] Pipe's brother Gershon was contributing most of the money needed to publish the materials; the YIVO promised to allocate the rest. Weinreich felt that if Cahan would not answer in a timely fashion, they would edit the collection in Vilne.[37] Cahan warmly replied to Pipe's collection, suggesting that many genres of folk song be included, not just love songs.[38] Pipe replied that there was not enough money to produce such a large-scale collection. Cahan recommended publishing the songs in the *YIVO-bleter*, and Pipe agreed to the suggestion. Cahan finally sent back his commentary on the songs and indicated which songs he thought should be published. The number of songs that Cahan deleted shocked Pipe. Pipe had recorded many of the texts from his father, and from other family and friends. Now Cahan was telling him that they sang the songs imperfectly or wrong. Pipe, as the fieldworker who had heard the songs and believed them to be competently performed, was stymied. He eventually agreed with Cahan's deletions; yet, he was determined to understand why Cahan had edited so exclusively.[39]

Pipe returned to Sanok in the summer of 1936, and read Yitskhok Shiper's article, "Introduction to Jewish *Folkskentenish*," at Cahan's suggestion.[40] "Folkskentenish" was a literal translation of the German term

"Volkskunde," knowledge or science of the folk. Pipe wrote a lengthy letter to Cahan in which he discussed and questioned basic concepts of folklore. Pipe was confused by Shiper's limitation of the terms "folk-lore" and "folkskentenish" to the lower classes. This limitation disturbed Pipe, and he countered, as someone who had conducted extensive field-work, that, "In fact, folklore exists not only among the lower classes . . . but even among those who have a higher status. I would say among the whole people. Does not the whole people use or create jokes and proverbs and others? Certainly, yes. They are therefore, co-creators of folklore."[41] Pipe was guided not only by his experience on this question; Yiddish folklorists, particularly the Warsaw group, had been expanding the class dimension of the "folk" since before the First World War. Shiper, depending heavily on German folkloristics, was out of touch with the Yiddish side of this issue. In Cahan's reply which came months later, he, too, the most conservative of Yiddish folklorists, began to have doubts that the "folk" equaled the "lower classes," and he agreed with Pipe.[42]

In the same letter, Pipe asked other fundamental questions: What is an authentic folk song? If the folk sings a song from literature, is that not a folk song? And why does the folk have more right to add or to subtract from a song than the folklorist? Pipe had always recorded the texts faith-fully; yet, since Cahan had changed his unaltered texts for print, he was confused.[43] Cahan replied that his own views on folklore and folk song had evolved and were still changing; there were many unanswered ques-tions on the nature of folklore. He explained that the fact that the folk sang the songs made them folk songs. Literary songs could thus become folk songs and vice versa. Pipe's direct line of questioning had turned Cahan's view on these issues around completely from his earlier views. In terms of "correcting" mistakes, Cahan wrote, there were no set rules. "One must know intuitively how to go about it."[44] He asked Pipe to send him some texts; he would explain why they were not included in his collection of Yiddish folk songs from Galicia. Cahan's comments about some of these songs reveal his rigid editorial policy and his notion of a literary standard for Yiddish folk songs.[45] Cahan set up a dichotomy of the performed song and the written song. In his paradigm, the folk often sang the songs incorrectly, and it was up to the folklorist to edit the song so that it could appear in its "written form."[46] Pipe never chal-lenged Cahan on this point, though his sending the songs back to Cahan to explain the "improvements" was a protest of sorts. Pipe, by that time, had become as experienced a fieldworker as Cahan, and his intuition told him something was amiss when the folklorist viewed the folk as a ruiner of the texts.

Pipe was not completely satisfied with Cahan's reply, and observed, "Perhaps it's really impossible to give a clear definition" of a folk song.[47] Pipe's own folkloristic ego began to break away from Cahan's influence at this time. Cahan had always emphasized the need to prioritize collecting folklore; the old was more important than the new. Pipe believed that both old and new should be collected, since the new would be old in twenty years. This was the approach of many of the Yiddish folklorists, such as Lehman and Bastomski, who had collected revolutionary songs and texts from the First World War. The correspondence between Cahan and Pipe filled a theoretical gap in Pipe's folkloristic education; it was also a break for Pipe, who worked many hours at cataloging the YIVO archives and not enough at pondering folklore theory. Pipe studied the Soviet Yiddish folklorists, who had recently raised important theoretical issues, particularly on the nature of workers' songs.[48] He generally agreed with Cahan in his distrust of Soviet Yiddish folklore scholarship, though on some issues he was more open.

Pipe began to write reviews during the summer of 1936. One result of his efforts was a cover article in *Literarishe bleter* that honored I. L. Cahan for his fortieth year of folklore activities.[49] Pipe had hoped to study folk medicine when he returned to YIVO as a second-year *aspirantr*. Weinreich advised him to look at other genres of children's folklore, so he could become an expert in one subfield.[50] The first major article written by Pipe, and the only folk song collection printed in his lifetime, was finally published in *YIVO-bleter* in early 1937.[51] This was a rare publication of a collection of texts in a journal that had printed monographs almost exclusively. In his introduction, written in March 1936, almost a year before publication, Pipe made it clear that he expected 129 songs from his collection of 840 to be published, as well as some of the music to the songs. However, only 45 songs were published, in two parts, with no musical notes. Cahan drastically cut the number to be published, though Pipe's pleadings finally convinced him to allow 10 additional songs.[52]

The fieldwork experience occupied much of Pipe's introduction. While this aspect of folklore was to some degree discussed by other Yiddish folklorists, no other Yiddish folklorist used his family as his prime informants. In these fieldwork narratives, however, no mention was made of his family. Pipe collected in the evenings, except for the "stubborn ones," who knew that he worked during the day and so intentionally told him they were available only at that time. He used various methods to "elicit" folklore: "There are a few individuals (mostly among the young) who understand the thing. Only an explanation is necessary and they sing for you gladly. For others, you have to sing something to them for the singer often complains that he does not know or remember anything. Therefore one must have one's one repertory. Among the poor people, money brings the best results, since, 'I won't make a fool of myself for nothing.'"[53] When even money did not help, he resorted to other means to gain the folk's trust—buying the products they sold, or engaging them in long conversations on other matters. At one point, Pipe devised an intricate scheme. He befriended the desired singer's neighbor, and when the singer visited her neighbor, she found Pipe listening to the woman sing. She then began to sing as well. To Pipe's surprise, the neighbor knew many more songs than the original informant. As was the case with other Yiddish folklorists, Pipe also felt the danger of doing fieldwork among the "folk." A jealous husband entered unexpectedly during one fieldwork session and complained to his family of "a strange young man who supposedly came on account of songs."[54] The images of deception and ignorance of the people did not escape Pipe's reaction to his *zamlarbet* (collection work). Once again, the folklorist denigrated the folk while exalting the folklore, which had to be extracted against their wishes.[55]

Pipe's song collection included only love songs, which was no doubt due to Cahan's emphasis upon that genre.[56] The projected collection included ballads, wedding songs, and short songs as well. The Yiddish used was very close to standard Yiddish, with few dialectical features; however, the article does include a quick guide to the Sanok pronunciation of Yiddish words.[57] The work was to remain the only collection of folk songs from Galicia until the posthumous collection of Pipe's work, which had been kept by his brother Oyzer in Israel, published by Dov Noy and Meyer Noy in 1971.

In the same issue with the second part of the song collection, Pipe and Nekhame Epshteyn, another *aspirant*, reviewed a Soviet collection of children's games.[58] Here the authors decried the tendentious Soviet approach to folklore. The criticism focused on the poor classification of the games, a subject of which Pipe knew more than any other Yiddish folklorist.

In his next publication, Pipe examined I. L. Peretz's collection of folk songs.[59] This contained no theoretical analysis or conclusion; only a cross-indexing with other Yiddish folk song collections. He continued his work on children's songs and published an introductory article in late 1937 on his second year's work in the *Aspirantur*.[60] As in his work with children's games, the main goal was to classify the materials; in this case, a collection of 1,427 children's songs. Most of the article was devoted to detailing the difficulties of differentiation among the preliminary categories, which had been based on the subject of the song. He postponed the issue of the origin of the texts for a later date, highlighting the positivist agenda over that of the "survivalists," such as Shiper. Pipe concluded that his materials would eventually aid not only the folklorist, but also the child psychologist, as well as the modern Yiddish school.

Nakhmen Blumental, a literary critic and a folklorist, found serious fault with Pipe's thematic categories of children's songs.[61] The reviewer recommended that the songs be systematized according to their psychological function—that is, according to which needs the songs fulfilled at the time. A number of the song themes, he complained, did not relate to what they "accomplished." When Oyzer suggested that Blumental had a point, Pipe answered that psychological categories were "misleading." Each scholar proposed his or her own categories. "It's easier to make theoretical classifications than on the basis of the actual material. My division is built on the basis of the materials."[62]

In his third year at YIVO, Pipe was given a salary and made a research associate. For the *Aspirantur* Pipe researched the subject *Dos kunstlid in dem folks moyl* (The art song among the folk). Prompted by his correspondence with Cahan over the issue, and by recent Soviet scholarship, Pipe chose a subject for the first time that, on the face of it, was not a large classificatory project.[63] After some initial research, Pipe realized that all Yiddish folk song collections included, unknowingly, songs of literary origin. Weinreich suggested he use the historic-geographic approach, as Walter Anderson had done in his analysis of a Yiddish folk song.[64] As a result, Pipe once again classified materials, this time the variants of the song. He never wrote on his original interest in the dynamics of the folklorizing process. The written result of this topic was his study on one song of literary origin, "Der arbeter" (The worker), by the socialist poet Dovid Edelshtat(1866–92), first published in 1889.[65]

Pipe had sent out his own questionnaire on this song in early 1938 and had amassed thirty-four variants from twenty-four towns.[66] Pipe analyzed the language of the song, how certain words changed from the original, and why. Otherwise, the main accomplishment of the work was its compartmentalization of variants. Since the origin, the ur-text, was known, this was an interesting use of the historic-geographic method. His goal was to identify the main types of the folklorized version through a lexical analysis. Pipe drew no theoretical conclusions, but was satisfied with the presentation of the materials from which one could draw such conclusions. The folklore literature that he cited for the study were German works by Hans Naumann and John Meir that analyzed folklorized art or literary songs. Pipe, however, made no mention of a central framework that these works had conceived in which these songs were "crippled" as they "sank" to the lower classes. Pipe had already read of these views through Shiper's article on *folkskentenish*, and as his letter to Cahan indicated, he rejected them.[67]

After I. L. Cahan died suddenly on April 3, 1937, Pipe wrote that, "he [Pipe] was walking around in a daze."[68] In his fourth year in the *Aspirantur*, 1938–39, Pipe had two goals. One was to edit and prepare I. L. Cahan's literary inheritance for print, including the planned volume of Yiddish folklore. The other was to work on riddles in Cahan's collection. Pipe acknowledged that his mentor had helped him publish his first collection of songs, and had been generous with his time. By this time, in terms of his outlook on folklore, Pipe had evolved beyond Cahan's nineteenth-century romantic nationalist outlook. He had read and was affected by Soviet Yiddish folkloristics. He had also read the Polish and German folklore literature, knew what he liked and disliked about it, and was poised to write crucial theoretical works on Yiddish folklore.

Pipe's final theoretical analysis was his twenty-eight-page review of a collection of Yiddish folk songs by the Soviet Yiddish folklorist Z. Skuditski.[69] Here, in the tradition of Alfred Landau, whose reviews of scholarship were themselves major scholarly statements, he exhibited his profound knowledge of Yiddish folk song scholarship and, more importantly, his unrivaled familiarity with the nineteenth-century literary sources of Yiddish folk songs. Pipe's tone throughout this review was contentious, revealing a dislike of the ideology of Soviet Yiddish scholarship and, in his opinion, its use of propaganda rather than research. Pipe questioned Skuditski's search for Slavic roots and parallels to the folk songs while excluding a similar attempt to find German origins. Skuditski saw an ideological camaraderie between the working classes of the Jews and the Slavs. If that were true, Pipe asked, then what about the macaronic Slavic-Yiddish songs that were sung in religious circles? Those songs were definitely not from the working class. With his experience using the historic-geographic method, Pipe upbraided the author for making claims of origins before all the variants of a song had been compared in all the coterritorial languages. The second half of the review listed bibliographic references on the locations and descriptions of songs omitted in Skuditski's collection. So impressive was Pipe's criticism that one could say the review announced to the Yiddish folklore world that Pipe had assumed the mantles of I. L. Cahan and Alfred Landau and had been properly groomed by YIVO (especially Max Weinreich) to become the YIVO's folklorist in residence. The *Aspirantur* had been a success; it had trained a self-educated young man to join the ranks of folklore scholars around the world.

Pipe's last major work was his collection on "Napoleon in Yiddish Folklore."[70] He completed this work in August 1939. This was the first thematic study by Pipe in which he took materials on a given topic from numerous genres: tales, legends, jokes, riddles, games, counting out rhymes, nicknames, blessings, curses, material culture (a hat: napoleonkele; a pastry: a Napoleon). The materials were collected, at the request of the editor of the volume, using a questionnaire sent to the folklore correspondents over a three-month period. Pipe amassed 113 texts but made no conclusions based on the material, other than that the name Napoleon was still popular among Jews. Included were materials that supported Russia, and others that supported Napoleon. As was Pipe's style, his erudition emerged in the endnotes and parallels.

As Pipe prepared to return to Sanok, in August 1939, he wrote Oyzer of his plan to marry Nekhame Epshteyn that winter.[71] Only two more letters arrived from Pipe via Romania to his brothers in Israel. He was killed in the German extermination camp of Zaslaw, near Sanok, in 1943, at the age of thirty-six. He had an opportunity to escape, but would not leave his parents.

In the four years of his Vilne residence, from August 1935 to August 1939, Shmuel Zaynvil Pipe emerged from hundreds of YIVO folklore collectors in the field to become the leading YIVO folklorist. As a fieldworker, as in his scholarly work, he was indefatigable. Pipe recorded folk songs from 151 informants from forty locations in Galicia, of all ages.[72] As a *zamler* he was representative of many other diligent YIVO fieldworkers in his zeal for the collection process, his eagerness to see his materials published, and his feeling of being part of the "folk" that he had recorded. However, unlike other YIVO *zamlers* and even folklorists such as Shmuel Lehman, who had no interest in writing about the materials, Pipe did not stop at the *zamler* stage of his development. For Lehman, the act of presenting "the joys of Yiddish" was an end in itself. Pipe sought to be educated in the world of folklore studies. Initially his experience in the Hashomer Hatsair camps, and then his contacts with I. L. Cahan in New York and Max Weinreich in Vilne, energized his quest for knowledge. As an archivist of the EC, he surrounded himself with the largest Yiddish folklore archive in the world and familiarized himself with those materials. After two years of essentially systematizing and arranging the folk texts, he arrived at a point where he could enter into a scholarly dialogue with the top Soviet Yiddish folklorists. He had just begun to find his own voice in Jewish folkloristics when the war broke out.

Nekhame Epshteyn

The other *aspirant* who became an intricate part of the Ethnographic/Folklore Commission was Nekhame Epshteyn. She was born in 1898 in Lodz and attended a Russian school. She became a leading activist in the Yiddish cultural movement as a teacher in the secular Yiddish schools in Vilne after 1922.[73] Epshteyn was a Yiddish poet, reviewer, and writer. She worked often as a translator from Polish into Yiddish, and her first connection to Jewish folklore may have been her translation of Regina Lilienthal's article on the evil eye in *Yidishe filologye*.[74] Another account gives her meeting with I. L. Cahan at the YIVO seminar in 1930 as the inspiration to study folklore and particularly jokes.[75] After her meeting with Cahan, he asked her to oversee the publishing of his first book of folktales, which was published in Vilne in 1931.[76] He had planned to produce a series of folkloristic books in Yiddish with her assistance.

Epshteyn entered the *Aspirantur* during the first year, 1935–36, and remained an *aspirant* for all four years of its existence. Before this, she had already researched Yiddish jokes and was on the Ethnographic Commission. She reviewed Dr. Immanuel Olsvanger's collection of Yiddish folklore in 1932.[77] This impressive collection received a warm reception in Epshteyn's review, though she criticized Olsvanger's tendency to draw out the jokes in a "cutesy" fashion. She accepted the dictum that brevity is the soul of wit. Olsvanger, however, in retrospect captured the performance style of the Yiddish joke more accurately than did any other folklorist, and in effect disproved that notion of humor for Jews. A good Jewish joke teller will take his or her time during the joke, not cut it short to get to the point.

In her first and second year at the *Aspirantur*, Epshteyn worked, probably at Weinreich's suggestion, on "Jewish folk humor." During the first year, she concentrated on the taxonomy of the humor material in the EC archive. Both folklore *aspirants*, Pipe and Epshteyn, undertook such organizational work in the beginning, for the EC archive was in need of serious sorting. One must also consider, though, that Weinreich, their supervisor, envisioned the work of the folklorist as not much more than classification and comparison, given his philological approach. At that point in the history of folklore studies, Weinreich was in step with the rest of folklore scholarship. If Walter Anderson, one of the world's leading folklorists and a friend of YIVO, was Weinreich's model of what a folklorist was and should be, then this was understandable. The historic-geographic method promoted exactly this type of work; much of the folklore world was preoccupied with the accumulation and comparison of texts at this time.

Epshteyn's long-term plan was to research a massive project on "Jewish Folk Humor." The work was to contain an introduction, three chapters, and a collection of Yiddish jokes. Only the second chapter, on classification, was ever printed. In this classic article, "How to Classify the Yiddish Joke,"[78] she looked at 1,300 joke texts in the EC archive and arranged them according to their *levush* (garb, "the environment around the persons") and *tendents* (goal, what were they really laughing at?). She divided the material into three large groups: the first was a variety of subjects—family, Jews and non-Jews, Hasidim—twelve all together; the second was humorous sayings; the third was jokes attributed to famous jokesters, such as Motke Khabad. The items in the category "humorous sayings" did not poke fun at anybody, but were examples of word play, often in question-and-answer form. Epshteyn established the category on famous pranksters, for she observed that the jokes were a separate, closed category. She also observed several similar qualities among all Jewish jokesters and pranksters. Epshteyn's tripartite division of her corpus was an innovation in Jewish humor research. Until her work, the leading collectors and researchers, especially Alter Druyanov and J. Ch. Ravnitzki, employed subject headings as in Epshteyn's first category.[79] Immanuel Olsvanger did not even divide his jokes according to subject.[80] At no time during her research did Epshteyn attempt a psychological analysis of the materials, as had Alter Druyanov in his work on Jewish folk humor,[81] or a cultural historical contextualization, as in Olswanger's work.[82] Methodologically, YIVO's approach discouraged any general conclusions on the subject until all the materials were in order and had been classified.

During this time, Epshteyn prepared her very extensive notes on the humor material to be included in the EC's collection, *Yidisher folklor.*[83] Her detailed footnotes were rivaled only by those of Druyanov in the back of each of his three volumes of jokes. The notes examined variants from Jewish and non-Jewish sources and other texts in the YIVO archives. They were comparative only, and in no case did the researcher offer her own opinion on origin or interpretation.

During the 1938–39 year, Epshteyn worked with Pipe on the literary heritage of I. L. Cahan. In this collaboration, Pipe was to arrange the songs, and Epshteyn the folktales.[84] Of the planned six-volume "Collected Works of I. L. Cahan," the EC published one volume of folktales, *Yidishe folksmayses* (Yiddish folktales), which was compiled by Epshteyn and edited by Weinreich.[85] The work was published after the outbreak of the war, when Vilne returned briefly to an independent Lithuania. There were no notes or commentary to the texts, and a one-page preface explained that all notes to the tales would be published in the final volume of the collected works.

Though all of Epshteyn's published work was of a comparative nature, in her unpublished reports to the *Aspirantur* she exhibited an interest in theoretical issues and had begun to think about the nature of Yiddish jokes, and what caused certain texts to be widely distributed while others were not. In her first report on Jewish jokes in the *Aspirantur,*

"Variants and Parallels in Jewish Jokes," she reported how startled she was when she compiled the archival material and discovered the large number of variants of some jokes in oral and written sources.[86] She saw interesting interchanges between texts from printed joke collections and from joke tellers and observed that "joke dissemination was a non-stop circulation from teller to printed source and visa-versa."[87] Epshteyn also discussed the process of localization and modernization of jokes. The former process involved telling the joke with local people as the characters, while the latter process caused the same joke to change from one generation to the next. Because of these processes, while the same essential joke might be told, the "point" could change dramatically. Epshteyn was also aware of, and inquisitive about, the fact that the same motifs that were found in jokes were also found in proverbs, nicknames, and other genres. She concluded her report with the conviction that no matter how one approached Jewish jokes, through a historic-geographic method or with a psychological one, one still needed as many versions of texts as possible. Only after all the parallels had been brought together could one proceed further.

In this one surviving report, one can see that Epshteyn was an astute and promising folklorist and could have contributed much to Yiddish folkloristics had the war not ended that possibility. The *Aspirantur* had trained her well and she developed a sensitivity to the scholarly issues of her day in folklore. Unlike Pipe, she had an advanced education and was not a devoted *zamler*. Whereas Pipe drifted into Yiddishism and folklore at the same time, Epshteyn had been active as a Yiddishist for years before her interest in folklore. For her, one may surmise, the study of Yiddish folklore was an extension of her other Yiddish cultural activities. Once she began to study the field, and with encouragement from I. L. Cahan and Max Weinreich, she became fascinated with the subject. If, as Lucy Dawidowicz wrote, Epshteyn's "greatest asset was her sense of humor," then the study of Jewish humor would have been reflexive, just as Pipe's collection of folklore permitted him to study his family, friends, and self.[88]

In August 1939 she remained in Vilne, while her fiancé, Pipe, returned to Sanok. While the Germans occupied Lithuania, she lived in the Vilne ghetto. She escaped, but was captured and shot at Ponary at the end of the summer of 1942.[89]

Yidisher folklor

The final product of the YIVO Ethnographic Commission was *Yidisher folklor*, published in 1938 after many years of preparation and editing.[90] I. L. Cahan had been the editor of the volume, but had died the year before its publication. The commission had had enough material for this volume after its first year of collecting in 1926 and had planned and announced earlier versions of this collection.[91] Cahan edited many of the texts during his visit to YIVO in 1930, and by 1931 the EC had prepared the material for publication. However, Cahan had not finished (or even really started) his notes to the materials when he died six years later. When the secretary of the commission, Kh. Khayes, left, the work was at a standstill. According to Pipe, Khayes was dismissed after writing to Cahan in America that the money he set aside for the folklore volume had been spent on other things. Cahan wrote to YIVO to complain, and Khayes was let go in 1935. Zelig Kalmanovitsh, one of the leaders of YIVO, told Pipe that Cahan would probably never send his comments; such was Cahan's reputation as a procrastinator and perfectionist who printed just a small fraction of his available material.[92] The *aspirants* finished most of the incomplete materials.

Yidisher folklor was divided into five genres: songs, legends and tales, jokes and humorous tales, *purim-shpiln*, and folk remedies and omens. A sixth section included musical notations to the songs and *purim-shpiln*. This section was followed by scholars' notes on three genres: Pipe on the songs, Epshteyn on the jokes, Pipe and Shiper on the *purim-shpiln*. The most popular genre, the proverb, was missing from the volume. Khayes had prepared a collection of similes, but it was not published. Cahan had envisioned this first volume to be followed by a volume on each genre.[93]

Though the publication of the volume had a long and tortuous history, YIVO desperately wanted to print it, for it was a "thank you gift" to the folklore *zamlers* after thirteen years of unpaid fieldwork. At the end of the volume, YIVO printed two lists: one of the 138 points of origin of the folklore material (with a map); the other of the 311 *zamlers* who had contributed to the work. The volume was a testament to the collaborative effort that marked the Ethnographic/Folklore Commission and made it the most successful branch of YIVO.[94] This work followed in the tradition of the first major Yiddish folk song collection by Ginsburg and Marek in 1901, which included 376 texts sent in by fifty correspondents.[95] The lists were also a means of exhibiting the pan-Polish, if not pan-Eastern European, influence of the YIVO institute.

Upon closer analysis of the song section, however, the illusion that this collection was a balanced reflection of Yiddish folklore throughout Poland evaporated. Despite years of efforts to have collectors send in the music with the texts, the song section evidenced the failure of this endeavor. Only 40 percent of the song texts have melodies. The song collection is also overwhelmingly disproportionate in terms of geographic distribution. Of the 203 folk song texts, 140 are from the Lithuanian town of Podbroz. Seventy-six of the 88 melodies are also from Podbroz, collected almost entirely by Aron and Khaye Engeltsin. Was this small town in Lithuania really the Yiddish folk song capital of Poland?

The songs section manifested the editorial hand of I. L. Cahan. It began with "Ballads," a genre that Cahan regarded as especially important, for it included the oldest songs in the Yiddish folksinger's repertory. The scholarship on the ballad was also an internationally interconnected one, and Cahan strove to make Yiddish folkloristics part of that discussion. The songs had few dialectic features, though more had been transcribed in the originals by the collectors.[96] The YIVO policy was to allow only those dialectic features that were necessary for a rhyme. Only one version of most of the songs was printed—another sign of Cahan's influence, for the New York folklorist wanted to display only the "best" of Yiddish folklore. This view contradicted what the EC had written repeatedly to the zamlers: every version is important.

The largest song category, numbering forty-two texts, was "libe lider" (love songs), another of Cahan's pet song genres. Other smaller sections were of "tants lider" (dance songs), "khosn-kale un khasene lider" (groom-bride songs and wedding songs), "vig lider" (cradle songs; not one melody included), "familyen lider" (family songs), "soldatn unrekrutn lider" (soldier and draft songs), "milkhome lider" (war songs), "arbeter lider" (work songs), "shpot lider" (mocking songs), "humoristishe lider" (humorous songs), "ganovim lider" (thieve's songs; only two included), "religyeze lider" (religious songs), "Purim lider" (Purim songs), and "Lider vegn mentshns goyrl" (songs on people's fate). Except for the love songs, the number of songs in each section seemed to have been arbitrary, and not to have indicated any correlation with the actual ratio of these song genres to folksingers' repertories. For example, the family songs section contained only eight songs, whereas in the Soviet collections, where they were also called *shteyger* (way of life) songs, they comprised a major song genre.[97]

S. Z. Pipe's extensive notes compared variants with the Yiddish folk song literature, which was not very large at the time, as well as with scarcer sources, such as song sheets, plays, and nineteenth-century chapbooks. Pipe, like his mentor Cahan, immediately assumed that if an older printed version of a folk song text could be found, then that folk song was a folklorized version of that original source.[98] Neither Pipe nor Cahan envisioned the possibility that the printed version could have used a current folk song as its source, which was sometimes the case. Pipe also quoted numerous collectors' comments when the information helped clarify the performance context, especially with the dance and wedding songs. The song collection was a disappointment, given the number of songs in the EC archive. Pipe's notes, though restricted to comparisons with other Yiddish collections, were an example of excellent scholarship.

The tales and legends section included 26 wondertales, or *marchen*, and 134 legends. As with the ballad genre, the *marchen* were highlighted above other tales, for it was this genre which was at the center of international folktale scholarship. Cahan considered secular folktales as Jewish as any of the more overtly religious tales.[99]

Pipe had collected six of the tales.[100] Surprisingly, none of the tales collected by the great Grodne collector Berl Verblunski appeared. He had sent in dozens of tales, many of which have survived in the YIVO archives.[101] Though the EC held him in high esteem, Cahan referred to him as a "terrible falsifier," and as a result, one presumes, his tales were not printed.[102] The tale section seemed to have been quickly edited. The absence of commentary reinforces this notion. So the section of tales, like the song section, was a disappointment for a commission that had hundreds of tales and songs available.

On the other hand, the collection of legends was a fine contribution to an undercollected genre in Yiddish folklore.[103] The first two questionnaires that the EC distributed in November and December 1925 were on legends, and the response was a good one. Almost all of the included texts were local legends of old synagogues, churches, treasures, supernatural creatures, and the origin of town names. A few described famous personalities, such as Rothschild and Napoleon. They had little relation to traditional Yiddish and Hebrew religious legends or exempla, which had been widely published in chapbooks. In the Yiddish folklore literature, there had been very little analysis of local legends, aside from S. Ansky's article on old synagogues.[104] Unfortunately, no one added notes or commentary for the legends in *Yidisher folklor.*

The next section, "Vitsn un vitsike mayselekh" (Jokes and witty tales), included eighty jokes divided according to the famous jokesters Motke Khabad, Hershele Ostropolyer, and Froyim Graydinger. The majority are uncategorized. This section was put together by Nekhame Epshteyn, probably before her classification of Yiddish jokes had been constructed. This meager collection of jokes was improved considerably by her extensive notes.

The *purim-shpiln* section included sixteen plays and was the largest single collection of the genre up to that time. Pipe contributed six of the plays. No *shpiln* on biblical themes were included, for YIVO planned a separate volume for them.[105] The collection included the music for several plays, as well as comments by Pipe and Shiper. Pipe's notes examined the songs, and Shiper's much more detailed comments looked at the history of each *shpil* and attempted to date them.[106]

The final section of omens and remedies included only texts related to animals and plants. Khayim Khayes put this section together before his dismissal. This is the most useful collection of this sort, thanks to its systematization by animal and plant. If the number of texts reflects the actual occurrence of these beliefs and remedies, then one can see which animals played a more important part in folk belief among Jews. The items under dog, fish and bird, rooster, and frog were the most numerous. Again, no commentary was printed, though a Mr. Paskvinski in Vilne had collated the beliefs in the EC archives and compared them to Talmudic sources. According to the *Yedies,* he had found eight hundred parallel beliefs in the Talmud. The plan to publish this in a separate volume never materialized.[107]

The volume concluded with a list of the collectors, collecting circles, and informants (*afgeber*) and which items each contributed. This final list encapsulated the real significance of the publication: it was an important symbolic gesture of gratitude by the EC to those who had helped. As a scholarly work, it was uneven. The collections of legends, *purim-shpiln,* and folk beliefs were the only genres that did not dissatisfy. The work was edited in haste, though it was at least ten years in the making. The EC and Cahan envisioned *Yidisher folklor* as the beginning of a series of volumes of Yiddish folklore, not the end. There is no reason to doubt that without the interruption of the war a year later, YIVO would have printed many more such volumes.

Naftuli Vaynig

Throughout the 1930s, one of the leading folklorists associated with the YIVO EC was Naftuli Vaynig. Born in Tarnow in 1897 and raised in a Polish-speaking home, he studied Slavic languages and philosophy at the University of Cracow. Vaynig often drew from his familiarity with Polish folkloristics for his Jewish folklore work. He was not only a folklorist, but an outstanding literary critic who wrote important essays even in the Vilne ghetto shortly before his deportation to a death camp in Estonia.[108] Though closely associated with YIVO, Vaynig often worked alone and outside the YIVO circle, and should be considered a folklorist both within and outside of YIVO's influence.

Vaynig's folklore work began with two publications, the coauthored *What is Jewish Ethnography?* and his lengthy study of a Polish folk song about Jews in the third volume of *Yidishe filologye*.[109] One sees in these two works that Vaynig was interested in parallels to primitive civilizations and in the cross-fertilization of Polish and Jewish folklore.

He became a frequent reviewer of Polish folklore works in the *YIVO-bleter*, and wrote the obituary for the folklorist Benyomin Wolf Segel.[110] In his writings he avoided the term "folklore," which he associated with only oral genres, and preferred to use the term "ethnography," which he believed covered all of the folk culture.

Vaynig became active in the *Yidishe gezelshaft far landkentnish—Zydowski Towarzystwo Krajoznawcze* (Jewish Geographic Society), an organization that had sections including art, kayaking and skiing, and "ethnographic circles" in many locations throughout Poland.[111] Many of the members in these ethnographic circles were the same as those in the YIVO's *Zaml-krayzn* (collectors' groups), and the two circles often worked together. Vaynig wrote an article explaining the "essence and notion of ethnography" for the society's bilingual Yiddish-Polish journal, *Landkentnish*.[112] Ethnography, he declared, had "emancipated itself as an independent discipline with its own territory and separate research methods."[113] In the essay, which repeats much of his 1929 handbook for YIVO, he enumerated the genres that comprise ethnography, but added no bibliography. Compared to the YIVO publication, the *Landkentnish* essay spent much more time on the role of the collector and on the fieldwork experience. Vaynig proposed questionnaires for the circles, without mentioning any of the EC's work over the previous ten years. His participation in the *Yidishe gezelshaft far landkentnish* was perhaps an attempt to direct ethnographic research his own way. Vaynig implied that one of the problems with YIVO's method of collecting was that the fieldworkers collected the texts, provided little contextual information, and then sent the materials away to the YIVO archive without having learned anything themselves about Jewish ethnography. Vaynig suggested that the ethnographic circles discuss the collected materials in order to develop an "ethnographic intuition."[114] Members could even lecture on specific aspects of their work. This kind of activity was in stark contrast to the centralization of the YIVO organization. The YIVO was not successful in its presentation of itself as a "folk's organization." Vaynig and the *Yidishe gezelshaft far landkentnish* sought to make the study of ethnography and folklore more enjoyable, more social, and more educational.

Though active in social organizations, Vaynig was primarily a scholar, and he wrote many longer and shorter pieces on Jewish folklore. He authored one of the few articles on the history of Yiddish folkloristics, "The History and Problems of Yiddish Paremeology," which had originally been presented as a lecture at the YIVO ten-year anniversary conference in August 1935.[115] The title promised much more than was delivered, for Vaynig's brief historical overview was primarily an appeal to publish a Yiddish proverb dictionary and a theoretical discussion of what should be included in such a project. Historically, he divided Yiddish proverb scholarship into three stages: pre–Ignaz Bernstein, Bernstein, and post-Bernstein. He based the division of proverb collections methodologically upon whether the scholars used a key word system (*shlogvort*) or alphabetically arranged the texts. Vaynig rarely printed collections; he consistently concerned himself with theory and methodology. This was rare among Yiddish folklorists of his time.

He was also an exceptional folklorist of the genres of custom and belief; this was not surprising in lieu of his emphasis upon those fields in the YIVO handbook. In the Vilne journal *Sotsyale meditsin* in 1937, he printed two articles on these genres. The first, on "Epidemic-Weddings" (*mageyfe-khasenes*), analyzed the phenomenon of marrying off poor, often handicapped Jews on the cemetery to ward off an epidemic (usually cholera).[116] Vaynig printed excerpts from Yiddish literature and ethnographic sources to show the basic characteristics of the custom. He then compared elements of the custom with non-Jewish sources to show the magical thought and practice inherent in the rite, and its affinities to the folklores of other cultures. He continued this analysis in a larger context in the next issue in an article entitled "Jewish Cures and Remedies during Epidemics," in which he arranged all the known literature on the subject to arrive at the magical principles involved.[117]

His interest in medicinal issues and folklore continued with a study on *parkhes* (Jews afflicted with favus).[118] This was a topic considered too distasteful for most folklorists; yet, Vaynig accumulated much material and proceeded to delineate the basic folk practice to cure the illness, providing the first study dealing only with the disease.[119]

Vaynig returned to oral genres in "Historical Motifs in the Yiddish Folksong."[120] He maintained that while other categories of songs were collectively created, historical songs were the result of individual efforts. He took issue with Hans Naumann's rejection of historical songs as creations of higher literature. Among Jews, Vaynig argued, the writer of the historical folk song was one of the folk and not from the higher classes.[121] Vaynig observed that the images and verses of pogrom songs often were repeated and applied to different locations. Israel Zinberg made a similar analysis in reference to old Yiddish prose literature; however, Vaynig was interested in not only the literary aspect of folklore, but also the social dynamics involved in the creation and dissemination of folklore.[122] This was why he was drawn to Naumann's *Gesunkenes Kulturgut* theory, though as a Yiddishist folklorist he could not fully accept the idea that the lower classes had little creative power.

It is unfortunate that so little is known of Vaynig's relationship to the YIVO. He seems to have been in the center of the EC's activities in the late 1920s, but then concentrated his efforts elsewhere in the 1930s. He was an outstanding representative of a new generation of Yiddish folklorists who were not content to collect materials, but sought to analyze those materials and to write more theoretical studies, keeping abreast with folklore scholarship.

The YIVO *Zamlers*

The hundreds of far-flung collectors, or *zamlers*, who contributed materials to the YIVO were the component that made the Ethnographic/Folklore Commission the amazing success that it was. Throughout the 1930s, the EC continued to collect folklore materials, to issue occasional questionnaires, and to keep in touch with its network of correspondents. The surviving papers of the YIVO Ethnographic Commission, which are now housed at the YIVO Institute for Jewish Research in New York, include hundreds of letters from *zamlers* to the EC from the years 1928 to 1931. Several themes continually resurface in the correspondence, most of them of a practical nature. The *zamlers* had no money for postage to mail the texts they had collected. Some even hoped to get paid for their work: "I have much material. I can send it to you three to four times a week. However, I want a small payment for it, up to forty zlotys a month. And you will receive from me very valuable materials. If you agree, then write immediately. You don't have to send me postage stamps anymore. I will use the money from the pension for you. I conclude my writing now sure that you will do this. In any case, please answer yes or no."[123] Another leitmotif found among the letters of the *zamlers* was the desire to see their materials published. The EC secretary[124] answered one such letter this way:

> The goal of our folkloristic collection work is not only to collect, but also to edit and to publish the material that is very vital for our research. But you understand that from the fieldworker's transcription to being published is a great middle stage of classification, ordering, researching and comparing the material from one Jewish area with another, from our folklore to similar folklore of the peoples around us and to establish influences from both sides. In order for our work to be complete, we must collect a large amount of material; therefore, today, the most important thing is to collect.[125]

Many correspondents, as mentioned earlier in the chapter, asked for official certificates from YIVO authorizing them to carry out their work. Some even feared the police without one. Dozens of requests were made for *What is Jewish Ethnography?*

The fieldworkers also needed reassurance that their collections were worthy. They had entered a new field of folklore and did not know what was expected of them. The YIVO EC was a success in its accumulation of folklore and in activating hundreds of people who had been alien to the ethnographic fieldwork experience. Financial difficulties for YIVO, as for all of Polish Jewry, limited publications and organizational growth. Nevertheless, the EC was one of the largest networkings of field-workers in the history of folklore, and proved that the Yiddish nationalist fervor of the "ordinary guy" could be expressed in terms of collecting folklore.

Conclusion
The Jewish Folklorist and the Yiddish Nation

As the popular interest in the YIVO Ethnographic Commission demonstrated, the study and collection of folklore was not limited to small intellectual circles in Warsaw and Vilne, but was relevant to thousands of Jews in Poland. The letters from *zamlers* in the field indicate that at least one reason for this fascination with collecting Yiddish folklore was that it allowed easy access into publishing and proximity to a scholarly field. All one had to do was to record a few proverbs, songs, or customs from one's family and friends (or from one's own memory).[1] Of course, this easy access was not the only reason the Ethnographic Commission was more popular than other sections such as linguistics and demography. The appeal of folklore was also in its nationalist character—in its interpretation and representation of the Polish Jews as a "Yiddish nation."

The Jews of the interwar period were unlike any other generation in the history of the Jewish diaspora. The historian Ezra Mendelsohn has dubbed this period the "golden age of diaspora Jewish politics," for never had such a large percentage of Jews in Eastern Europe been politically active in a Jewish nationalist endeavor. The reasons for this were manifold: externally, the anti-Semitism of Polish society and the poor economic conditions created a desperate situation for Jews.[2] Internally, the Jews were quickly secularizing and entering into the modern world. Joining political parties seemed "almost an inevitable event"[3] for the Jewish youth of Poland. Mendelsohn concludes that though their political activities ultimately did little to ameliorate their plight, the Jews in interwar Poland would have experienced an even "bleaker" life, had it not been for the hope raised by their involvement in nationalist aspirations.[4] While this assertion is quite true, his other statement, that all the Jewish "isms" "proved impotent to one degree or another in the face of Polish reality and the international situation,"[5] is too cynical. Certainly, Yiddishists did not accomplish all that they had intended; few cultural and political movements ever do. Yet, they did lay the necessary groundwork for a secular, Yiddish-language-based movement which accomplished much in a short time frame in the fields of literature, education, linguistics, and folklore. Much of the Yiddish cultural work that continued after the Holocaust in Israel and in diaspora Jewish communities around the world relied upon the theoretical and material advances (books and resources) developed before the war in Poland.

To return to I. J. Trunk's discussion of humanism and Yiddishism presented in the introduction, the combination of Yiddishism and folklore allowed the Jews of the interwar generation to "know themselves." This knowledge was situated in the present, not the past—not "who we were," but "who we are." The Warsaw circle included in this "we" the Jewish underworld, the prostitutes and pimps, and the workers, for those groups represented the "Yiddish" nation in all its shades of good and bad. The Jews had moved rapidly from *shtetl* to city, and Lehman, Graubard, Prilutski, and the others delved right into the thick of urban life to record the folklore in this new environment. While one of America's leading folklorists, Richard M. Dorson, still had to ask, "Is There a Folk in the City?" in the 1960s, the Yiddish folklorists never questioned the "folkness" of the Jews in the urban centers of Warsaw, Vilne, and Lodz.[6]

The folkloric attempt to know oneself, however, posits a "they" or "other" to be studied and a "we," the folklorist. The very notion of folklore, dating from Herder's thinking, establishes this division in its visualization of a "folk" separate from the rest of the nation. Michael Herzfeld writes of the Greek folklorists, "Their willingness and ability to think in terms of studying folklore are some measure of the distance which actually separated them from the rural people."[7] In the case of Yiddish folklorists, the dichotomy was not urban versus rural, for there were no Jewish peasants. The "other" who served as informants for the folklorists and collectors were often friends and family. Sometimes, the "other" was oneself (as with Lehman, for example). Kipnis, on the other hand, obtained most of his folk songs from friends who were well-known intellectuals and could hardly be conceived of as belonging to the romantic notion of "folk."

During the course of this work, I have often stopped to analyze the occasional annotations or narratives describing the fieldwork of the Polish Jewish folklorists as the collectors themselves presented it. This has been done in order to highlight the complex relationship between the folk, the folklorist, and the collected folk text. Often the folklorist felt endangered by the folk from whom he was collecting. The folklore, which was a reflection of the greatness of the Yiddish language, was the "gold," which should belong to the folklorist, not the folk. The collection of folklore represented a power struggle. The narratives reveal that the folk, ironically, was a hindrance to the folklorists' nationalist agenda. This dynamic between the scholar or collector and the "other" exists not only in our example, but for the entire history of folkloristics and anthropology.[8] In nineteenth-century romantic terms, it was the folk poetry, which the folk created communally, that was aesthetically prized, not the folk itself.

The Yiddish folkloristic activities that have served as the focus of this examination of Yiddish folklore studies—the Warsaw circle, the S. Ansky Vilna Jewish Historical-Ethnographic Society, and the Ethnographic Committee of the YIVO Institute for Jewish Research—approached Yiddish folklore with both aesthetic and positivist criteria. At the turn of the century, the influential writer Peretz emphasized the aesthetic value of Yiddish folk poetry. His reworking of folk texts was to serve, he hoped, as the inspiration for a national cultural renaissance. The Warsaw folklorists perpetuated Peretz's perspective with a stress on the beauty of the texts. They deemphasized the importance of classification and comparison. Only Prilutski showed a serious interest in textual variants from other languages; yet, even then, he did not do so for the sake of historical reconstruction, but for the prestige of the Yiddish version, as if to say we, the Jews, have our version, too. The members of the AVJHES also sought to collect and publish Yiddish folklore in order to publicize the aesthetic qualities of the texts, but became more concerned with the use of those texts as historic and ethnographic documentation.

With the creation of YIVO and its EC, Yiddish folklore study in Poland turned to a scientific approach. It is no coincidence that Max Weinreich, the driving force of YIVO, was primarily a historical linguist, while Noyekh Prilutski, the head of the Warsaw group, was a master dialectician. This paralleled their respective approaches to folklore. The EC, led by Weinreich, sought survivals among the folk that would help historical research. Prilutski encouraged the accurate transcription of the texts so that the Yiddish language could be seen in all its multiple variants. Prilutski was satisfied with diversity as an end product of research; Weinreich wanted the collected texts to lead to a single origin. Young YIVO folklorists such as Pipe turned to the historic-geographic method for this purpose.

The problem remained, though, that if the Yiddish folklorist were to find "survivals," from what "past" or tradition would they have survived? On the one hand, Yiddishism represented an abandoning of Jewish tradition: it was not based on religion and was thoroughly modern in orientation. It dissociated itself from the classic Jewish civilization in Israel. On the other hand, the study of folklore was, in a sense, the study of traditions. Was Yiddishist folklore, therefore, a contradiction in terms?

For the Yiddish folklorists in interwar Poland, the uneasiness of being modern nationalists yet looking at traditions of the past emerged in the prioritizing of folklore genres that were collected. In the literature, oral folklore—folk songs and proverbs in particular—far outnumber the non-oral genres such as custom, belief, or material culture. In defining a Yiddish nation, the Jewish folklorists' vision was a synchronic one; envisioning a Yiddishland alongside emerging nations in post–First World War Europe. By centering on the Yiddish language, the spoken language of the masses and the tradition-bearers, and not on the Hebrew language or on the religion, the folklorists could more easily have a sense that their collecting was for a new, modern nation with no ancient roots, and that they were important in building this nation. The collected materials, the folklore, would essentially be the basis from which this nation would be defined.

Notes

Introduction

1. "Undzer veg" (Our path), *Di yidishe velt* 1 (1912): 1.
2. Benedict Anderson, *Imagined Communities: Reflections On the Origin and Spread of Nationalism* (London: Verso, 1983), 15.
3. See Anderson, *Imagined Communities*, 136. See also Ernest Gellner, *Nations and Nationalism* (Ithaca: Cornell University Press, 1983), 106–7; E. J. Hobsbawm, *Nations and Nationalism since 1780: Programme, myth, reality* (Cambridge: Cambridge University Press, 1990), 110–11.
4. Hobsbawm, *Nations*, 110–11.
5. J. Trunk, "Yidishizm un yidishe geshikhte: polemishe shrift," *Amol in a yoyvl: zamlbukh* 2 (1931): 185.
6. See Giuseppe Cocchiara, *The History of Folklore in Europe* (Philadelphia: ISHI, 1981), 168–84; and, more concisely, Ernst S. Dick, "The Folk and Their Culture: The Formative Concepts and the Beginnings of Culture," in *The Folk: Identity, Landscapes and Lores*, ed. Robert J. Smith and Jerry Stannard (Lawrence: Department of Anthropology, University of Kansas, 1989), 11–28.
7. Statistics of census in Joseph Marcus, *Social and Political History of the Jews in Poland 1919–1939* (Berlin: Mouton, 1983), 16.
8. William Wilson, "Herder, Folklore and Romantic Nationalism," *Journal of Popular Culture* 6 (1973): 819. Other studies of folklore and the use of the past in nation building include: Richard M. Dorson, "The Question of Folklore in a New Nation" *Journal of the Folklore Institute* 3, no. 3 (December 1986): 277–98; William Wilson, *Folklore and Nationalism in Modern Finland* (Bloomington: Indiana University Press, 1975); Michael Herzfeld, *Ours Once More: Folklore, Ideology, and the Making of Modern Greece* (Austin: University of Texas Press, 1982); Brynjulf Alver, "Folklore and National Identity," in *Nordic Folklore*, ed. Reimund Kvideland and Henning K. Sehmsdorf (Bloomington: Indiana University Press, 1989), 12–22; Henry Senn, "Folklore Beginnings in France, The Academie Celtique: 1804–1813" *Journal of Folklore Institute* 18, no. 1 (December–January 1981):23–31; James W. Fernandez, "Folklore as an Agent of Nationalism," *African Studies Bulletin* 5, no. 2 (May 1962): 3–8. For a general introduction to Herder's thought see:

F. M. Barnard, *Herder's Social and Political Thought: From Enlightenment to Nationalism (Oxford: Clarendon Press, 1965).*

9. Trunk, "Yidishizm," 183.

10. Lucy S. Dawidowicz, *From That Place and Time: A Memoir 1938–1947* (New York: W.W. Norton, 1989), 7.

11. On the Chernovitz conference see Emanuel S. Goldsmith, *Architects of Yiddishism at the Beginning of the Twentieth Century: A Study in Jewish Cultural History* (Rutherford, N.J.: Fairleigh Dickinson University Press, 1976), 183–222; Joshua A. Fishman, "Attracting a Following to High-Culture Functions for a Language of Everyday Life: The Role of the Tshernovits Language Conference in the 'Rise of Yiddish,'" in *Never Say Die: A Thousand Years of Yiddish in Jewish Life and Letters,* ed. Joshua A. Fishman (The Hague: Mouton, 1981), 369–94.

12. Dan Miron has written on the problem of writing in Yiddish during the *Haskala,* specifically on the Yiddish/Hebrew writers and their inner and outer ambivalence with the language. See Dan Miron, *A Traveler Disguised: A Study in the Rise of Modern Yiddish Fiction in the Nineteenth Century* (New York: Schocken Books, 1973), 1–66.

13. See Goldsmith, *Architects of Yiddishism,* 45–46.

14. I. M. Lifshits, "Di daytsh yidishe brik," *Kol-Mevaser* (1867), 239–41. Reprinted in *"Kol-Mevaser": Selections from the Years 1863–1869* (Jerusalem, 1964).

15. See, for example, Nokhem Shtif, "Ditrikh fun bern: yidishkeyt un veltlekhkeyt in der alter yidisher literatur," *Yidishe filologye* 1 (1924): 1–11, 112–22, which traces Yiddishism back to the Yiddish literature of the Middle Ages.

16. See Jonathan Frankel, *Prophecy and Politics: Socialism, Nationalism, and the Russian Jews, 1862–1917* (Cambridge: Cambridge University Press, 1981), 258–87, on the new combination of socialism and Jewish nationalism based on Yiddish and a diaspora existence.

17. *Encyclopaedia Judaica,* s.v. Zhitlowsky, Chaim.

18. Frankel, *Prophecy and Politics,* 285.

19. These folklorists are discussed further in chapter 2.

20. See Jacob Lestschinsky, "Dubnow's Autonism and his 'Letters on Old and New Judaism,'" in *Simon Dubnow: The Man and His Work: A Memorial Volume on the Occasion of the Centenary of His Birth (1860–1960),* ed. Aaron Steinberg (Paris: French Section of the World Jewish Congress, 1963), 77.

21. See Hans Kohn, *Pan-Slavism: Its History and Ideology* (New York: Bantam, 1960).

22. This is most forcefully documented by Stephan Horak, *Poland and Her National Minorities, 1919–39* (New York: Vantage Press, 1961).

23. Arthur P. Coleman, "Language as a Factor in Polish Nationalism," *Slavonic Review* 13 (1934): 156. See also Peter Brock, "Polish Nationalism," in *Nationalism in Eastern Europe,* ed. Peter F. Sugar and Ivo J. Lederer (Seattle: University of Washington Press, 1969), 315.

24. See Alexander Posern-Zielinski, "The Forming of Polish Ethnography as

an Independent Discipline of Science (until 1939)," in *Historia Etnografi Polskiej,* ed. Witold Armon et al. (Wroclaw: Zaklad narodowy Imienia Ossolinskich Wydawnictwo Polskiej Akademii Nauk, 1973), 326–32. See also Mark W. Kiel, "Vox Populi, Vox Dei: The Centrality of Peretz in Jewish Folkloristics," *Polin* 7 (1992): 88–120 on Jews and Polish folklore studies.

25. Yoysef-Yehude Lerner, "Di yidishe muze: Yidishe folkslider," *Hoyzfraynd* 2(1889): 182–98. Ed. Mordkhe Spektor.

26. See Lerner's entry in *BDMYL* 5(1963): 362–66. Steven J. Zipperstein writes that Lerner "may have" converted. See *The Jews of Odessa: A Cultural History, 1794–1881* (Stanford, Calif.: Stanford University Press, 1985), 146.

27. According to Zalmen Reyzen, the Yiddish writer H. D. Nomberg should be credited with the neologisms, "Yiddishists" and "Yiddishism." See *Yidishe filologye* 1 (1924): 97. Reyzin does not mention in which essay Nomberg suggests them, and I could not find the specific work, though most of Nomberg's essays were written during the first decade of the twentieth century. On Vanvild, see chapter 2.

28. Lerner, "Di yidishe muze," 184.

29. Ibid., 184.

30. On this debate, see David G. Roskies, "Ideologies of the Yiddish Folksong in the Old Country and the New" *Jewish Book Annual* 50 (1992–93): 148–50.

31. See Lerner, "Di yidishe muze," 197. On Mikhl Gordon see *BDMYL* 2 (1958): 129–34.

32. See Dick, "Folk and Their Culture," 11–28.

33. Lerner, "Di yidishe muze," 186.

34. Ibid., 190. Predicting the future based upon the shapes formed by poured wax was a folk custom among Eastern European Jews.

35. For the appropriation of folkloric forms by the literary world because of their eternal quality or immortality, see Susan Stewart, "Notes on Distressed Genres," in *Crimes of Writing: Problems in the Containment of Representation* (Oxford: Oxford University Press, 1991), 69.

36. A reference to Exodus 3:5.

37. On Spektor (1858–1925) see *BDMYL* 6 (1965): 518–27. The collection was printed in *Yidishes folksblat* 6 (1886).

38. Avrom-Yitskhok Bukhbinder, "Yidishe simonim (zabobones)," *Hoyzfraynd* 2: 249–58, see entry in *LYL* 1 (1926): col. 236–37.

39. Dan Miron, "Folklore and Anti-Folklore in the Yiddish Fiction of the Haskala," in *Studies in Jewish Folklore: Proceedings of a Regional Conference of the Association for Jewish Studies Held at the Spertus College of Judaica, Chicago, May 1–3, 1977,* ed. Frank Talmage (Cambridge, Mass.: Association for Jewish Studies, 1980), 219–50.

40. Bukhbinder, "Yidishe simonim," 257.

41. I[gnaz]. B[ernstein]., "Yidishe shprikhverter," *Hoyzfraynd* 5 (1895). Separate pagination at end of volume, 1–48.

42. Mordkhe Spektor, "foreword" to B[ernstein]., 2.

43. Ibid., 2.

44. See Simon Dubnow, *Nationalism and History: Essays on Old and New Judaism*, ed. Koppel Pinson (Philadelphia: Jewish Publication Society, 1958).
45. See H. D. Nomberg, *A literarisher dor: vegn I. L. Perets* (A literary generation: On I. L. Peretz) (Warsaw: Levin-Epshteyn, n.d.), 15.
46. Dr. Gershon Levin. *Perets: a bisl zikhroynes* (Peretz: A few memoires) (Warsaw: Yehudia, 1919), 45–46. On singing in Peretz's circle see I. L. Cahan, "I. L. Perets vi a zamler fun yidishe folkslider: bamerkungen tsu zayne kolektsyes" (I. L. Peretz as a collector of Yiddish folksongs: Comments on his collections) *YIVO-bleter* 12, nos. 1–3 (1937): 280–85; Kiel, "Vox Populi," 88–120; and Roskies, "Ideologies," 145.
47. See Kiel, "Vox Populi," 105–6. On Peretz's influence on the Warsaw Yiddish folklorists see chapter 2.
48. Peretz had a notebook of recorded folk songs dated 1896. See I. L. Peretz, "Dos yidishe lebn loyt di yidishe folkslider (Jewish life according to Yiddish folksongs)," *YIVO-bleter* 13, nos. 1–2 (1937): 291.
49. S. M. Ginzburg and P. S. Marek. *Yidishe folkslider in rusland*, photo-offset of the 1901 edition (Ramat-Gan: Bar-Ilan University Press, 1991).
50. Ibid., 25.
51. Ibid., 31.
52. For a history of Jewish folklore studies at this time outside of the Yiddish-speaking world, see Barbara Kirshenblatt-Gimblett, "Problems in the Historiography of Jewish Folkloristics" (paper presented at conference on "Folklore and Social Transformation: A Dialogue of American and German Folklorists," Bloomington, Ind., November 1–3, 1988). See also Kiel, "Vox Populi."
53. Ignaz Bernstein, *Judische Sprichworter und Redensarten* (Warsaw: n.p., 1908).
54. See chapter 2 for a more detailed discussion of Bernshteyn's influence on the Yiddish folklorists.
55. See discussion on this point in chapter 2.
56. This collection is discussed in chapter 2.
57. See translated published minutes of Expedition in *Gal-Ed* 6 (1982) (Isaiah Trunk, "Homer bilti-yada shel 'mishlahat An-ski' ba-shanim 1912–1916"), where Ansky promotes Hasidic folklore as the essence of Jewish culture. For Peretz's influence on Yiddish and Hebrew literature, see Mark Kiel, "A Twice Lost Legacy: Ideology, Culture and the Pursuit of Folklore in Russia until Stalinization (1930–1931)" (Ph.D. diss., Jewish Theological Seminary, 1991), especially chapter 2, "Bialik and the Transformation of Agadah into Folklore." On Ansky see entry in *LYL* 1 (1928): col. 125–41. In English, see David G. Roskies, "S. Anski and the Paradigm of Return," in *The Uses of Tradition: Jewish Continuity in the Modern Era*, ed. Jack Wertheimer (New York: Jewish Theological Seminary, 1992), 243–60.
58. See, for example, S. Ansky, "Der yidisher folks-gayst un zayn shafung (The Jewish folk spirit and its creativity)," in *Folklor un ethnografy*, vol. 15 (Warsaw: Farlag An-ski, 1925), 15–28. Ansky claimed that Jewish folklore was unique because it lacked violence.

59. See examples in I. L. Cahan, *Shtudyes vegn yidisher folksshafung* (Studies in Yiddish folklore), ed. Max Weinreich (New York: YIVO, 1952), 17–19.
60. I. L. Cahan, *Yidishe folkslider: mit melodien* (Jewish folksongs: With airs), 2 vols. (New York: International Library, 1912).
61. Shmuel Niger, ed., *Der pinkes: yorbukh fun der geshikhte fun der yidisher literatur un shprakh, far folklor, kritik un bibliografye* (The record book: Yearbook for the history of Yiddish literature and language, folklore, criticism and bibliography) (Vilne: Kletskin, 1913).
62. Ber Borokhov, "Di oyfgabn fun der yidisher filologye," in Niger, *Der pinkes,* 1.
63. The two collections are L. B., "Folkslider: farshriben fun L. B." in Niger, *Der pinkes,* 398; Khaye Fayn, "Yidishe folkslider: gezamlt fun khaye fayn," in Niger, *Der pinkes,* 399–410. I. L. Cahan's review was published under a pseudonym, L. Vilenski [I. L. Cahan], "Yidishe folkslider," in Niger, *Der pinkes,* 356–65.
64. See Kirshenblatt-Gimblett, "Problems in the Historiography," 4–6.

Chapter 1

1. Others in this circle included the Yiddish writer Y. Perle, Sore Kornvayzer (Perle's future wife), Miriam Khmelnitski, and A. Kh. Sheps (Almi's brother?). See A. Almi, "Epizodn fun a literarishn fargangenhayt" (Episodes from a literary past), *Nyu-yorker vokhnblat,* August 28, 1942, 7.
2. See *Encyclopaedia Judaica,* s.v. "Poland."
3. On this work by Peretz, see Ruth R. Wisse, *I. L. Peretz and the Making of Modern Jewish Culture* (Seattle: University of Washington Press, 1991), 83–86.
4. I. L. Peretz, *Briv un redes fun I. L. Peretz* (The letters and speeches of I. L. Peretz), ed. Nakhman Meisel (New York: YKUF, 1944), 371, 382–83.
5. Jacob Shatsky, "Peretz-shtudyes," *YIVO-bleter* 28 (1946): 63.
6. Chone Shmeruk, "Aspects of the History of Warsaw As a Yiddish Literary Centre," *Polin: A Journal of Polish-Jewish Studies* 3 (1988): 142–55; Kiel, "Twice Lost Legacy," 140–71.
7. Dr. A. Mukdoni, *Oysland: mayne bageginishn* (Buenos Aires: Tsentral-farlag fun poylishe yidn in Argentina, 1951), 134.
8. Jacob Shatsky, "Yehude Leyb Kan (1881–1937): materialn far a biografye," in *Yorbukh fun Amopteyl,* A. Mukdoni and Jacob Shatsky, eds. (New York, Yiddish Scientific Institute-American Section, 1938), 16–18.
9. See Kiel, "Vox Populi," 93–96.
10. Shatsky, "Peretz-shtudyes," 62.
11. Regina Lilienthal, "Eyn hore," *Yidishe filologye* 1 (1924): 245–71.
12. A. Almi, "Fun amolikn varshe" (From Warsaw long ago), *Der poylisher yid* 2 (1944): 28–30.
13. Avrom Zak, *In onheyb fun a friling: kapitlekh zikhroynes* (In the beginning of a spring: Chapters of memoirs) (Buenos Aires: Tsentral farband fun poylishe yidn in Argentina, 1962), 113.

14. A. Almi, "Pinkhes Graubard: zikhroynes" (Pinkhes Graubard: Memoirs), *Der Tog* (New York), January 11, 1953, 8. Also: A. Almi, "Mitn oyer tsum folk" (Listening to the people), *Fraye arbeter shtime* (New York), September 23, 1955, 5.

15. M. Vanvild, ed., *Bay undz yidn: zamlbukh far folklor un filologye* (Among us Jews: Collection of folklore and philology) (Warsaw: Farlag Pinkhes Graubard, 1923). Each contribution to this volume will be examined seperately below, according to author.

16. See David G. Roskies, *A Bridge of Longing: The Lost Art of Yiddish Storytelling* (Cambridge: Harvard University Press, 1995), 230–31.

17. See entry in *BDMYL* 8 (1981): 29–31.

18. For example, see Efrayim Kaganovski, *Yidishe shrayber in der heym* (Yiddish writers at home) (Paris: Oyfsnay, 1956), 9–13; Z. Segalovitsh, *Tlometske 13: fun farbrentn nekhtn* (Tlometske 13: From the burnt past) (Buenos Aires: Tsentral farband fun poylishe yidn in Argentina,1946), 30; Isaac Bashevis Singer, "Vanvild Kava," in *Collected Stories of Isaac Bashevis Singer* (New York: Farrar Strauss Giroux, 1982), 580–86; and S. L. Shnayderman, personal communication, June 14, 1991.

19. Shmuel Lehman, *Arbet un frayhayt: zamlung fun lider vos zenen antshtanen in folk in der tsayt fun der frayhayts-bavegung in tsarish rusland* (Warsaw: Folklor-bibliotek, 1921).

20. Vanvild, *Bay undz yidn*, ii. This is apparently a reformulation of the criticism leveled by the Hebrew writer Joseph Hayyim Brenner at Ahad Ha-Am for his dismissal of folklore. See Dan Ben-Amos, "Nationalism and Nihilism: The Attitudes of Two Hebrew Authors Toward Folklore," *International Folkore Review* 1: 5–16. Brenner is quoted on page 10.

21. Vanvild, *Bay undz yidn*, iii.

22. See discussion following, in section on Lehman.

23. See entry on Almi in *BDMYL* 1 (1956): 108–9, and especially the bigraphical sketch in A. Almi, *Khezhbn un sakh-hakl: kapitlekh fun mayn seyfer hakhayim* (Account and reckoning: Chapters from my book of life] (Buenos Aires: G. Kaplanski,1959), 9–12.

24. See A. Almi, *Momentn fun a lebn* (Moments from a life) (Buenos Aires: Tsentral farband far poylishe yidn, 1948).

25. Noyekh Prilutski, *Yidishe folkslider*, vol. 1, *Religyeze un yontifdike* (Warsaw: Bikher far ale, 1911–12).

26. For detailed description of this woman, see Almi, *Momentn fun a lebn*, 77–79.

27. Noyekh Prilutski, *Yidishe folkslider*, vol. 2, *Lider un mayselekh fun toyt; Balades un legendes mit un on a muser-haskol* (Yiddish folksongs, vol. 2, Songs and tales about death; Ballads and legends with and without a moral) (Warsaw: Bikher far ale, 1913–14).

28. A. Almi, *1863: Yidishe povstanye-mayselekh* (Warsaw: Goldfarb, 1927). Povstanye means "insurrection" in Polish.

29. For extensive historiographic literature on this event, see David Hundert and Gershon C. Bacon, *The Jews in Poland and Russia: Bibliographical Essays*

(Bloomington: Indiana University Press, 1984), 180. See also Magdalena Opalski and Israel Bartal, *Poles and Jews: A Failed Brotherhood* (Hanover, N.H.: Brandeis University Press, 1992). In Yiddish literature, the uprising was treated most notably by Joseph Opatoshu in his novel, *1863* (Vilne: Kletskin farlag, 1926).

30. Almi, *1863,* iii.
31. Ibid., 90. *1863* was translated into Polish by S. Hirszhorn: *Legendy Zydowdkie o Powstaniu—1863* (Warsaw: Widawnictwo E. Gitlina, 1929).
32. On Prilutski's interest in variants, see following section on Prilutski.
33. See I. L. Cahan, *Yidishe folkslider,* lx.
34. It is not mentioned, for example, in Uriel Weinreich and Beatrice Weinreich, *Yiddish Language and Folklore: A Selective Bibliography for Research* (The Hague: Mouton, 1959); neither is it mentioned in Haim Schwarzbaum, *Studies in Jewish and World Folklore* (Berlin: Walter De Gruyter, 1968).
35. A. Almi, *Di reyd fun buda* (The words of Budda) (Vilne: Kletskin, 1927); A. Almi, *Far di likht* (Before the light) (Warsaw: n.p., 1927).
36. Almi, *1863,* 13–17.
37. Ibid., 39–44.
38. "Di shtrof far libe" (The punishment for love), in ibid., 100–105.
39. *LYL* 2 (1927): 210. The historian Jacob Shatsky (1893–1956) contradicts this description ("He came from a poor family. He was deeply rooted in the lower classes of Warsaw and thus became interested in Jewish folklore as a boy") in "Shmuel Lehman: 1886–1941," *YIVO-Bleter* 18 (1941): 80–83. Since the authors themselves supplied much of the information for Zalmen Reyzen's *LYL,* it is more reliable.
40. Melekh Ravitch, "Shmuel Lehman," in *Mayn leksikon,* vol. 2 (Montreal: n.p., 1947), 36–38.
41. Avrom Lis, "Shmuel Lehman—Der pioner fun yidishn folklor," *Di letste nayes* (Israel), September 18, 1959, 6.
42. Isaiah Trunk, "Shmuel Lehman," in *Geshtaltn un gesheenishn* (Figures and events) (Buenos Aires: Tsentral Farband fun poylishe yidn in Argentina, 1962), 47–50.
43. Nokhem Kapovitch, "Shmuel Lehman in Varshever geto" (Shmuel Lehman in the Warsaw Ghetto), *Di oystralishe yidishe nayes* (Melbourne), December 19, 1947, 7.
44. Ravitch, "Shmuel Lehman," 36. Ravitch was told this by Lehman.
45. Emanuel Ringleblum, *Ksovim fun geto* (Writings from the ghetto) (Tel-Aviv: Farlag I. L. Peretz, 1985), 2:176–78.
46. Trunk, "Shmuel Lehman," 49.
47. See "Shmuel Lehman," in *Doyres bundistn, tsveyter band,* ed. J. S. Hertz (New York: Undzer tsayt farlag, 1956), 252–53.
48. Noyekh Prilutski and Shmuel Lehman, *Noyekh Prilutskis zamlbikher far yidishn folklor, filologye un kulturgeshikhte* (Noyekh Prilutski's collections of Yiddish folklore, philology and cultural history), vol. 1 (Warsaw: Nayer farlag, 1912).

49. Shmuel Lehman and Noykeh Prilutski, "Yidishe shprikhverter, glaykhvert-lekh, rednsartn un tsunemenishn vegn lender, gegentn, shtet un shtetlkeh," in Prilutski and Lehman, *Noyekh Prilutskis zamlbikher*, vol. 1, 9–87.
50. Ber Borokhov, "Noyekh Prilutskis zamlbikher far yidishn folklor," in Niger, *Der pinkes*, 347–51. See discussion in Kiel, "Twice Lost Legacy," 35. Borokhov is primarily remembered as a founder of Marxist Zionism. See Jonathan Frankel, *Prophecy and Politics*, 329–64.
51. Borokhov, "Noyekh Prilutskis zamlbikher far yidishn folklor," 348.
52. Noyekh Prilutski, "Dos yidishe folksvort vegn medines un yeshuvim" (The Yiddish folktongue on countries and communities), in Prilutski, *Noyekh Prilutskis zamlbikher far yidishn folklor, filologye un kulturgeshikhte*, vol. 2 (Warsaw: Bikher far ale, 1917), 161–84.
53. Shmuel Lehman, "Shtot un land in der folksshprakh" (City and country in the folktongue), in Noyekh Prilutski and Shmuel Lehman, *Arkhiv far yidisher shprakhvisnshaft, literaturforshung un etnologye* (Archive for Yiddish Philology, Literary Research and Ethnology), vol. 1 (Warsaw: Nayer farlag, 1926–33), 256–83.
54. Prilutski and Lehman, *Noyekh Prilutskis zamlbikher*, vol. 1, 32.
55. Ibid., 33.
56. Ibid., 35.
57. Borokhov, "Noyekh Prilutskis zamlbikher far yidishn folklor," 349.
58. "Folkslider" collected by Pinkhes Graubard and Shmuel Lehman, in *Frishmans yubileyum-bukh: tsu zayn fuftsik-yorikn geburts-tog* (Warsaw: n.p., 1914), 205–15.
59. A later but well-known example is found in M. Bassein, ed., *500 yor yidishe poezye*, 2 vols. (New York: n.p., 1917). The editor printed a number of folk songs from I. L. Cahan's collection.
60. See *LYL* 1 (1926): 609.
61. Francis J. Child, *The English and Scottish Popular Ballads* [1884–1898], is noted in a footnote in Cahan, *Yidishe folkslider*, xxii. All the Yiddish folklorists knew Cahan's work well.
62. "Historically, the first artistic narrative poem in modern Yiddish literature." *BDMYL* 7 (1968): 239. "Monish" was first published in *Di yidishe bibliotek*, vol. 1 (Warsaw: n.p., 1891).
63. See Mark Slobin, "note" to "Folksongs in the East European Jewish Tradition from the Repertoire of Mariam Nirenberg," Global Village Music 117, sound recording.
64. Lehman, *Arbet un frayhayt*. The Folklor-bibliotek was initiated and funded by Graubard.
65. Ansky, "Der yidisher folks-gayst un zayn shafung," 15–28. This was a lecture that Ansky delivered in Vilne in 1918. It was published in *Der Vilner Tog* that same year.
66. Cahan, "Folksgezang un folkslid," (Folksinging and folksong: Comments on labor and freedom), in *Landoy-bukh: Dr. Alfred Landoy tsu zayn 75stn geboyrnstog dem 25stn november, 1925* (Vilne: YIVO, 1926), 139–54.

67. See "Aynlaytung" (Introduction) to Cahan, *Yidishe folkslider.*
68. This meant Lehman collected the materials from age seventeen to age twenty!
69. Lehman, *Arbet un frayhayt,* 2.
70. For a general overview of Cahan's attitude toward Yiddish folk songs see Itzik Gottesman, "I. L. Cahan: Adapting Yiddish Folkpoetry to 'World Literature'" (Talk held at the Annual Meeting of the American Folklore Society, Baltimore, October 1986).
71. Ayzik Rozentsvayg, *Sotsyale diferentsiyatse inem yidish folklor-lid* (Social differentiation in the Yiddish folksong) (Kiev: Farlag fun der alukraynisher visnshaftlekher akademye, 1934).
72. Rozentsvayg, *Sotsyale diferentsiyatse,* 50.
73. Jacob Shatsky, "Arbet un frayhayt," *Bikhervelt* 1 (1922): 48.
74. Jacob Shatsky, "Di naye dershaynungen in der yidisher folklor-literatur" (The new developments in the Yiddish folklore literature), *Dos naye lebn* 1, no. 11 (1923): 44–48.
75. Shloyme Bastomski, *Baym kval: materialn tsum yidishn folklor, yidishe folkslider* (At the source: Materials for Yiddish folklore, Yiddish folksongs) (Vilne: Di naye yidishe folkshul, 1923).
76. S. Niger, "Sotsyale lider fun folks-mentshn" (Social songs of the folk), *Der Tog* (New York), May 19, 1922: 11.
77. Shatsky, "Arbet un frayhayt," 48.
78. Lehman, *Arbet un frayhayt,* 177–78.
79. For a more recent contentious discussion of the nature of revolutionary songs, see Steve Siporin's review of *Avanti Popolo! Revolutionary Songs of the Italian Working Class* in *Journal of American Folklore* 389: 373–74 and Portelli's and Siporin's comments in *Journal of American Folklore* 393: 320–21. Unlike that discussion, no one attacked Lehman's collection as a political use of folklore.
80. Shmuel Lehman, "Di eyropeyishe milkhome: a zamlung fun yidishe folksvertlekh, anekdotn, rimozim, briv, gramen, lider, mayses un legendes, vos zaynen geshafn gevorn in der tsayt fun krig," in *Lebn: heftn far literatur, kunst, un publitsisdik* (Life: Periodical of literature, art, and current affairs), ed. Moyshe Shalit (Vilne: 1922), 3–28. A special issue devoted to World War One.
81. S. Ansky also published a short collection of First World War Yiddish folklore in the Vilne newspaper, *Der Tog,* in 1919. He concluded that the material revealed the "profound perspicacity of the Jewish folk spirit." See S. Ansky, "Yidishe milkhome-glaykhvertlekh" (Yiddish war sayings), in S. Ansky, *Folklor un ethnografye,* vol. 15 of *Gezamlte shriftn* (Warsaw: Farlag An-ski, 1925), 233–39.
82. Shmuel Lehman, "Ganovim un ganeyve: rednsartn, tsunemenishn, shprikhverter, fragn, gramen, anekdotn, un mayses," in Vanvild, *Bay undz yidn,* 43–92.
83. Pinkhes Graubard, "Gezangen fun tom . . . lider fun ganovim, arestantn, gasn-froyen" (Songs from the abyss) in Vanvild, *Bay undz yidn,* 17–42.

84. Vanvild, *Bay undz yidn,* iv.
85. Shmuel Lehman, *Ganovim-lider: mit melodyes* (Warsaw: Pinkhes Graubard, 1928).
86. I. L. Cahan, *Yidishe folksmayses: funem folksmoyl gezamlt* (Vilne: Yidishe folklor bibliotek, 1931).
87. See Beatrice Silverman Weinreich, "Four Yiddish Variants of the Master-Thief Tale," in *The Field of Yiddish: Studies in Yiddish Language, Folklore, and Literature,* ed. Uriel Weinreich, no. 3 (New York: Publications of the Linguistic Circle of New York, 1954), 199–213.
88. Lehman had his own form of transcription, which only he could read. In the Warsaw Ghetto, as he lay dying, a young folklore enthusiast was assigned to Lehman by the "Oyneg shabes" group to learn the transcription. See "Shmuel Lehman—the man—the institution," in Ringleblum, *Ksovim fun geto,* vol. 2.
89. Lehman, "Ganovim un ganeyve," 80.
90. A. Litvin took many photographs, but they never appeared in his magnum opus, *Yidishe neshomes* (Jewish souls), 6 vols. (New York: Yidishe folksbildung, 1916).
91. Shmuel Lehman, "Di kinder velt: gramen, lidlekh, hamtsoes un shpiln," in Vanvild, *Bay undz yidn,* 113–49.
92. Roskies, *A Bridge of Longing,* 231.
93. A. Landau, "Spiele der judischen Kinder in Ostgalizien," *Mitteilungen zur judischen Volkskunde* 3 (1899): 40–49.
94. Cited in Max Weinreich's review of *Bay undz yidn, Bikher-velt* 2, no. 6 (1923): 480.
95. Shmuel Lehman, "Treyfene skhoyre," 153–54. For English translation and analysis of these plays, see Barbara Kirshenblatt-Gimblett, "Contraband: Performance, Text and Analysis of a *Purim-shpil,*" *Drama Review* 3 (1980): 5–16.
96. Shatsky, "Arbet un frayhayt," 44–48.
97. Weinreich, review of *Bay undz yidn,* 478–84.
98. Ibid., 479.
99. See chapter 4.
100. *Landoy-bukh.*
101. Lehman, *Ganovim-lider.*
102. Heinrich Heine, "The Romantic School," in *The Romantic School and Other Essays,* ed. Jost Jermand and Robert C. Holub (New York: Continuum, 1985), 86.
103. Yiddish literature had already "discovered" the colorful side of the Jewish underworld. See, for example, Joseph Opatoshu, *Roman fun a ferd ganef* (Novel of a horse thief) (New York: n.p., 1917). The jargon of the Jewish underworld had been well known since the mid-nineteenth century; see Friedrich Christân Benedict Ave-Lallemant, *Das deutsche Gaunerthum in seiner social-politischen, litterarischen und linguistischen Ausbildung,* 4 vols. (Leipzig: Brockhaus, 1858–62).

104. S. Bastomski, review of *Ganovim-lider, Bikher-velt* 1 (1929): 60.
105. Prilutski and Lehman, *Arkhiv*.
106. Both *Zamlbikher* (1912) and Prilutski's *Yidishe folkslider*, vol. 2 (1913) were published by Nayer farlag.
107. Letter from S. Z. Pipe, Vilne, to his brother Oyzer in Israel, August 20, 1935, in S. Z. Pipe, *Yiddish Folksongs from Galicia: The Folklorization of David Edelstadt's Song "Der arbeter"; Letters*, Folklore Research Center Studies vol. 2, ed. Meir Noy and Dov Noy (Jerusalem: The Hebrew University of Jerusalem, Institute of Jewish Studies, Folklore Research Center, 1971), 483.
108. Shmuel Lehman, "Elye-hanovi in der folks fantazye: mayses un legendes" (Elijah the Prophet in the folk fantasy: Tales and legends), in Prilutski and Lehman, *Arkhiv*, 115–78.
109. For an exemplary comparative type and motif analysis of Lehman's Elijah tales, see Haim Schwarzbaum, *Studies in Jewish and World Folklore*, 6–14.
110. B. W. Segel printed an early collection; see his "Elijah der Prophet: eine Studie zur juddischen Volks-und Sagenkunde," *Ost und West* 1904: 477–88, 675–80, 807–12. For bibliography see Beatrice Silverman Weinreich, "Genres and Types of Yiddish Folk Tales about the Prophet Elijah," in *The Field of Yiddish: Studies in Language, Folklore, and Literature, Second Collection*, ed. Uriel Weinreich (The Hague: Mouton, 1965), 202–31; and Schwarzbaum, *Studies in Jewish and World Folklore*, 318. See also Avrom Menes, *Fun Undzer Altn Kval: Elye Hanovi* (New York: CYCO, 1955).
111. Shmuel Lehman, "Gazlen-shpil," in Prilutski and Lehman, *Arkhiv*, 287–91.
112. Shmuel Lehman, "Folks-mayselekh un anekdotn mit nigunim," in Prilutski and Lehman, *Arkhiv*, 355–432.
113. Schwarzbaum, *Studies in Jewish and World Folklore*, 82.
114. Z. Kalmanovitch, review of *Arkhiv far yidisher shprakhvisnshaft, literaturforshung un etnologye*, *YIVO-bleter* 5 (1937):384–87.
115. Only one other work has been published on this genre: Meir Noy, ed., *East Euoprean Jewish Cante Fables*, Israel Folktale Archives, publication series no. 20 (Haifa: n.p., 1968).
116. Two of Lehman's texts have been translated into English. Tale no. 4 appeared as "Two Songs for Three Hundred Rubles" in Nathan Ausbel, *A Treasury of Jewish Folklore* (New York: Crown Publishers, 1948), 349–53. Tale no. 6 appeared as "Two Cows for a Melody" in Beatrice Silverman Weinreich, ed., *Yiddish Folktales* (New York: Pantheon Books, 1988), 231–32.
117. See *Shmuel Lehman: zamlbukh* (Warsaw: Published with the aid of the Union of Yiddish Writers and Journalists in Warsaw, 1937).
118. Also see I. Rappaport, "A groyser folklorist vos iz aleyn geven a shtik folklor" (The folklorist who was himself part of the folklore), *Fraye arbeter shtime* (New York), July 23, 1948, 5. The author believes that Lehman traveled so widely throughout Poland that the "folk" had developed their own folklore on the folklorist.
119. *YIVO-bleter* 4–5 (1937): 454–62.

120. Shmuel Zaynvil Pipe, letter to his brother Oyzer, August 28, 1935, in Pipe, *Yiddish Folksongs*, 483.
121. "Committee to Enable the Publication of the Collections of the Folklorist Shmuel Lehman," letter to the Yiddish writer Melekh Ravitch, Warsaw, 1937. Papers of Melekh Ravitch, National Archives at the National Library, Jerusalem.
122. Unidentified letter to Melekh Ravitch, March 20, 1938. Papers of Melekh Ravitch, National Archives, National Library, Jerusalem.
123. Shmuel Lehman,"Sotsyaler moment inem yidishn shprikhvort," *Literarishe bleter* 45 (1935): 728.
124. M. Vanvild, "An ideal fun a folklorist," *Literarishe bleter* 7 (1932): 107.
125. *Shmuel Lehman: zamlbukh*, 20–23.
126. Ibid., 23.
127. Ibid., 24–26.
128. Ibid., 27.
129. Compare with I. L. Cahan's fear of the folklorist being duped with non–folk songs by informants eager to please: see I. L. Cahan, "Peyrushim oyf 24 lider" (Comments on twenty-four songs), in *Shtudyes vegn yidisher folksshafung*, 180.
130. See John A. Lomax, *Adventures of a Ballad Hunter* (New York: Macmillan, 1947).
131. S. Z. Pipe, letter to Oyzer Pipe, August 28, 1935, in Pipe, *Yiddish Folksongs*, 486.
132. Rappaport, "A groyser folklorist," 5.

Chapter 2

1. See *BDMYL* 2 (1958): 339 and *LYL* 1 (1926): 609–10.
2. See Ezra Mendelsohn, *Zionism in Poland: The Formative Years, 1915–1926* (New Haven, Conn.: Yale University Press, 1981), 136–61. There were many splits in the Poale-Zion Party; generally speaking, the further to the left one found oneself, the more supportive one was of Yiddish.
3. Pinkhes Graubard, "In yene teg" (In those days), in *Pinkes Sochaczew*, ed. A. S. Stein and G. Weissman (Jerusalem: Former Residents of Sochaczew in Israel, 1962), 330–35.
4. The story of Graubard's trip to Israel was described in A. Almi, "Pinkhes Graubard: zikhroynes," 8.
5. Avrom Zak, *In onheyh fun a friling*, 113.
6. Ber I. Rozen, *Portretn* (Buenos Aires: Tsentral farband fun poylishe yidn in Argentina, 1956), 74.
7. P. Graubard, "Shmuel Lehmans oytser: tsu zayn 30-yoriker folkloristisher arbet" (Shmuel Lehman's treasure: To his thirty years of folklore work), originally published in *Di nayer folkstsaytung* (Warsaw), February 5, 1932. Reprinted in *Shmuel Lehman: zamlbukh*, 27–31. Graubard dates the meeting to 1910.

8. I. Friedman, "Pinkhes Graubard," in *Pinkes Sochaczew*, ed. A. S. Stein and G. Weissman (Jerusalem: Former Residents of Sochaczew in Israel, 1962), 274. The relationship between Ansky and Graubard is extensively described in Graubard's book of memoirs, *An Ander Lebn* (Warsaw: Kultur-lige, 1928).
9. Prilutski, *Yidishe folkslider*, vol. 1.
10. Pinkhes Graubard, ed., *Literarishe shriftn: zamlbukh no. 1* (Warsaw: n.p., n.d.). The copy of this journal at the YIVO Institute has a partially torn cover; therefore no publishing date was found. The date given in *LYL* is 1912.
11. Ibid., 27.
12. Prilutski, *Yidishe folkslider*, vol. 1, 1.
13. Graubard, *Literarishe shriftn*, 27.
14. Ibid., 28.
15. *Frishmans yubileyum-bukh*. No editor or publisher is mentioned on the title page. *LYL* 1 (1926): 609 provided the information that Graubard published this work.
16. Pinkhes Graubard, "Folkslider—fun P. Graubards zamlungen," in *Frishmans Yubileyum-bukh*, 205–13.
17. Pinkhes Graubard, *Fun nont un vayt: zamlung fun literatur un folklor* (From near and far: Collection of literature and folklore) (Warsaw: Pinkhes Graubard, 1914). Both *LYL* and *BDMYL* give 1912 as the date. The cover says 1914.
18. Graubard, *Fun nont un vayt*, inside back cover. This "call" implies that an earlier correspondence had been established.
19. Noyekh Prilutski, *Noyekh Prilutskis zamlbikher*, vol. 2.
20. Pinkhes Graubard, "Gezangen fun tom . . . lider fun ganovim, arestantn, gasn-froyen," in Vanvild, *Bay undz yidn*, 18–41.
21. Vanvild, *Bay undz yidn*, iii.
22. Shatsky, "Arbet un frayhayt," 46.
23. Weinreich, review of *Bay undz yidn*, 478.
24. Graubard, "Shmuel Lehmans oytser," 28.
25. Ibid., 29.
26. Ibid., 30
27. The word "balabatim" literally means "bosses," or "the heads of the household." In this case, the word indicates the "establishment," the Jewish middle and upper-middle class. See Graubard, "In yene teg," 334.
28. Noyekh Prilutski, "Di ershte yidishe shprakh konferents," reprinted in *Der yidisher gedank in der nayer tsayt*, ed. A. Menes (New York: Congress for Jewish Culture, 1957), 261–64.
29. For history of this newspaper, see Mendl Mozes, "Der moment (1910–1939)," in *Yidishe prese in varshe* (New York: Congress for Jewish Culture, 1956), 241–98. For a monograph on the Yiddish press in Warsaw in the early years of the century and on the founding of *Der Moment*, see D. Druk, *Tsu der geshikhte fun der yidisher prese: in rusland un polyn* (To the history of the Yiddish press: In Russia and Poland) (Warsaw: Farlag zikhroynes, 1920).
30. Mikhl Veykhert, *Zikhroynes*, vol. 2 (Tel-Aviv: Menora, 1961), 60.

31. Mark W. Kiel, "The Ideology of the Folks-partey," *Soviet Jewish Affairs* 2 (1975): 75–89.
32. Noyekh Prilutski, "Draysik yor literarishe tetikeyt fun Noykeh Prilutski" (Thirty years of literary activity for Noyekh Prilutski), *Literarishe bleter*, May 1, 1931, 1–3.
33. Ibid., 1.
34. Avrom Zak, *In kenigraykh fun yidishn vort: eseyen un dermonungen* (In the kingdom of the Yiddish word: Essays and memoirs) (Buenos Aires: YIVO, 1966), 54.
35. Zak, *In onheyb fun a friling*, 113.
36. A. Almi, "Noyekh Prilutski," in *Mentshn un ideyen* (Warsaw: Farlag M. Goldberg, 1933), 202. Compare with previously mentioned analogy of Yiddish folklorists to bees in section on Lehman.
37. Almi, *Momentn fun a lebn*, 125.
38. Prilutski, *Yidishe folkslider*, vol. 1.
39. Ibid., iii.
40. Ibid., vii.
41. Noyekh Prilutski, "Folks khad-gadye: a bletl folklor" (The folk's *khad-gadye*: A page of folklore), *Passover Supplement* to *Undzer lebn*, no. 85 (1910): 11–12.
42. Prilutski, *Yidishe folkslider*, vol. 1, viii.
43. Ibid., x.
44. See, for example, Leo Weiner, "Aus der Russisch-Judischen Kinderstube," *Mitteilungen zur judischen Volkskunde* 2 (1898): 40–49; and Alfred Landau, "Kinderratsel aud Galizien," *Mitteilungen zur judischen Volkskunde* 7 (1901): 87–88.
45. Prilutski, *Yidishe folkslider*, vol. 1, xi.
46. In the final footnote to the "foreword," Prilutski mentioned ten more volumes that were planned for publication: "Ballads, ballad-like songs and moral tales in verse," "historic songs," "lullabies," "songs by orphans," "children and *kheder* songs," "love songs," "bride and groom songs," "family songs," "social songs," and "satiric songs." Of these, only the volume on "ballads" would be printed.
47. See, for example, text number 33, which is referred to as a variant of 32 but is significantly different.
48. "A characteristic of German folklore studies has been the collecting of parallels and the writing of annotations. . . . Collecting analogues and annotating folklore, of course, are activities which others than German scholars have performed, but more of this kind of work has been done in Germany than elsewhere." See Archer Taylor, "Characteristics of German Folklore Studies," *Journal of American Folklore* 74 (1961): 297.
49. *Mitteilungen zur judischen Volkskunde*, 4 (1899): 123 and 7 (1901): 84–85.
50. Prilutski, *Yidishe folkslider*, vol. 1, 19.
51. Ibid., 83.
52. Ibid., 86.

53. I. L. Cahan, "Yidishe folkslider," in Niger, *Der pinkes,* 364–65.
54. Listen to T. Bikel's famous version on his record, *Theodore Bikel Sings Jewish Folk Songs,* Electra 141. See furthur discussion in section on Menakhem Kipnis.
55. Prilutski, *Yidishe folkslider,* vol. 1, 110.
56. Cahan, "Yidishe folkslider," 361.
57. S. Ansky, review of *Yidishe folkslider,* vol. 1, by Noyekh Prilutski, *Evreiskaia Starina* 4 (1911): 591–94.
58. Cahan, "Yidishe folkslider," 355–66.
59. Prilutski and Lehman, *Noyekh Prilutskis zamlbikher,* vol. 1.
60. Noyekh Prilutski, "Polemik—a tshuve eynem a retsenzent," in Prilutski and Lehman, *Noyekh Prilutskis zamlbikher,* vol. 1, 154–79.
61. Borokhov, "Noyekh Prilutskis zamlbikher far yidishn folklor," 351.
62. Prilutski and Lehman, *Noyekh Prilutskis zamlbikher,* vol. 1, 157. The ethnomusicologist A. Z. Idelsohn, twenty years later, had no problem including *Got fun avrom* as a Yiddish folk song. See A. Z. Idelsohn, *The Folk Song of the East European Jews,* vol. 9 of *Thesaurus of Hebrew Oriental Melodies* (Leipzig: Friedrich Hofmeister, 1932), 4, 205.
63. Prilutski and Lehman, *Noyekh Prilutskis zamlbikher,* vol. 1, 159.
64. Ibid., 164.
65. Ibid., 167.
66. I. L. Cahan, "Dos yidishe folkslid," in Cahan, *Yidishe folkslider,* v–lx.
67. Prilutski and Lehman, *Noyekh Prilutskis zamlbikher,* vol. 1, 167.
68. Ibid., 168.
69. Ibid., 170–71.
70. Ibid.,173.
71. Borokhov, "Noyekh Prilutskis zamlbikher far yidishn folklor," 352.
72. Prilutski and Lehman, *Noyekh Prilutskis zamlbikher,* vol. 1, 7–8.
73. See chapters 3 and 4.
74. See Noyekh Prilutski, "Shmuel Lehman," in *Shmuel Lehman: zamlbukh,* 67.
75. "*Nokhvort,*" in Prilutski and Lehman, *Noyekh Prilutskis zamlbikher,* vol. 1, 81–87.
76. Ibid., 86
77. Noyekh Prilutski, "Purim-shpiln," in Prilutski and Lehman, *Noyekh Prilutskis zamlbikher,* vol. 1, 88–125.
78. Ibid., 98.
79. Dr. S. Weissenberg printed a *shpil* in Yiddish in the Roman alphabet. See his "Das purimspiel von Ahasverus und Esther," in *Mitteilungen zur judischen Volkskunde* 7 (1904),1: 1–26.
80. N. Prilutski, *Yidishe folkslider,* vol. 2.
81. Ibid., 38. In summing up his analysis of one song, he writes, "The distribution of the songs, the large number of variants and fragments, as well as its general character and several linguistic points convince us that the work must be included among the Yiddish folksongs."
82. Ibid., 11–12.

83. Ibid., 32.
84. See Eleanor Gordon Mlotek, "International Motifs in the Yiddish Ballads," in *For Max Weinreich on His Seventieth Birthday: Studies in Jewish Languages, Literature, and Society* (The Hague: Mouton, 1964), 209–28. She discusses the wide dispersion of many of the songs included in this section.
85. Prilutski, *Yidishe folkslider,* vol. 2, 82, 87. I can find no treatment of the spoken elements in Yiddish song performance.
86. See Mlotek, "International Motifs," 223–25 for a fuller treatment and bibliography on the Yiddish riddle song.
87. Prilutski, *Yidishe folkslider,* vol. 2, 107–10; and Mlotek, "International Motifs," 225–28.
88. Prilutski, *Yidishe folkslider,* vol. 2, 104.
89. Anon. review of *Yidishe folkslider,* vol. 2, by Noyekh Prilutski, *Vokhenblatt* (Warsaw) no. 82, April 5, 1914, 16.
90. Alfred Landau, "Bamerkungen tsu Noyekh Prilutskis *yidishe folklslider,"* *Yidishe Filologye* 1 (1924): 151–60.
91. Ibid., 153.
92. Prilutski, *Noyekh Prilutskis zamlbikher,* vol. 2.
93. For a linguistic analysis and overview of the work, see Marvin I. Herzog, "Grammatical Features of Markuze's *Seyfer Refues (1790),"* in *The Field of Yiddish: Studies in Language, Folklore and Literature, Second Collection,* ed. Uriel Weinreich (The Hague: Mouton, 1965), 49–62.
94. Noyekh Prilutski, "Dr. Moyshe Markuze: a yidishist fun 18tn yorhundert" (Dr. Moyshe Markuze: A Yiddishist from the eighteenth century), in Prilutski, *Noyekh Prilutskis zamlbikher,* vol. 2, 1–56.
95. Dan Miron, "Folklore and Anti-Folklore," 220.
96. Noyekh Prilutski, "Purim-shpiln," 88–125.
97. Prilutski, *Noyekh Prilutskis zamlbikher,* vol. 2, 126.
98. Noyekh Prilutski, "Dos yidishe folksvort," 161–73.
99. Noyekh Prilutski, *Dos gevet: dialogn vegn shprakh un kultur* (Warsaw: Farlag kulturlige, 1923), 253.
100. Ibid., 8–13.
101. A. Almi, *Humoristishe shriftn,* vol. 1, *Parodyes* (Warsaw: A. Gitlin, 1928), 115–18.
102. Prilutski and Lehman, *Noyekh Prilutskis zamlbikher,* vol. 1, 173.

Chapter 3

1. *LYL* 1 (1926):668–69; *BDMYL* 2 (1958):229–31.
2. Khayim Leyb Fuks, "Yitskhok Katsenelsons shtub," *Yidishe shriftn* 2, nos. 5–6 (1947):12–13.
3. See Rokhl Oyerbakh, "Hershele (Danilevitsh)," *Yidishe shriftn* 2, nos. 5–6 (1947): 15–16.
4. Yitskhok Katsenelson, "Di khronik fun Hersheles toyt" (The story of Hershele's death), in *Yidishe geto-ksovim, Varshe 1940–1943* (Israel: Ghetto

Fighter's House and Hakibbutz Hameuchad Publishing House, 1984), 476–78.

5. Yitskhok Katsenelson, "Ya mam lidlekh" (I have poems), in Katsenelson, *Yidishe geto-ksovim*, 479–83.

6. Yoysef Papirnikov, "Hersh Danilevitsh," in *Heymishe un noente* (Tel Aviv: Farlag Perets, 1958), 217–21.

7. I. H. Radoshitski, "Hershele-der lodzher trubador," in *Lodzher yizker-bukh* (New York: Fareynikte reytungs komitet far der shtot lodzh, 1943), 119–21.

8. Tsipore Katsenelson-Nakhumov, *Yitskhok Katsenelson: zayn lebn un shafn* (Buenos Aires: Tsentral farband fun poylishe yidn in Argentina, 1948), 171.

9. See entry on Koltsov in *Handbook of Russian Literature*, ed. Victor Terras (New Haven, Conn.: Yale University Press, 1985), 230–31.

10. Dr. Mordkhe Schaechter, oral communication.

11. Hershl Danilevitsh, *Hersheles lider: ershter zamlung* (Pietrokov: n.p., 1907). The cover states Lodz as place of publication, the title page Pietrokov. This rare book is not even in the YIVO Institute's library in New York. A copy has found its way to the Gratz College Library in Philadelphia.

12. Ibid. Found on untitled page following title page.

13. Ibid., 3.

14. Hershl Danilevitsh, "Mi bemayim: poeme fun kantonistn lebn", in *Haynt yoyvl-bukh (1908–1938)* (Warsaw: n.p., 1938), 61. The female folkpoet of Lodz, Miriam Ulianover, has a poem printed on the same page.

15. Hershl Danilevitsh, "Fun'm folks-moyl: rekrutn un soldatn lider, retenishn, anekdotn," in Vanvild, *Bay undz yidn*, 95–110.

16. See ibid., 103–4. The four songs printed as "rent songs" are all variants of the same song but are not marked as such.

17. See the recordings of the comedians Dzigan and Schumacher, both Lodz Jews.

18. See Mlotek, "International Motifs," 222–23, for a discussion and complete bibliography of this ballad in Yiddish.

19. S. Ansky, "Yidishe folks-retenishn," in Ansky, *Folklor un ethnografye*, 223–29.

20. Vanvild, *Bay undz yidn*, 108.

21. Weinreich, review of *Bay undz yidn*, 479.

22. Ibid.

23. Yitskhok Shiper, *Geshikhte fun yidisher teater-kunst un drama* (Warsaw: Kultur-lige, 1927), 2:256–64.

24. Ibid., 256.

25. Ibid., 3:193.

26. Cited in Kiel, "Twice Lost Legacy," 160–61.

27. Danil Leybl, "Shiva shirey am" (Seven folk songs), *Reshumot* 6 (1930): 435–42.

28. *LYL* 3 (1929): 645–49.

29. Menakhem Kipnis, "Berditchever khazones," *Der shtral* 1 (1910) 18 Adar: 27–28.

30. Menakhem Kipnis, "In a malarusishn dorf," *Der shtral* 1, no. 35 (1910): 17–20 and continues in *Der shtral* 1, no. 36: 15–21.
31. "A khor fun yidn," *Der shtral* 1, no. 8 (1910): 30. The title intentionally calls attention to the fact that it is not "a yidisher khor" (a Jewish choir), but a "choir of Jews."
32. Menakhem Kipnis, "Fun zey iz keday tsu visn" (One should know about them), in *Shmuel Lehman: zamlbukh*, 72–77.
33. Menakhem Kipnis, *60 yidishe folkslider mit notn: fun M. Kipis un Z. Zeligfelds repertuar* (Warsaw; A. Gitlin, n.d. [1918]); idem, *80 yidishe folkslider: fun Z. Zeligfelds and M. Kipnis repertuar* (Warsaw: A. Gitlin, n.d. [1925]); idem, *Khelemer mayses* (Warsaw: Sz. Cukier, 1930).
34. *LYL* 3 (1929):648–49.
35. Quoted in *BDMYL* 8 (1981):195.
36. See Lucjan Dobroszycki and Barbara Kirshenblatt-Gimblett, eds., *Image Before My Eyes: A Photographic History of Jewish Life in Poland 1864–1939* (New York: Schocken Books, 1977) for several photographs and a history of Jewish photography in Poland. Also see Raphael Abramovitch, ed., *The Vanished World* (New York: Forward Association, 1947) for more examples of Kipnis's photographs.
37. Efrayim Kaganovski, *Yidisher shrayber in der heym*, 426.
38. Details of Kipnis's life in the ghetto are found in Janus Turkow, *Farloshene shterns* (Extinguished stars), vol. 1 (Buenos Aires: Tsentral farband fun poylishe yidn in Argentine, 1953), 137–42.
39. For a typical description of Kipnis's popularity in the countryside, see I. J. Trunk, *Poyln: zikhroynes un bilder* (Poland: Memoirs and episodes) (New York: Undzer tsayt, 1953), 7:49–54.
40. Text and melody in Kipnis, *60 yidishe folkslider*, 15–16.
41. Zak, *In onheyb fun a friling*, 212–13.
42. Melekh Ravitch, *Mayn leksikon* (Montreal: n.p., 1941), 231–32.
43. Turkow, *Farloshene shterns*, 138.
44. See H. D. Nomberg, "Der pedler geyt," in *Dos bukh felyetonen* (The book of feuilletons) (Warsaw: Kh. Bzozhe, 1924), 328–33, for the general interest in Yiddish folk songs in Warsaw.
45. Kipnis, *60 yidishe folkslider*, unpaginated last page.
46. Ibid., unpaginated last page.
47. Ibid., 60.
48. Ibid., 16.
49. Ibid., 89–90.
50. Ibid., 117–18.
51. See Mlotek, "International Motifs," 221–22.
52. See Uriel Weinreich's summary of the analysis on this genre, "Di forshung fun 'mishshprakhike' yidishe folkslider" (The research of macaronic Yiddish folk songs), *YIVO-bleter* 34 (1950): 282–88.
53. Kipnis, *80 yidishe folkslider*.

54. I. L. Cahan, "Folkslid un folkstimlekh lid," in *Shtudyes vegn yidisher folksssha-fung*, 194–201.
55. Kipnis, *80 yidishe folkslider*, 39.
56. Ibid., 51.
57. Ibid., 56.
58. Ibid., 58.
59. Ibid., 44–47.
60. Prilutski, *Yidishe folkslider*, vol. 2, 5–15. Three variants are given, but Kipnis is the first to provide a melody as well as a new variant.
61. Kipnis, *Khelemer mayses.*
62. Henekh Kon, "Menakhem-Mendl Kipnis, Folkzinger," *Tog Morgn Zhurnal*, August 25, 1967, 9.
63. Kipnis, *Khelemer mayses*, untitled first page.
64. For an overview of Chelm folklore studies, see Dov Sadan, "Araynfir tsu Khayim Zeltsers khelmyade" (Introduction to Chaim Zeltser's Chelm world), in Chaim Zeltser, *Shtern afn yarid oder khelm: di festung fun khokhme* (Stars at the fair or Chelm: The fortress of wisdom) (Tel Aviv: Farlag Yisrol Bukh, 1985), 7–18; and Dov Sadan, "Khokhmey khelm," *Yeda-Am* 2 (1954): 229–32.
65. See "Khelemer naronim" (Fools of Chelm), in Prilutski, *Noyekh Prilutskis zamlbikher*, vol. 2, 187–202.
66. Bastomski collected and published Chelm tales in many issues of *Der khaver* and *Grinike beymelekh*, the children's journals he edited, in Vilne in the 1920s and 1930s.
67. *Nisim veniflues: kuriozn un bilder—ershtes bikhl*, (Warsaw: n.p., 1930).
68. Menakhem Kipnis, "Reb Khayem Sholem der toyter geyt shtarbn: a folkstim-lekhe ertseylung," in *Haynt yoyvl-bukh (1908–1938)* (Warsaw: n.p., 1938), 97–99.
69. P. Sherman, "A fardinstfuler yubeleyum" (A deserved honoree), *Di khazonim velt* 1, no. 1 (1934): 2–3.
70. Ibid., 2.
71. See Ezra Mendelsohn, *Zionism in Poland*, 58, 60, 66. The Mizrachi Party in Russia was founded in 1902. See also Ehud Luz, *Parallels Meet: Religion and Nationalism in the Early Zionist Movement, 1882–1904* (Philadelphia: JPS, 1988), 227–56.
72. See *LYL* 1 (1926):1090–94.
73. Yehude Elzet, "Zakrutshiner balebatim" and "Plinsker kolekotnikes," in Pri-lutski, *Noyekh Prilutskis zamlbikher far yidishn folklor*, vol. 2, 184–86 and 210–12.
74. Yehude Elzet, "Miminhagei yisrael: Kovetz minhagim shelo nizkeru od o shelo nitbaru adayin kkol tsorham," *Reshumot* 1 (1918): 335–77.
75. Yehude Elzet [Zlotnik], *Der vunder-oytser fun der yidisher shprakh: folkstim-lekhe rednsartn, glaykhvertlekh un anekdotn* (Warsaw: Levin-Epshteyn, 1918–1920).

76. See Kiel, "Twice Lost Legacy," 48. Kiel states that Elzet's "folkloristic interests were related to his religious and political calling." Though this might be true of his Hebrew writings, his Yiddish writings reflect some basic beliefs in Yiddish literature shared by secular Yiddishists.
77. Yehude Elzet, *Der vunder-oytser fun der yidisher shprakh: davenen* (The wonderful treasure: Prayer) (Warsaw: Levin-Epshteyn, 1918), 1–2.
78. Ibid., 3.
79. See introduction to Yehude Elzet, *Der vunder-oytser fun der yidisher shprakh: malokhes un bal-malokhes* (The wonderful treasure of the Yiddish language: Trades and tradespeople) (Warsaw: Levin-Epshteyn, 1920), 3–14.
80. Ibid., 39–41.
81. Yehude Elzet, *Der vunder-oytser fun der yidisher shprakh: der mentshlekher kerper* (Warsaw: Levin-Epshteyn, 1920); idem, *Der vunder-oytser fun der yidisher shprakh: yidishe maykholim* (Warsaw: Levin-Epshteyn, 1920).
82. Elzet, *Yidishe maykholim*, 5–8.
83. Ibid., 122.
84. Letter from Elzet to unknown "Herr," n.d. [1941?] from New York. From Papers of Yehude-Leyb Zlotnik in Folklore Research Center, Hebrew University, Jerusalem.
85. Elzet mentions his first volume of *Vunder-oytser* (1918) in a footnote. Vanvild wrote in the introduction to *Bay undz yidn* that the volume was ready in 1917. See above.
86. Yehude Elzet, "Idiotizmen: materialen far der frazeologye fun der yidisher shprakh" (Idiomatic Expressions: Materials for a Phraseology of the Yiddish Language), in Vanvild, *Bay undz yidn*, 189–206.
87. Vanvild, *Bay undz yidn*, i.
88. Elzet, "Idiotizmen," 189.
89. See Yehude Elzet, *Studies in Past Jewish Domestic Life*, vol. 1 of *One Hundred Years Ago* (Montreal: n.p., 1927).
90. *BDMYL* 3 (1960):655.
91. Yeshaye Zlotnik, *Leksikon fun yidishe khokhmes: gute verter fun kluge yidn* (Warsaw: n.p., 1930).
92. Rabbi Yeshaye Zlotnik, *Yomim-toyvim folklor: ershter teyl* (Warsaw: n.p., 1930).
93. Alter Druyanov, "Hahalatsa hayehudit haamamit," *Reshumot* 1 (1918):303–57. See also Kiel, "Twice Lost Legacy," 56–74.
94. Zlotnik, *Yomim-toyvim*, vi–vii.
95. Ibid., vii.
96. Ibid., viii.
97. Ibid., ix.
98. Rabbi Yeshayne Zlotnik, *Khumesh-folklor*, vol. 1, *Seyfer breyshis* (Warsaw: n.p., 1937); idem, *Khumesh-folklor*, vol. 2, *Shmoys, vayikra* (Warsaw: n.p., 1938); idem, *Khumesh-folklor*, vol. 3, *Bamidbar, dvorim* (Warsaw: n.p., 1938).
99. Zlotnik, *Khumesh-folklor*, vol. 3, back cover.

Chapter 4

1. Hirsh Abramovitsh, *Farshvundene geshtaltn: zikhroynes un siluetn* (Vanished figures: Memoirs and silhouettes) (Buenos Aires: Tsentral farband fun poylishe yidn in Argentina, 1958), 171–73.
2. The Jewish Historical-Ethnographic Society evolved from the earlier Historical Ethnographic Commission founded in 1892. The emphasis upon ethnography was thus clearly not an innovation of Vilne historians; that credit is due Simon Dubnow and his circle in St. Petersburg. The ethnographic element, though, was introduced into Vilne at the time of the First World War, as indicated by Shalit. See Kiel, "Twice Lost Legacy," 366–78; and Abraham G. Duker, " 'Evreiskaia Starina'—A Bibliography of the Russian-Jewish Historical Periodical," *Hebrew Union College Annual* 8–9 (1931–32): 525–603.

    There was, of course, a parallel non-Jewish Polish tradition of learned societies. See Lech Trzeciakowski, "The Role of Learned Societies in the Development of Polish Culture during the Period of the Partitions," *East European Quarterly* 22, no. 3 (1988): 291–303.
3. Ezra Mendelsohn, *The Jews of East Central Europe Between the World Wars* (Bloomington: Indiana University Press, 1983), 213–25.
4. The full name in Yiddish reads, "Di vilne yidishe historish-etnografishe gezelshaft afn nomen fun S. Ansky, Z'l." Some references and publications left off the "Jewish" in the name of the organization; however, the "Statutes" (in Polish) in the YIVO archives include "Zydowskiego" in the name. The "Statutes" are not dated.
5. See entry in *LYL* 1 (1926): 133–34.
6. In Yiddish, *Libhober fun yidishn altertum*. See A. I. Goldshmidt, "Di Vilner historish-etnografishe gezelshaft un ir muzey" (The Vilner Historic-Ethnographic Society and its museum), in *Vilner almanakh*, A. I. Grodzenski, ed. (Vilne: Ovnt-kurier, 1939; reprint, New York: Moriah Offset Co., 1992), 189–94 (page citations are to the reprint edition).

    The *Encylopaedia Judaica*, s.v. "Museums" states that this museum opened in 1920. For a history of the museum, see Khaykl Lunski, "Di yidishe historish-etnografishe gezelshaft," in *Pinkes: far der geshikhte fun vilne in di yorn fun milkhome un okupatsye*, ed. Zalmen Reyzen (Vilne: AVJHES, 1922), 862–63.

    The imporant Polish Ethnographic Museum in Cracow was established as a public institution in 1911. One could thus claim that both Jewish and Polish nationalists endeavored to make private collections open to the people during this prewar period. See Stanislaw Lorentz, *Museums and Collections in Poland 1945–1955* (Warsaw: Polonia Publishing House, 1956), 23.
7. A. I. Goldshmidt, "Di historish-etnografishe gezelshaft afn nomen fun S. Ansky," *Literarishe bleter* 46 (1932): 736. Ansky emphasized the need for all of the folk to see their treasures in museums; see S. Anksy, "Di yidishe folksretenishn," *Gezamlte shriftn* 15 (1929): 227–45.

8. Vilne Society of Lovers of Jewish Antiquities, "An afruf vegn yidishn muzey," *Di yidishe velt* 10 (1913): 147.
9. Ibid., 148.
10. "Likht un shotn—Der oyfruf vegn yidishn muzey," *Di yidishe velt* 10 (1913): 126–29.
11. Lunski, "Di yidishe historish-etnografishe gezelshaft," 862.
12. See "Statutes" (in Polish) in collection of the AVJHES at the YIVO Institute for Jewish Research in New York.
13. Lunksi, "Di yidishe historish-etnografishe gezelshaft," 855–56.
14. Ibid., 862–63.
15. Ibid., 855.
16. Moyshe Shalit, "Vegn fareynikn di historish-etnografishe gezelshaft mit dem yidishn visnshaftlekhn institut," *Literarishe bleter* 39 (1928): 763.
17. For complete listing, see Moyshe Shalit, "Der An-ski arkhiv—Zayn inhalt un vert," *Literarishe bleter* 16 (1929): 313. Some of Ansky's materials from this museum are found in the collection of the AVJHES at the YIVO Institute for Jewish Research in New York.
18. Hirsh Abramovitsh, "Farshvundene yidishe parnoses," *Fun noentn over* 1 (1937): 46–51, 212–25.
19. A. Sutskever, "Dov Sadan: 1902–1989," *Goldene keyt* 128 (1990): 5.
20. Hirsh Abramovitsh, "Der biblioteker," *Literarishe bleter* 1, no. 58 (1925): 4.
21. Biograpical details from *BDMYL* 5 (1963): 14–16.
22. See correspondence with S. Niger, papers of S. Niger, YIVO Archives.
23. (Vilne, 1917). *Yeda Am* published thirty anecdotes in Hebrew, translated from the Yiddish, collected by Lunski on Ayzik Kharif. "Anecdotes of the Great Rabbi Ayzl Kharif: Rabbi in Slonim," *Yeda Am* 1 (1962): 75–89. The introduction states that the texts were taken from Lunski's "literary inheritance."
24. Khaykl Lunski, *Fun vilner geto: bilder un geshtaltn geshribn in shvere tsaytn* (From the Vilne Ghetto: Portraits and figures described in hard times) (Vilne: Fareyn fun di yidishe literatn un zhurnalistn in vilne, 1920).
25. Khaykl Lunski, "Vilner kloyzn un der shulhoyf," in *Vilner zamlbukh* 2 (1920): 56–72. A *kloyz* is a small house of study, often designed for a particular occupation or other social group. Lunski enumerates thirty but there were more than one hundred in Vilne.
26. Khaykl Lunski, *Legendes vegn vilner goen, reb elye bar shloyme zalmen z'l: geklibn fun menthsn un sforim fun Kh. Lunski* (Vilne: Farlag di naye yidishe folkshul, 1924).
27. Abramovitsh, "Der biblioteker," 4.
28. Khaykl Lunksi, "Iserlins yidish," *Yidishe filologye* 1 (1924): 288–302; and "Yidish bay r'yankev Vayl," in *Landoy-bukh* (Vilne: YIVO, 1926), 285–88.
29. Moyshe Shalit, *Af di khurves fun milkhomes un mehumes: pinkes* (Vilne: Gegnt-komitet YEKOPO, 1931).
30. Khaykl Lunski, "Olkenik: a shtetl mit legendes," in Shalit, *Af di khurves*, 434–43.

31. Yoysef Vinyetski, "Zhetler folklor," in Shalit, *Af di khurves*, 430–34.
32. Khayim-Khaykl Lunski, *Geoynim un gdoylim fun noentn over: sipurim un agodes fun zeyer lebn un shafn* (Vilne: n.p., 1931).
33. N. Vaynig, "Khaykl Lunski," *Literarishe bleter* 12 (1933): 188.
34. Abramovitsh, "Der bibloteker," 3. Lunski was a supporter of Hebrew University and sent hundreds of his collected *sforim* (religious books) to that institution. See entry in *LYL* 1 (1927): 95–96.
35. On this interest by cantors in nonreligous music see Mark Slobin, *Chosen Voices: The Story of the American Cantorate* (Urbana: University of Illinois Press, 1989), 20–21.
36. See *LYL* 1 (1926): 367–69.
37. Editor's note to A. M. Bernshteyn's "Mayne taynes tsu khazones" (My gripes against cantorial music) in *Di khazonim velt* 1 (May 1934): 19.
38. For the most detailed biography, see Meyer Bernshteyn, "A. M. Bernshteyn: zikhroynes fun mayn bruder" (A. M. Bernshteyn: Memoirs of my brother), in special A. M. Bernshteyn issue of *Di khazonim velt* 1 (1934): 15–17. For an evalution of his accomplishments see in same issue, P. Sherman, "A. M. Bernshteyn: tsu zayn tsveyter yortsayt, dem tsentn siven" (A. M. Bernshteyn: To his second *yorstayt,* the tenth of sivan), *Di khazonim velt* 1 (1934): 1–4.
39. See "complete" list of his compositions in *Di khazonim velt* 1, May 1934, 6–8. Two hundred and five is the number given in his entry in Macy Nulman, *Concise Encyclopedia of Jewish Music* (New York: McGraw-Hill, 1975), 32–33.
40. Moyshe Shalit, foreword to A. M. Bernshteyn, *Muzikalisher pinkes: nigumim-zamlung fun yidishn folk-oytser* (Musical record: Collection of melodies from the Jewish folk-treasure) (Vilne: Vilner yidisher historish-etnografishe gezelshaft af dem nomen fun S. Ansky z'l, 1927), 1:1.
41. Compare to a similar opinion by Max Eisikovits on *nigunim:* "From a musical point-of-view, they unquestionably constitute the most original and noble aspect of Jewish folklore." In his *Songs of the Martyrs: Hassidic Melodies of Maramures* (New York: Sepher-Hermon Press, 1980), preface page.
42. Bernshteyn, *Muzikalisher pinkes*, xvii–xix.
43. Ibid., xix.
44. Ibid., xx.
45. Ibid.
46. See Eisikovits, *Songs of the Martyrs,* unpaginated last page of introduction, in which similar experience with Hasidim in Hungary in 1938 is recounted: " 'These are *niggunim kedoshim,*' said the Rebbe. 'How do you expect us to sing these hallowed melodies just any time?' "
47. Bernshteyn, *Muzikalisher pinkes*, xxii.
48. Yisroel Gladshteyn, review of *Muzikalisher pinkes, Bikher-velt* 4 (1929): 61.
49. Bearing in mind that much of the information of Reyzin's *LYL* of 1928 came from the writers, 1912 would seem accurate.
50. Letter dated November 8, 1913, in Papers of S. Niger, YIVO Institute for Jewish Research, New York.
51. Shloyme Bastomski, *Yidishe folksretenishn* (Vilne: Di naye yidishe folkshul,

1917). I have examined the second editon of 1920. S. Ansky reviewed a second edition of 1919. I believe all the editions are the same except for the addition of the Ansky review to the 1920 edition. Bastomski, in a footnote to Ansky's review, admits that the mistakes the reviewer pointed out in 1919 have remained in the 1920 edition. If he did not correct the mistakes, he probably did not change anything else either.

52. Ibid., 1.
53. Ansky, *Folklor un ethnografye*, 227–28.
54. Bastomski, *Yidishe folksretenishn*, 1.
55. Ibid., 1–2.
56. For a structural analysis of the riddles, see Jennifer Dowling, "Riddles and Riddle Parodies: Shloyme Bastomski's Yidishe Folksretenishn," in *History of Yiddish Studies: Winter Studies in Yiddish*, vol. 3, ed. Dov-Ber Kerler (Chur, England: Harwood Academic Publishers, 1987).
57. Shloyme Bastomski, *Yidishe sprikhverter far shul un heym* (Vilne: Di naye yidishe shul, 1920).
58. Ibid., 1.
59. Ibid., inside back cover.
60. Ibid.
61. S. Bastomski, *Baym kval: yidishe shprikhverter, vertlekn, glaykhvertlekh, rednsartn, farglay khenishn, brokhes, vintshenishn, Kloles, kharomes, simonim, sgules, zababones*, edited by Zalmen Reyzen and the Folklore Section of the Vilner historish-ethnografisher gezelshaft (Vilne: Di naye yidishe folkshul, 1920).
62. Ibid., ii.
63. Ibid.
64. Ibid., iii.
65. Ibid., iv.
66. Ibid.
67. Ibid., v.
68. Ibid. See also Kiel, "Twice Lost Legacy," 394, and Roskies, "S. Ansky and the Paradigm of Return," for Ansky's ideas on returning folklore to the folk.
69. The complete title reads, *Der kundes: zamlungen fun retenishn, rebusn, oyf-gabn, kuntsn, shpiln, sharadn, numer 1: serye: kinder-literatur n.19* (Vilne: Di naye yidishe farlag, 1921).
70. Shloyme Bastomski, "Materialn tsum yidishn folklor," in *Pinkes: far der geshikhte fun Vilne in di yorn fun milkhome un okupatsye*, ed. Zalmen Reyzen (Vilne: AVJHES, 1922).
71. Shloyme Bastomski, *Baym kval: materialn tsum yidishn folklor, yidishe folk-slider*.
72. S. Bastomski, "Materialn tsum yidishn folklor." This is an introduction to his work, *Baym kval: materialn tsum yidishn folklor, yidishe folkslider*. See also introduction to Cahan, *Yidishe folkslider*.
73. Yitskhok Broydes (1880–1946) was a cofounder of AVJHES. He published a

series of Vilne legends in the local newspapers. He emigrated to Palestine in 1923. See *LYL* 1 (1926): 410.

74. These guidelines do not appear in Ansky's collected works in Yiddish. They are similar to the guidelines in S. Ansky et al., *Dos yidishe etnografishe program*, ed. L. I. Shternberg (Petrograd: Publication of the Jewish Ethnographic Expedition, named for Baron Hertz Gintsburg, an independent section of the Jewish Historic-Ethnographic Society, 1914), 13–15.

75. S. Ansky, "Klolim: vi azoy tsu farshraybn verk fun folksshafung," in Bastomski, *Baym kval: materialn tsum yidishn folklor, yidishe folkslider*, 23. This point is taken verbatim from Ansky et al., *Dos yidishe etnografishe program*, 15.

76. Ignaz Bernstein, *Erotica et Rustica* (Warsaw: n.p., 1908).

77. Item numbers four and five in the first section are variants of songs found in the Ginzburg-Marek collection. There are many other examples.

78. S. Bastomski, review of *Gavonim-lider*, by Shmuel Lehman. Discussed in chapter 2.

79. Bastomski, *Baym kval: materialn tsum yidishn folklor, yidishe folkslider*, inside cover.

80. Interview conducted with Sheskin at his home, Brooklyn, New York, May 29, 1991.

81. S. Bastomski, *Yidishe folksmayses un legendes*, vol. 1, Legendes vegn besht (Yiddish folktales and legends, vol. 1, Legends of the Besht) (Vilne: Naye yidishe folkshul, 1925).

82. Ibid., 4.

83. Letter dated June 6 [1925 or 1926], Papers of S. Niger, YIVO Institute for Jewish Research, New York.

84. Letter dated August 15 [1925 or 1926], Papers of S. Niger, YIVO Institute for Jewish Research, New York.

85. Bastomski, *Yidishe folksmayses*, 6.

86. S. Ansky, *Khurbn galitsye*, volumes 4, 5, and 6 of his *Gezamlte shriftn* (collected works) (Warsaw, Vilne, New York: S. Shreberk, 1925).

87. Shloyme Bastomski, *Purim-shpiln: a) Yoysef-shpil (mekhires yoysef) b) Akheshverush-shpil* (Vilne: Di naye yidishe folkshul, 1926), 4.

88. A. Damesek, "Dray naye kindertsaytungen" (Three new children's newspapers), *Literarishe bleter* 6 (1927): 105.

89. *Yidishe vitsn*, vol. 1, *1) vegn orem un raykh, 2) vegn ligns* (Yiddish jokes, vol. 1, 1) about poor and rich, 2) about lies) (Vilne: Di naye yidishe folkshul, 1931).

90. Shloyme Bastomski, *Mayselekh vegn Motke Khabad*, vol. 1 (Vilne: Grininke beymelekh, 1938); idem, *Mayselekh vegn Motke Khabad*, vol. 2 (Vilne: Grininke beymelekh, 1940); idem, *Mayselekh vegn khelemer naronim*, vol. 1 (Vilne: Grininke beymelekh, 1938); idem, *Mayselekh vegn khelemer naronim* vol. 2 (Vilne: Grininke beymelekh, 1940); idem, *Mayselekh vegn khelemer naronim*, vol. 3 (Vilne: Grininke beymelekh, 1940); idem, *Peysekhdike vitsn un vertlekh* (Vilne: Grininke beymelekh, 1940).

91. See Dr. I. Rubin, "Akshonim (S. Bastomski)" (Stubborn people), *Literarishe bleter* 29 (1929): 568.

Chapter 5

1. For a summation of Miese's life and work and the impact of his talk at Chernovitz, see Goldsmith, *Architects of Yiddishism*.
2. I. Efren, "Organizatsye," *Di yidishe velt* 11 (1913): 152–56.
3. Ber Borokhov, "Di oyfgabn fun der yidisher filologye," 1–22.
4. Ber Borokhov, "Gramatishe frumkeyt" (Grammatical strictness), *Di yidishe velt* 12 (1913): 147–53.
5. Bal dimyen [Nokhem Shtif], "Der pinkes," in *Literatur un lebn: di yidishe velt* (April 1914): 247–61; (May 1914): 395–410.
6. A. Vilner [S. Niger], "Vegn dem rayon tsu shafn a yidishn universitet" (On the idea to establish a Jewish university), *Literatur un lebn* 6 (1914): 126–34.
7. For a survey of Yiddish encyclopedia projects, see Y. Yashunski, "Pruvn fun yidishe entsiklopedias," *Bikher-velt* 1 (1922): 127–32; and Nakhmen Mayzel, "Forgeyer fun der algemeyner entsiklopedye in yidish," *Literarishe bleter* 12 (March 15, 1935): 170–71.
8. For example, the announcement of a planned encyclopedia in *Literatur un lebn: di yidishe velt* (December 1914): 118.
9. Dr. A. Gliksman, "Neo-haskole: a vort vegn undzer folks-universitetn," *Literarishe-bleter* 1 (January 9, 1925): 1–2.
10. Ibid., 2.
11. This dichotomy is most obvious in YIVO's course of action in standardizing Yiddish orthography in the 1930s, which effected a powerful anti-intellectual backlash that is still felt today in Yiddish intellectual circles.
12. See Alfred Abraham Greenbaum, *Jewish Scholarship and Scholarly Institutions in the Soviet Union, 1918–1953* (Jerusalem: Hebrew University of Jerusalem, Centre for Research and Documentation of East European Jewry, 1978), 27–28.
13. The full title reads *Yidishe filologye: tsvey khodoshimdike bleter far shprakhvisnshaft, literaturforshung, un etnografye.*
14. Max Weinreich and Zalmen Reyzin, "A briv tsu ale yidishe filologn" (A letter to all Yiddish philologists) *Teolit: teater un literatur* 1 (1923): 48.
15. Nokhem Shtif, "Ditrikh fun Bern," 1–11.
16. Noyekh Prilutski, "Shpet-loshn" (Mocking language), 33–45, A[lfred Landau], "Miluim ts M. Vaynraykhs *Shtaplen*" (Supplement to M. Weinreich's *Shtaplen*), 55–61; F. Alfabet, "Materialn tsu a idiotikon fun shtetl pyask" (Materials for a regional glossary from the town of Pyask), 61–72; M[oyshe] Lerer, "Miluim tsu N. Prilutskis *Gevet*" (Supplement to N. Prilutski's *gevet*), 72–74; all in *Yidishe filologye* 1 (1924).
17. Noyekh Prilutski, "Grins af shvuos," *Yidishe filologye* 1 (1924): 87–89.
18. Khane Perlshteyn and Borukh Kats, "Tsvey aktuele folkslider," *Yidishe filologye* 1 (1924): 94.
19. See chapter 2.
20. Elye Sosnovik, "Materialn tsu der yidisher folksmeditsin in vaysrusland," *Yidishe filologye* 1 (1924): 160–62; Max Weinreich, "Tsu der kharakteristik

fun undzere folksgleybenishn: onmerkungen tsu E. Sosnoviks artikl" (To the nature of our folk belief: Remarks on E. Sosnovik's article), *Yidishe filologye* 1 (1924): 168–76.

21. Max Grunwald, "Aus Hausapotheke un Hexenkuche," *Mitteilungen zur jud-ischen Volkskunde* 5 (1903): 19.
22. Lilienthal, "Eyn hore," 256–71.
23. For a detailed summary of the founding of YIVO see Zosa Szajkowski, *YIVO and Its Founders: Catalogue of the Exhibition on the Occasion of the Fiftieth Anniversary of the YIVO Institute for Jewish Research* (New York: YIVO Institute for Jewish Research, 1975).
24. Nokhem Shtif, "Vegn a yidishn akademishn institut," in *Di organizatsye fun der yidisher visnshaft* (Vilne: Tsentraler Bildung Komitet and Vilbig, 1925), 9.
25. Ibid., 9.
26. Shtif, *Di organizatsye fun der yidisher visnshaft*, 28.
27. Max Weinreich, "Vilner tezisn vegn yidishn visnshaftlekhn institut," in *Di organizatsye fun der yidisher visnshaft* (Vilne: Tsentraler Bildung Komitet and Vilbig, 1925).
28. Ibid., 37.
29. Tcherikover quoted in Szajkowksi, *YIVO and Its Founders*, 14.
30. Dr. Max Weinreich, "Der yidisher visnshaftlekher institute," in *Vilne*, ed. J. Jeshurin (New York: Workmen's Circle—Branch 367, 1935), 323.
31. Max Weinreich, "The Language of the Way of the Shas," in *History of the Yiddish Language*, trans. Shlomo Noble (Chicago: University of Chicago, 1980), 175–246. *Shas* means six and refers to the six books of the Talmud.
32. "Yedies fun yidishn visnshaftlekhn institut," *Literarishe bleter* 75 (1925): 159–60.
33. "Klolim far zamler fun etnografishn material," *Literarishe bleter* 81 (1925): 255.
34. Ibid., 255.
35. An undated "Rules" is in the Collection of the YIVO Ethnographic Commission, YIVO Institute, New York. It seems to be a late 1925 or early 1926 version.
36. Handwritten letter from Max Weinreich, Collection of the YIVO Ethnographic Commission, YIVO Institute, New York.
37. Typewritten letter from the EC, n.d. Collection of the YIVO Ethnographic Commission, YIVO Institute, New York.
38. "Yedies fun yidishn visnshaftlekhn institut," *Literarishe bleter* 83 (1925): 288.
39. "Yedies fun yidishn visnshaftlekhn institut," *Literarishe bleter* 81 (1925).
40. "Yedies fun yidishn visnshaftlekhn institut," *Literarishe bleter* 85 (1925): 319. The Vilne Goan (1720–97) was the leading Talmudist and commentator of his time and a fierce opponent of Hasidism.
41. See Lunski, *Legendes vegn vilner goen*.
42. See Almi, A. *1863*.
43. A reference to the legend of Karmelin is in Lifshe Schaechter-Widman's memoirs, *Durkhgelebt a velt* (New York: Lifshe Vidman Bukh Komitet,

1973), 17. During the flood in her town, a hundred years earlier, the wealthiest Jew, Nekhemye Karmelin, refused to let go of his chest of gold and drowned. People sang a folk song about the incident. Dobosh was a Ukrainian Robin Hood–type bandit.

44. "Yedies fun yidishn visnshaftlekhn institut," *Literarishe bleter* 88 (1925): 32.

45. See chapter 3, 139–40 for discussion of Dubnov and Ansky's use of the term "ethnographic."

46. "Di oyfgabn fun der yidisher etnografye," *Literarishe bleter* 89(1925):47–48. Khayim Khayes (?–1941) was the first secretary of the EC. He was killed by the Gestapo in Vilne. His role in the EC and works will be discussed later in this chapter. Biographical details from *BDMYL* 3 (1960): 730. Entry does not mention that he was born in Kolomey, Galicia.

47. "Yedies fun yidishn visnshaftlekhn institut," *Literarishe bleter* 90 (1926): 64–65.

48. See Yitskhok Shiper, *Geshikhte*.

49. Max Weinreich, *Mekhires yoysef* (Berlin: Vostok, 1923).

50. "Yedies fun yidishn visnshaftlekhn institut," *Literarishe bleter* 93 (1926): 112.

51. "Yedies fun yidishn visnshaftlekhn institut," *Literarishe bleter* 97 (1926): 176.

52. "Yedies fun yidishn visnshaftlekhn institut," *Literarishe bleter* 99–100 (1926): 218. The Passover questionnaire was incorporated unchanged as the first part of the "Peysakh a mol un haynt" (Passover past and present), which appeared as an insert in *Yidisher folklor,* 1 (January 1954), New York, published by the Y. L. Cahan Folklore Club of the Yiddish Scientific Institute (YIVO).

53. Ansky et al., *Dos yidishe etnografishe program.* One section of this on death rituals, "Der toyt in dem yidishn folksgloybn," was published in *Filologishe shriftn,* vol. 2 (Vilne: YIVO, 1928), 89–100.

54. "Yedies fun yidishn visnshaftlekhn institut," *Literarishe bleter* 99–100.

55. "Yedies fun yidishn visnshaftlekhn institut," *Literarishe bleter* 103 (1926): 273.

56. "Yedies fun yidishn visnshaftlekhn institut," *Literarishe bleter* 107 (1926): 339–40.

57. Since the holiday of Shvuos is associated with the harvest, Jews decorated their homes with *reyzelekh* (little roses) and other designs cut from paper.

58. On *Og melekh,* see Numbers 21:33.

59. "Yedies fun yidishn visnshaftlekhn institut," *Literarishe bleter* 107 (1926): 406–9.

60. "Yedies fun yidishn visnshaftlekhn institut," *Literarishe bleter* 111 (1926): 406–9.

61. Alfred Landau, "Spiele der judischen kinder in Ostgalizien, 51–59.

62. "Yedies fun yidishn visnshaftlekhn institut," *Literarishe bleter* 119 (1926): 539–40.

63. Mates Olitski, "A shosey in shtetl" (A highway in town), *Jewish Daily Forward* (New York), May 5, 1989.

64. "Yedies fun yidishn visnshaftlekhn institut," *Literarishe bleter* 125 (1926): 636–38.

65. "Yedies fun yidishn visnshaftlekhn institut," *Literarishe bleter* 131 (1926): 740–41.
66. "Yedies fun yidishn visnshaftlekhn institut," *Literarishe bleter* 133 (1926): 775.
67. Ibid., 776.
68. "Yedies fun yidishn visnshaftlekhn institut," *Literarishe bleter* 17–18, no. 1 (1927).
69. "Yedies fun yidishn visnshaftlekhn institut," *Literarishe bleter* 13 (April 1, 1927): 256–57.
70. "Yedies fun yidishn visnshaftlekhn institut," *Literarishe bleter* 33 (1927): 584.
71. "Yedies fun yidishn visnshaftlekhn institut," *Literarishe bleter* 50 (1927): 989.
72. See Barbara Kirshenblatt-Gimblett, "Toward a Theory of Proverb Meaning," *Proverbium* 22 (1973): 821–27.
73. *2 yor arbet far dem yidishn visnshaftlkehn institut, 1925–1927* (Vilne: Yidisher visnshaftlekher institut, 1928), 26–29.
74. Ibid., 28–29.
75. *Filologishe shriftn* (Studies in philology), 3 vols. (Vilne: YIVO, 1926, 1928, 1929).
76. *Landoy-bukh: Dr. Alfred Landoy tsu zayn 75stn geboyrnstog dem 25stn november, 1925* (Vilne: YIVO, 1926). See "Bibliografe fun Dr. Alfred Landaus shriftn" in *Landoy-bukh*, 4–10. Bibliographic supplement in *Studies in Philology*, vol. 2, ed. Max Wienreich and Zalmen Reyzen (Vilne: B. Kletskin, 1927), 485–86.
77. B. Pet and B. Rabinovitch, "Fun di leksikologishe zamlungen fun vilner lerer-seminar" (From the lexigraphic collections of the Vilne Teachers' Seminary), in *Landoy-bukh*, 307–14.
78. Dr. Alfred Landau, "Bamerkungen tsum yidishn folklor: vegn S. Bastomskis zamlungen" (Comments on Yiddish folklore: On S. Bastomski's collections), in *Landoy-bukh*, 13–22.
79. See chapter 2.
80. I. L. Cahan, "Folksgezang un folkslid."
81. Max Weinreich, "Lantukh: di geshikhte fun a heymishn nitgutn" (Lantukh: A Jewish hobgoblin), in *Landoy-bukh*, 217–36. English version in *YIVO Annual of Jewish Social Science* 2–3 (1947–48): 243–51.
82. Rabbi Shloyme Yitzhaki, born in France in 1040, died in Troyes in 1105, was a great commentator on the Talmud and Bible.
83. Dr. Bernard Wachstein, "Di oysbreyterung fun Ignats Bernshteyns lebens-verk" (The expansion of Ignatz Bernshteyn's life's work), in *Landoy-bukh*, 28–38; Dr. Shmuel Weissenberg, "Di tsunemenishn fun yidn in Yelisavet-grader krayz" (The nicknames of the Jews in the Elisabethgrad region), in *Landoy-bukh*, 79–90.
84. Shmuel Lehman, "Libe lider fun ganovim" (Lovesongs of thieves), in *Landoy-bukh*, 291–398; Shmuel Rubinshteyn, "Shprikhverter un rednsartn" (Proverbs and sayings), in *Landoy-bukh*, 411–26. Rubinshteyn was a social-

ist/leftist writer who published numerous articles on folklore. See *BDMYL* 8 (1981):424–25.

85. Isaac Rivkind (1895–1968). See *BDMYL* 8 (1981): 442–43.
86. Isaac Rivkind, "Der bal-malokhe in an alt yidish lid" (The artisan in an old Yiddish song), in *Landoy-bukh*, 42–50; Eli Sosnovik, "Dem raboyne shel oylems tanoyim" (God's betrothal), in *Landoy-bukh*, 37–42; Dr. Arthur Goldmann, "Di vakhnakht bay viner yidn onheyb 15tn yorhundert" (The *Vakhnakht* of the Jews in Vienna in the fifteenth century), in *Landoy-bukh*, 91–94.
87. Kh. Khayes, "Gleybungen un minhogim in farbindung mit toyt" (Beliefs and customs related to death), in *Filologishe shriftn* 2 (1928):281–328.
88. Regina Lilienthal, "Przesady zydowskie" (Jewish superstitions), *Wisla* 12, 14, 18 (1898, 1900, 1904); idem, "Zycie pozagrobowe w wyobrazeniu" (The afterlife in Jewish folk imagination), *Lud* 8 (1902).
89. Dr. Adam Fiszer, *Zwyczaje pogrzebowe ludu polskietgo* (Polish folk customs of the afterlife) (Lvov: n.p., 1921).
90. Khayes, "Gleybungen," 282.
91. Tsvi Shpirn, "Di role fun nemen in undzer mame-loshn" (The role of names in our mother tongue), in *Filologishe shriftn* 2 (1928):175–86.
92. Max Weinreich. "Tsu: lantukh, di geshikhte fun a heymishn nitgutn," *Filolgishe shriftn* 2 (1927): 494–500.
93. Walter Anderson, "Dos lid fun der mobilizatsye" (The song of the mobilization) in *Filologishe shriftn* 2 (1928): 401–14. On Anderson see Kurt Ranke, "Walter Anderson (1885–1962)," *Fabula* 5 (1962): unpaginated first page.
94. For a concise contemporary overview of the Finnish method, see Archer Taylor, "Precursors of the Finnish Method of Folk-lore Study," *Modern Philology* 25 (1927–28): 481–91, and the classic article by Anderson himself, "Geographisch-historische Methode," in *Handwörterbuch Des Deutschen Märchens*, ed. Lutz Mackensen (Berlin: Walter De Gruyter & Co., 1934), 2:508.
95. For a detailed recounting of Anderson entering the schools and speaking with the children, see Stith Thompson, ed., *Four Symposia on Folklore: Held at the Midcentury International Folklore Conference, Indiana University, July 21–August 4, 1950* (Bloomington: Indiana University Press, 1953), 58–59.
96. Anderson, "Dos Lid," 413–14.
97. I base this observation on many letters from the *zamlers* to the EC central office in Vilne asking for copies of the publications to help them in their work. Many could not afford stamps, much less a large academic volume. Letters in Collection of Ethnographic Commission in YIVO Institute for Jewish Research, New York.
98. Dr. Yitskhok Shiper, "Di nayste matone funem yidishn visnshaftlekhn institut" (The newest gift from the Yiddish Scientific Institute), *Literarishe bleter* 5, no. 9 (March 2, 1929): 187.
99. See, for example, a "Special Publication" printed by the Vilne Communist newspaper *Etyudn* that was handed out to delegates at YIVO's tenth

anniversary convention, in August 1935: "We pose the question: What has the Yiddish Scientific Institute, which in its founding declaration promised with great fanfare to serve the Jewish masses, done to help the bitter struggle that these masses are leading to hold onto the remnants of their economic and cultural positions?"

100. *Filologishe shriftn,* vol. 3 (Vilne: Kletskin, 1929).
101. Ansky et al., *Dos yidishe etnografishe program.*
102. S. Ansky, "Death in Jewish Folk Belief," in *Filologishe shriftn* 3 (1929): 89–90.
103. Dr. I. Tsoller, "Lilis," in *Filologishe shriftn* 3 (1929): 121–42.
104. M. Gromb, "Gasn un hoyf reklame" (Street and courtyard advertising), in *Filologishe shriftn* 3 (1929): 283–96.
105. Ibid., 285–86.
106. Henry Mayhew, *London Labour and the London Poor,* 4 vols. (1861–62; reprint, New York: Dover Publications, 1968).
107. Naftuli Vaynig, "Dos poylishe folkslid 'Wojna zydowska' " (The Polish folk song, "The Jewish War"), in *Filologishe shriftn* 3 (1929): 411–66.
108. *Filologishe shriftn* 3 (1929): unpaginated first page.
109. Two volumes of *Pinkes* were published by the American Section of the YIVO Institute: vol. 1 in 1927, vol. 2 in 1929 (New York: Friends of the *Yidisher visnshaftlekher institute,* American Section).
110. *The Yiddish Scientific Institute, Account of Two Years Organizing Work [sic] (1925–1927)* (Vilne: YIVO, 1927), 26–27.
111. *Report of the Conference of the Yiddish Scientific Institute: Held in Vilne From the 24th to the 27th of October 1929* (Vilne: YIVO, 1930), 65.
112. "Yedies fun yidishn visnshaftlekhn institut," *Literarishe bleter* 40 (1927): 792.
113. See Khayim Loyke, "Berl Verbliunski—Der grodner folklor zamler: fartseykhensihn" (Berl Verblunski—The Grodne folklore collector: Notes), *Grodner opklangen* (1975): 61–62.
114. "Yedies fun yidishn visnshaftlekhn institut," *Literarishe bleter* 48 (1930): 792.
115. Oral communication from fellow Grodne *zamler* Khayim Sheskin, May 29, 1991. According to Loyke, he handed out candies, not money.
116. "Yedies fun yidishn visnshaftlekhn institut," *Literarishe bleter* 31 (1928): 612.
117. The "Folklore Volume" was first announced in *The Yiddish Scientific Institute, Account of Two Years,* 23. More details are given in "Yedies fun yidishn visnshaftlekhn institut," *Literarishe bleter* 31 (1928): 610.
118. I. L. Cahan, ed., *Yidisher folklor* (Vilne: YIVO, 1938).
119. "Yedies fun yidishn visnshaftlekhn institut," *Literarishe bleter,* 28 (1930): 4.
120. *Report of the Conference of the Yiddish Scientific Institute,* 68. One expedition to Burgenland, Hungary, was apparently all ready to go, but lack of funds prevented it. YIVO did announce an expedition into the city of Lublin to document historic buildings and sites, but it was under the sponsorship of a historic commission. See "Yedies fun yidishn visnshaftlekhn institut," *Literarishe bleter* 52 (1929): 1026.
121. *Etnografishe anketes. Heft 1: yon-toyvim* (Vilne: YIVO, 1928).
122. Ibid., 4.

123. In some areas, one fed the birds on Shabes-shire (a Sabbath in winter). Tisha Bav is the ninth day of the month of Av, a national day of mourning (during the summer). Khamishe Oser Bishvat, also called Tu Beshvat, is the fifteenth day of the month of Shvat, a semi-holiday in winter to mark the beginning of spring in Israel. The fifteenth day of the month of Kislev, in winter, was a special day for the Khevre Kadishes (the burial societies).

124. *Etnografishe anketes*, 8–9.

125. *Vos iz azoyns yidishe etnografye? Hantbikhl farn zamler* (Vilne: YIVO, 1929). No author is given on the booklet itself. However in Vaynig's article, "Organizatsye un arbet fun an etnografishn krayz" (Organization and labor for an ethnographic circle), *Landkentnish* 2 (1934): 5–18, the author listed himself and Khayes as coauthors of the work.

126. One could also include in this category of folklore handbooks the important *A Handbook of Irish Folklore* by Sean O Suilleabhain which is "an encyclopedia of Irish, and indeed, of West European tradition as well" (1942; reprint, Hatboro, Pa.: Folklore Associates, 1963), iii.

127. Kaarle Krohn, *Folklore Methodology* (1926; reprint Austin: University of Texas at Austin, 1971.

128. *Vos iz azoyns*, 5.

129. For an anti-Hebraist position in regard to Yiddish folklore, see Vanvild, *Bay undz yidn*, ii.

130. *Vos iz azoyns*, 6.

131. Ibid., 10.

132. See the work of Lehman and Graubard on the Jewish underworld in chapters 2 and 3.

133. *Vos iz azoyns*, 12. Compare this point with (Dov) Bernard Heller, "Tasks of Jewish Ethnography and Folklore in General, and in the Holy Land in Particular," *Tsiyon* 4 (1930): 73. Heller has two seperate points on settlements and houses. Most of his description of ethnography is taken up by material culture.

134. *Vos iz azoyns*, 14.

135. E. B. Tylor, *Primitive Culture*, 2 vols. (London: J. Murray, 1871). J. G. Frazer, *The Golden Bough*. 3rd ed. (London: Macmillan, 1911–15). See letter from I. L. Cahan to Nekhame Epshteyn, April 24, 1931, in Cahan, *Shtudyes vegn yidisher folksshafung*, 292–94. Both New York and Vilne folklorists knew the work. Khayes considered translating *The Golden Bough* and Cahan considered translating Tylor's work for his planned Yiddish Folklore Library Series.

136. See Cocchiara, *History of Folklore in Europe*, 292–94; George Stocking, *Race, Culture and Evolution* (New York: Free Press, 1968), 78–90. For history of term "survival" and debate on its impact see entry in Hultkrantz, *International Dictionary*, 1:224–28; and Margaret T. Hodgen, *The Doctrine of Survivals: A Chapter in the History of Scientific Method in the Study of Man* (London: Allenson, 1936).

137. Letter from Cahan to Khayes, February 27, 1931, in Cahan, *Shtudyes vegn yidisher folksshafung*, 304–5.

138. Reb Dov-Ber and Reb Motele Chernobler were Hasidic Rabbis of the late eighteenth and early nineteenth centuries.
139. Letter from Cahan to Khayes, February 27, 1931, in I. L. Cahan, *Shtudyes vegn yidisher folksshafung*, 306.
140. *Vos iz azoyns*, 17.
141. Cahan, *Yidishe folkslider*. See discussion in chapter 2 on Prilutski.
142. For a review of theories on the superiority of Jewish humor see Dan Ben-Amos, "The Myth of Jewish Humor," *Western Folklore* 32 (1973): 112–31.
143. The riddle genre was singled out as stemming from primitive sources. The lack of comparisons with primitive peoples is notable for folk drama, since the fundamental work on the genre, Shiper, *Geshikhte*, printed much on the parallels with other folk traditions, ancient and more recent.
144. *Sforim* in Yiddish usually denotes books in Hebrew/Aramaic. The handbook, however, also includes women's Yiddish prayers and Yiddish translations of the Bible (also for women).
145. This was a prime interest of coauthor Vaynig, as discussed previously.
146. *Vos iz azoyns*, 22.
147. Ibid., 27. See also discussion of genre in chapter 2.
148. James A. Matisoff, *Blessings, Curses, Hopes, and Fears: Psycho-Ostensive Expressions in Yiddish* (Philadelphia: ISHI, 1979).
149. *Der yivo—zayne oyfgabn un oyftuen*. (Buenos Aires: YIVO argentia opteyl, 1932), 10.

Chapter 6

1. See undated letter from Khayim Khayes to I. L. Cahan, in Cahan, *Shtudyes vegn yidisher folksshafung*, 304–5.
2. See undated letter (1933?) from Khayes to Cahan, in Cahan, *Shtudyes vegn yidisher folksshafung*, 311.
3. See Nekhame Epshteyn's introduction to Cahan's "Tsu hilf dem zamler" (Instructions for the folklore collector), in Cahan, *Shtudyes vegn yidisher folksshafung*, 141. For an appreciation of this document and Cahan's contribution to folkloristics see Richard Bauman, "Y. L. Cahan's Instructions on the Collecting of Folklore," *New York Folklore Quarterly* 18 (1962): 284–89; Ruth Rubin, "Y. L. Cahan and Jewish Folklore," *New York Folklore Quarterly* 11 (1955): 34–45; Gottesman, "I. L. Cahan"; Jacob Shatsky, *Yehuda Leyb Cahan* (New York: YIVO, 1938); and Max Weinreich, Afterword to Cahan, *Shtudyes vegn yidisher folksshafung*, 352–70.
4. See photograph of seminar group reprinted in Pipe, *Yiddish Folksongs*, 410.
5. See Gottesman, "I. L. Cahan."
6. I shall still refer to it as EC in the following pages.
7. First announced in *Literarishe bleter* 8 (1934): 124. See "Der yivo farmest zikh af groyser tetikeyt" (YIVO prepares for a big event), *Literarishe bleter* 11, no. 38 (1934): 1–2. Tsemakh Shabad (1864–1935) was a community leader

and doctor in Vilne. He was also Max Weinreich's father-in-law. See entry in *BDMYL* 8 (1981): 517–18.
8. Pipe, *Yiddish Folksongs*. For his childhood, see Gershon Givoni-Pipe, "The Life History of My Brother, In View of His Letters"; and Berl Rabach, "Reminiscences of My Youth from Sonik," in Pipe, *Yiddish Folksongs*, 23–47, 50–52.
9. See reminiscences of his brothers on this point in Pipe, *Yiddish Folksongs*, 19, 75–77.
10. Founded in Galicia during the First World War. See Ezra Mendelsohn, *Zionism in Poland*.
11. S. Z. Pipe, letter to Oyzer Pipe, August 8, 1928, in Pipe, *Yiddish Folksongs*, 364–65.
12. S. Z. Pipe, letter to Oyzer Pipe, March 10, 1929, in ibid., 376.
13. S. Z. Pipe, letter to Oyzer Pipe, July 4, 1929, in ibid., 387.
14. S. Z. Pipe, letter to Oyzer Pipe, March 18, 1929, in ibid., 377.
15. S. Z. Pipe, letter to Oyzer Pipe, November 12, 1929, in ibid., 396.
16. S. Z. Pipe, letters to Oyzer Pipe, January 10 and January 24, 1930, in ibid., 403–4.
17. S. Z. Pipe, letter to Oyzer Pipe, July 24, 1932, in ibid., 411.
18. S. Z. Pipe, letter to Oyzer Pipe, September 8, 1932, in ibid., 420.
19. S. Z. Pipe, letter to Oyzer Pipe, May 7, 1933, in ibid., 437.
20. S. Z. Pipe, letter to Oyzer Pipe, October 6, 1932, in ibid., 424.
21. S. Z. Pipe, letter to Oyzer Pipe, November 16, 1934, in Pipe, *Yiddish Folksongs*, 457.
22. S. Z. Pipe, "Lebns-bashraybung," in papers of the YIVO *Aspirantur*, YIVO, New York.
23. S. Z. Pipe, letter to I. L. Cahan, October 5, 1935, in Pipe, *Yiddish Folksongs*, 499.
24. Pipe, *Yiddish Folksongs*, 475–85. Letter dated August 20, 1936. See protocols of these debates in *The International Conference of The Yiddish Scientific Institute: On Its 10th Anniversary, held in Vilne from the 14th to the 19th of August 1935* (Vilne: YIVO, 1936), esp. 114–26.
25. K. Wehrhan, *Kinderlied und Kinderspiel* (1909; reprint, Gloucester, Mass.: Peter Smith, 1970).
26. *Gesunkenes Kulturgut* (sunken cultural materials) proposed that folklore began as "high culture" and sank down to the folk level. Hans Naumann coined the term in 1902, but a similar idea, *Rezeptionstheorie*, was espoused by John Meier. See Cocchiara, *History of Folklore in Europe*, 528–37; Ake Hultkrantz, ed., *International Dictionary of Regional European Ethnology and Folklore* (Copenhagen: Rosenkilde and Bagger, 1960), 1:158–59; Otto Ranke, "Hans Naumann: Mann und Werk," *Hessische Bletter fur Volkskunde* 46 (1955): 1–7.
27. Protocols of Pipe's first report, reprinted in Pipe, *Yiddish Folksongs*, 495–98.
28. S. Z. Pipe, letter to I. L. Cahan, January 22, 1936, in Pipe, *Yiddish Folksongs*, 514. See also Dawidowicz, *From That Place and Time*, 91–92.
29. I. L. Cahan, letter to S. Z. Pipe, January 10, 1936, in Cahan, *Shtudyes vegn yidisher folksshafung*, 320–21.

30. Pipe, *Yiddish Folksongs,* 518–24.
31. S. Z. Pipe, letter to Oyzer Pipe, March 16, 1936, in ibid., 529.
32. S. Z. Pipe, letter to Oyzer Pipe, June 5, 1936, in ibid., 538.
33. S. Z. Pipe, "Yidishe kindershpiln" (Jewish children's games), *YIVO-bleter* 10 (1936): 39–47.
34. Cited in ibid., 40. See also Regina Lilienthal, *Dziecko zydowkie* (Jewish games) (Cracow, 1927).
35. I. L. Cahan, "Tsum ofkum fun yidishn tantslid" (The development of the Jewish dance song), in Cahan, *Shtudyes vegn yidisher folksshafung,* 88–98.
36. Zalmen Reyzin, letter to I. L. Cahan, October 15, 1935, in Pipe, *Yiddish Folksongs,* 501.
37. S. Z. Pipe, letter to Oyzer Pipe, October 16, 1935, in ibid., 502.
38. I. L. Cahan, letter to S. Z. Pipe, November 20, 1935, in ibid., 316–19.
39. S. Z. Pipe, letter to I. L. Cahan, March 13, 1936, in ibid., 527.
40. Yitskhok Shiper, "Araynfir-verter in der folkskentenish" (Introduction to *folkskentenish*), *Landkentnish* 1 (1933): 61–71, esp. 65–66. "Folkskentenish" is a Yiddish translation of the German "volkskunde." The term "folklore," Shiper argued, referred only to the "spiritual treasures of the lower classes." His term "folkskentenish" included the entire culture of the lower classes.
41. S. Z. Pipe, letter to I. L. Cahan, June 19, 1936, in Pipe, *Yiddish Folksongs,* 542.
42. I. L. Cahan, letter to S. Z. Pipe, October 7, 1936, in Cahan, *Shtudyes vegn yidisher folksshafung,* 335–41.
43. S. Z. Pipe, letter to I. L. Cahan, June 19, 1936, in Pipe, *Yiddish Folksongs,* 543.
44. Cahan, *Shtudyes vegn yidisher folksshafung,* 340.
45. See "Peyrushim af 24 lider" (Comments on twenty-four songs), in Cahan, *Shtudyes vegn yidisher folksshafung,* 171–93.
46. See ibid. This article is, in fact, a long letter to Pipe, undated, but probably written in the fall of 1936.
47. S. Z. Pipe, letter to I. L. Cahan, October 27, 1936, in Pipe, *Yiddish Folksongs,* 552.
48. See Z. Skuditski, "Vegn folklorishn arbeter-lid" (On Folkloric Worker's Song), in *Problemes fun folkloristik,* ed. Meyer Viner (Kharkov-Kiev: Melukhisher natsmindfarlag bam prezidium fun vutsik, 1932), 146–92; idem, "Araynfir," in *Folklor-lider: naye materialn-zamlung* ("Introduction" to *Folklore Songs: New Collection of Materials*), vol. 2 (Moscow: Emes, 1936). The copy of this latter work in the YIVO Archive in New York appears to have been Pipe's review copy, and his comments are written in the margins. See Sutskever-Katsherginski Collection, YIVO Institute, New York. On Soviet Yiddish Folkloristics, see Susan A. Slotnick, "The Contributions of the Soviet Yiddish Folklorists," *Working Papers in Yiddish and East European Jewish Studies,* vol. 20 (New York: YIVO Institute for Jewish Research, 1976); Paul Soifer, "Soviet Jewish Folkloristics and Ethnography: An Institutional History, 1918–1948," *Working Papers in Yiddish and East European Jewish Studies,* vol. 30 (New York: YIVO, 1978).
49. S. Z. Pipe, "Yehude Leyb Kahn: fertsik yor folkloristishe arbet" (Yehude-Leyb

Kahan: Forty years of folkloristic work), *Literarishe bleter* 4, no. 49 (1936): 1–2.

50. S. Z. Pipe, letter to Oyzer Pipe, July 11, 1936, in Pipe, *Yiddish Folksongs*, 545.
51. Shmuel Zaynvil Pipe and Oyzer Pipe, "Yidishe folkslider fun Galitsye" (Yiddish folk songs from Galicia), *YIVO-bleter* 11, nos. 1–2 (Jan–Feb 1937): 53–70; nos. 3–4 (Mar–April 1937): 252–69.
52. S. Z. Pipe, letter to Oyzer Pipe, January 5, 1937, in Pipe, *Yiddish Folksongs*, 563.
53. Pipe and Pipe, "Yidishe folkslider," 54. Cahan suggested that the folklorist have his or her own repertory in his 1930 YIVO seminar. See "Tsu hilf dem zamler," in Cahan, *Shtudyes vegn yidisher folksshafung*, 142–44 and Bauman, "Y. L. Cahan's Instructions on the Collecting of Folklore." See discussion of paying informants in general folklore practice in "The Collecting of Folklore" in Thompson, ed., *Four Symposia on Folklore* and compare the experience of Sean O Suilleabhain in Ireland: "the country people seem to realize instinctively that we are doing something important for them. . . . They have felt very much pleased to hand over the material" (Suilleabhain, *A Handbook of Irish Folklore*, 13–14).
54. Pipe and Pipe, "Yidishe folkslider," 55.
55. For Oyzer Pipe's reminiscences of the fieldwork experience, see Oyzer Paz-Pipe, "From the By-ways of Sanok, to the Roads of Israel," in Pipe, *Yiddish Folksongs*, 74–84.
56. See I. L. Cahan, "Vi alt zaynen undzere libe lider?" (How old are our love-songs) in Cahan, *Shtudyes vegn yidisher folksshafung*, 69–87.
57. Pipe and Pipe, "Yidishe folkslider," 56.
58. Nekhame Epshteyn and S. Z. Pipe, review of *Games of the Soviet Union*, by V. N. Vsevolodski-Gerngross et al., *YIVO-bleter* 11, nos. 3–4 (1937): 287–91.
59. S. Z. Pipe, "Di zamlungen yidishe folkslider fun I. L. Peretz" (I. L. Peretz's collections of Yiddish folk songs), *YIVO-bleter* 12, nos. 1–3 (1937): 286–90.
60. S. Z. Pipe "Yidishe kinderlidlekh" (Yiddish children's songs), *YIVO-bleter* 12, nos. 4–5 (1937): 494–507.
61. Nakhmen Blumental, "Dos tsveyte yor funem Tsemakh shabad aspirantur" (Second year of the Tsemakh Shabad Aspirantur), *Literarishe bleter* 13 (1938): 93–94.
62. S. Z. Pipe, letter to Oyzer and Gershon Pipe, March 22, 1938, in Pipe, *Yiddish Folksongs*, 606.
63. S. Z. Pipe, "S. Z. Pipe's Research Report: 'Art Song Among the Folk'—First Report," in Pipe, *Yiddish Folksongs*, 595–600. On Soviet scholarship, see Z. Skuditski, "Vegn folksiberarterungen fun Gotlobers lider" (On popular variations on Gotlober's songs), *Tsaytshrift* 5 (1931): 245–55. Cahan had prepared two essays on the topic, but they were not published until after his death: "Vegn dem folkslid fun a literarishn shtam" (On the folk song with a literary origin), in Cahan, *Shtudyes vegn yidisher folksshafung*, 202–9; and "Populer, ober nisht keyn folkslid" (Popular, but not a folksong), in Cahan, *Shtudyes vegn yidisher folkslid*, 210–14.

64. Walter Anderson, "Dos lid fun der mobilizatsye."
65. S. Z. Pipe, "Folklorizatsye fun D. Edelshatats 'der arbeter' " (Folklorization of D. Edelshtat's 'The Worker'), in Pipe, *Yiddish Folksongs*, 333–54.
66. See sample questionnaire in Pipe, *Yiddish Folksongs*, 612.
67. Hans Naumann, *Grundzuge der deutschen Volkskunde* (Leipzig: n.p., 1922); see also John Meier, *Kunstlied und Volkslied* (Halle a. S.: M. Niemeyer, 1906); idem, *Kunstlieder im Volksmund* (Halle a. S.: M. Niemeyer, 1906).
68. S. Z. Pipe, letter to Oyzer Pipe, April 8, 1937, in Pipe, *Yiddish Folksongs*, 583.
69. S. Z. Pipe, review of *Folklorlider*, by Z. Skuditski, *YIVO-bleter* 14 (1939): 339–67.
70. S. Z. Pipe, "Napoleon in Yidishn folklor" (Napolean in Yiddish folklore) in *Yidn in frankraykh: shtudyes un materialn* (The Jews in France: Studies and materials), vol. 1, ed. E. Tcherikower (New York: YIVO, 1942), 153–89.
71. According to Lucy Dawidowicz, they were married. However, they were only engaged. See Dawidowicz, *From That Place and Time*, 92.
72. Dov Noy, "The Path of S. Z. Pipe in Jewish Folkloristics," in Pipe, *Yiddish Folksongs*, 58.
73. See entry in *LYL* 2 (1927): 800–801.
74. Lilienthal, "Eyn Hore," 256–71.
75. Dawidowicz, *From That Place and Time*, 92.
76. I. L. Cahan, *Yidishe Folksmayses: funem folksmoyl gezamlt*. See letters from Cahan to Epshteyn in Cahan, *Shtudyes vegn yidisher folksshafung*, 284–303.
77. Nekhame Epshteyn, review of *Rosinkess mit Mandlen. Aus der Volksliteratur der Ostjuden: Schwanke, Erzählungen, Sprichwörter und Rätsel*, by Dr. Immanuel Olsvanger, *YIVO-bleter* 4, no. 1 (1932): 73–76.
78. *YIVO-bleter* 12 (1937): 102–11.
79. See their collections: Alter Druyanov, *Sefer Habedikhah vehakhidud* (Book of jokes and jests), 3 vols. (1922; reprint, Palestine: A. Drujanoff, 1935–38); J. Ch. Ravnitski, *Yidishe vitsn* (Jewish wit), 2 vols. (1922; reprint, New York: Moyshe Shmuel Shklarski, 1950).
80. Dr. Immanuel Olswanger, *Rosinkess mit Mandlen. Aus der volksliteratur der Ostjuden. Schwanke, Erzählungen, Sprichwörter und Rätsel* 2nd ed. (Basel: Verlag der Schweizerischen Gesellschaft für Volhskunde, 1931).
81. Alter Druyanov, "Jewish Folk Humor," *Reshumot* 2 (1922): 303–57.
82. I. Olswanger, "Aus dem Alltags- und Festleben der Ostjuden, in Olswanger, *Rosinkess mit Mandlen*, I–XLIV.
83. Nekhame Epshteyn, "Bamerkungen tsu di vitsn un vitsike mayselekh" (Comment on the jokes and humorous tales), in Cahan, ed., *Yidisher folklor*, 322–26.
84. Cahan, *Shtudyes vegn yidisher folksshafung*, 353. See Pipe's exact report on Cahan's materials, 353–59. Reprinted in Pipe, *Yiddish Folksongs*, 624–31.
85. I. L. Cahan, *Yidishe folksmayses* (Yiddish folktales), compiled by Nekhame Epshteyn, ed. Max Weinreich (Vilne: YIVO, 1940). This collection was subtitled "Volume 5 of the Collected Works of I. L. Cahan."
86. Nekhame Epshteyn, "Variantn un paraleln in yidishe vitsn: Oystsug funem

araynfir tsu der arbet, 'Yidishe vitsn' " (Variants and parallels in Jewish jokes: Excerpt from the introduction to the paper, "Yiddish Jokes"), unpublished essay, n.d. [end of 1937], papers of the YIVO *Aspirantur,* YIVO Institute for Jewish Research, New York.

87. Ibid., 3.
88. Dawidowicz, *From That Place and Time,* 92.
89. *BDMYL* 7 (1968): 24. Dawidowicz gives a slightly different account of her death, which I believe to be less informed. See Dawidowicz, *From That Place and Time,* 272.
90. Cahan, *Yidisher folklor.*
91. Ibid., ix.
92. S. Z. Pipe, letter to Oyzer Pipe, August 28, 1935, in Pipe, *Yiddish Folksongs,* 487.
93. Cahan, *Yidisher folklor,* xii.
94. For comments on the success of the EC in comparison to other YIVO sections, see *International Conference of the Yiddish Scientific Institute.*
95. See "Index of Correspondents and Their Locations," in Ginzburg and Marek, *Yidishe folkslider in rusland,* 79–84.
96. Examples of song text manuscripts sent in by EC collectors can be found in the papers of the YIVO Ethnographic Commission, YIVO Institute, New York.
97. See M. Beregovski, *Jidisher muzik-folklor* (Moscow: Meluxiser Muzik-Farlag, 1934): Skuditski, "Vegn folklorishn"; and idem, "Araynfir."
98. See his comments to song texts 199–200 in Cahan, *Yidisher folklor,* 309.
99. See Cahan's introductory note to *Yidishe Folksmayses: funem folksmoyl gezamlt,* in *Pinkes* 1:217 (New York: YIVO—American Section, 1927), and his posthumously published, "Vegn yidishe folksmayes," in Cahan, *Shtudyes vegn yidisher folksshafung,* 240–61.
100. These tales and other unpublished ones appeared in Hebrew translation in Shmuel Zaynvil Pipe, *Twelve Folktales from Sanok,* ed. Dov Noy. Israel Folktale Archives Publication Series no. 15 (Haifa: Haifa Municipality, Ethnological Museum and Folklore Archives, 1967). Noy provides cross-references and a motif and tale type index to the tales.
101. Eight of his tales have recently been printed in English translation. See Weinreich, *Yiddish Folktales.*
102. I. L. Cahan, letter to Max Weinreich, August 4, 1928, in Cahan, *Shtudyes vegn yidisher folksshafung,* 280.
103. Weinreich and Weinreich, *Yiddish Language and Folklore,* s.v. "Folktales."
104. S. Ansky, "Alte shuln un zeyere legendn," in Ansky, *Folklor un ethnografye,* 243–53. The article is almost entirely composed of the legends retold.
105. Cahan, *Yidisher folklor,* xii.
106. Ibid., 310–18.
107. "Yedies fun yidishn visnshaftlekhn institut," *Literarishe bleter* 4–5 (1934): 11.
108. Information from Avrom Sutskever's preface to N. Vaynig, "Naydus Studies," *Goldene keyt* 129 (1990): 57. This essay by Vaynig was written in the Vilne

ghetto in June 1943. Sutskever managed to save it. Vaynig also collected folklore in the ghetto and gave lectures on Jewish folklore.

109. *Vos iz azoyns* and Vaynig, "Dos poylishe folkslid 'Wojna zydowska.'"
110. N. Vaynig, review of *Wyncinanka zydowska w Polsce,* by Dr. Liza Franklowa, *YIVO-bleter,* 1, no. 4 (1931): 172–73. N. Vaynig, review of *Ze Studjow nad obrzedami weselnemi ludu polskiego. Czesc 1. Forma dramatyczna obrzedowosci weselnej,* by C. Baudouin de Courtenay-Ehrenkreutz, *YIVO-bleter* 5, no. 2 (1933): 163–65; N. Vaynig, "Benyumin Volf Zegel (1866–1931)," *YIVO-bleter* 3, no. 1 (1932): 91.
111. See Dobroszycki and Kirshenblatt-Gimblett, eds., *Image Before My Eyes,* 31.
112. N. Vaynig, "Organizatsye un arbet fun an etnografishn krayz."
113. Ibid., 5.
114. Ibid., 13.
115. N. Vaynig, "Geshikhte un problemen fun der yidisher paremiologye" (History and problems of Yiddish paremeology), *YIVO-bleter* 8 (1935): 356–70.
116. N. Vaynig, "Mageyfe-khasenes," *Sotsyale Meditsin* 10, nos. 9–10 (1937): 24–32.
117. N. Vaynig, "Refues un sgules bay yidn in tsaytn fun epidemyes" (Jewish cures and remedies during epidemics), *Sotsyale meditsin* 10, nos. 11–12 (1937): 25–31.
118. N. Vaynig, "Parekh-krankkayt in yidishn folklor" (The Parkh illness in Yiddish folklore), *Sotsyale meditsin* 11 (1938): 22–27.
119. On one particular custom involving *parkhes,* see Itzik Gottesman, "Ale parkhes keyn Mitsrayim! A Shabes-Hagodel Custom in Eastern Europe" (paper delivered at the American Jewish Studies Conference, Boston, Mass., December 19, 1989).
120. N. Vaynig, "Historishe motivn in yidishn folkslid" *Fun noentn over,* vol. 2 (1939), 79–83.
121. Ibid., 80.
122. Israel Zinberg, "Vanderendike motivn in yidishn folklor" (On wandering motifs in Yiddish folklore), *YIVO-bleter* 3 (1932): 330–36.
123. Aron Bam, letter to EC, summer 1928, Papers of the YIVO EC, YIVO Institute, New York. The YIVO denied his request but continued to send him postage.
124. Khayes in some cases, M.K. (?) in others.
125. EC, letter to B. Tishler, July 17, 1929, in Papers of the YIVO EC, YIVO Institute, New York.

Conclusion

1. For a parallel to the history of German folklore studies, see James R. Dow and Hannjost Lixfeld, eds., introduction to *German Volkskunde: A Decade of Theoretical Confrontation, Debate, and Reorientation (1967–1977)* (Bloomington: Indiana University Press, 1986), 6.

2. See Ezra Mendelsohn, "Aspects of Jewish Politics in Interwar Poland," in *Proceedings of the Conference on "Poles and Jews: Myth and Reality in the Historical Context,"* ed. John Micgiel, Robert Scott, and H. B. Segel (New York: Institute on East Central Europe, Columbia University, 1986), 203–22; also see Ezra Mendelsohn, "Jewish Politics in Interwar Poland: An Overview," in *The Jews of Poland Between Two World Wars*, ed. Yisrael Gutman, Ezra Mendelsohn, Jehuda Reinharz, and Chone Shmeruk (Hanover, N.H.: University Press of New England, 1989), 9–19. For the most gloomy portrait of the Jews in this period, see Celia S. Heller, *On the Edge of Destruction: Jews of Poland Between the Two World Wars* (New York: Columbia University Press, 1977); a more positive history, perhaps too much so, is Marcus, *Social and Political History of the Jews in Poland 1919–1939.*
3. Mendelsohn, "Aspects of Jewish Politics," 207.
4. Ibid., 222.
5. Mendelsohn, "Jewish Politics in Interwar Poland," 19.
6. Richard M. Dorson, "Is There a Folk in the City?" *Journal of American Folklore* 83 (1970): 185–216. For a brief history of urban folklore studies by British and American folklorists, see Barbara Kirshenblatt-Gimblett, "The Future of Folklore Studies in America: The Urban Frontier," *Folklore Forum* 16 (1984): 175–234, esp. 175–79.
7. Michael Herzfeld, *Ours Once More,* 8.
8. There is a large amount of literature on the subject of study as "other" in anthropological discourse, much of which is applicable to the field and history of folklore. See, e.g., George E. Marcus and Michael M. J. Fischer, *Anthropology as Cultural Critique: An Experimental Moment in the Human Sciences* (Chicago: University of Chicago Press, 1986); James Clifford and George E. Marcus, eds., *Writing Culture: The Poetics and Politics of Ethnography* (Berkeley and Los Angeles: University of California Press, 1986); Johannes Fabian, *Time and the Other: How Anthropology Makes Its Object* (New York: Columbia University Press, 1983); James Clifford, *The Predicament of Culture: Twentieth-Century Ethnography, Literature, and Art* (Cambridge: Harvard University Press, 1988). For an example of this type of literature that has folklore studies in mind, see Michael Herzfeld, *Anthropology through the Looking-Glass: Critical Ethnography in the Margins of Europe* (Cambridge: Cambridge University Press, 1987).

Bibliography

2 yor arbet far dem yidishn visnshaftlkehn institut, 1925–1927. Vilne: Yidisher visn-shaftlekher institut, 1928.

Abramovitsh, Hirsh. "Der biblioteker." *Literarishe bleter* 1, no. 58 (1925): 4.

————. *Farshvundene geshtaltn: zikhroynes un siluetn.* Buenos Aires: Tsentral far-band fun poylishe yidn in Argentina, 1958.

————. "Farshvundene yidishe parnoses." *Fun noentn over* 1 (1937): 212–25.

Abramovitch, Raphael, ed. *The Vanished World.* New York: Forward Association, 1947.

Alfabet, F. "Materialn tsu a idiotikon fun shtetl pyask." *Yidishe filologye* 1 (1924): 61–72.

Almi, A. *1863: Yidishe povstanye-mayselekh.* Warsaw: Goldfarb, 1927.

————. *A. Almi bukh: lekoved A. Almis vern a ben shivim.* Buenos Aires: Tsentral farband fun poylishe yidn in Argentina, 1962.

————. *Di reyd fun buda.* Vilne: Kletskin, 1927.

————. *Far di likht.* Warsaw, 1927.

————. "Fun amolikn varshe." *Der poylisher yid* 2 (1944): 28–30.

————. *Humoristishe shriftn.* Vol. 1 of *Parodyes.* Warsaw: A. Gitlin, 1928.

————. *Khezhbn un sakh-hakl: kapitlekh fun mayn seyfer hakhayim.* Buenos Aires: G. Kaplanski, 1959.

————. *Momentn fun a lebn.* Buenos Aires: Tsentral farband far poylishe yidn, 1948.

————. "Noyekh Prilutski." In *Mentshn un ideyen,* 202. Warsaw: Farlag M. Gold-berg, 1933.

Alver, Brynjulf. "Folklore and National Identity." In *Nordic Folklore,* ed. Reimund Kvideland and Henning K. Sehmsdorf, 12–22. Bloomington: Indiana University Press, 1989.

Anderson, Benedict. *Imagined Communities: Reflections on the Origin and Spread of Nationalism.* London: Verso, 1983.

Anderson, Walter. "Dos lid fun der mobilizatsye." *Filologishe shriftn* 2 (1928): 401–14.

————. "Geographisch-historische Methode." *Handwörterbuch des deutschen Märchens,* ed. Lutz Mackensen, Bard II. Berlin: Walter De Gruyter and Co., 1934/1940.

Ansky, S. "Alte shuln un zeyere legendn." In *Folklor un ethnografye,* vol. 15 of *Gezamlte shriftn.* Warsaw: Farlag An-ski, 1925.

———. "Death in Jewish Folk Belief." *Filologishe shriftn* 3 (1929): 89–90.

———. "Der yidisher folks-gayst un zayn shafung." In Ansky, *Folklor un ethnografye*, 15–28.

———. "Di yidishe folksretenishn." *Gezamlte shriftn* 15: 227–45.

———. *Folklor un ethnografye*. Vol. 15 of *Gezamlte shriftn*. Warsaw: Farlag An-ski, 1925.

———. *Khurbn galitsye*. Vols. 4, 5, and 6 of *Gezamlte shriftn*. Warsaw, Vilne, New York: S. Shreberk, 1925.

———. "Klolim: vi azoy tsu farshraybn verk fun folksshafung." In Bastomski, *Baym kval*, 23.

———. "Yidishe folks-retenishn." In Ansky, *Folklor un ethnografye*, 223–29.

Ansky, S., et al. *Dos yidishe etnografishe program. Ershter teyl: der mentsh*. Ed. L. I. Sternberg. Petrograd: Publication of the Jewish Ethnographic Expedition, named for Baron Hertz Gintsburg, an independent section of the Jewish Historic-Ethnographic Society, 1914.

Ashkenazi, Shloyme. "Oys dem porisover folklor." *Yidishe filologye* 1 (1924): 397–98.

Ave-Lallemant, Friedrich Christân Benedict. *Das deutsche Gaunerthum in seiner social-politischen, litterarischen und linguistischen Ausbildung*, 4 vols. Leipzig: Brockhaus, 1858–62.

A. Vilner [S. Niger]. "Vegn dem rayon tsu shafn a yidishn universitet." *Literatur un lebn* 6 (1914): 126–34.

Bal Dimyen [Nokhem Shtif]. "Der pinkes." *Literatur un lebn: di yidishe velt* (April 1914): 247–61; (May 1914): 395–410.

Barnard, F. M. *Herder's Social and Political Thought: From Enlightenment to Nationalism*. Oxford: Clarendon Press, 1965.

Bassein, M. *500 yor yidishe poezye*, 2 vols. New York: n.p., 1917.

Bastomski, Shloyme. *Baym kval: materialn tsum yidishn folklor, yidishe folkslider*. Vilne: Di naye yidishe folkshul, 1923.

———. *Baym kval: yidishe shprikhverter, vertlekh, glaykhvertlekh, rednsartn, farglaykenishn, brokhes, vintshenishn, kloles, kharomes, sgules, zabobones, etc.* Ed. Zalmen Reyzin. Vilne: Di naye yidishe folkshul, 1920.

———. "Materialn tsum yidishn folklor." In *Pinkes: far der geshikhte fun vilne in di yorn fun milkhome un okupatsye*, ed. Zalmen Reyzin. Vilne: AVJHES, 1922.

———. *Mayselekh vegn khelemer naronim*. 3 vols. Vilne: Grininke beymelekh, 1938, 1940.

———. *Mayselekh vegn Motke Khabad*. 2 vols. Vilne: Grininke beymelekh, 1938, 1940.

———. *Peysekhdike vitsn un vertlekh*. Vilne: Grininke beymelekh, 1940.

———. *Purim-shpiln: a) Yoysef-shpil (mekhires yoysef) b) Akheshverush-shpil*. Vilne: Di naye yidishe folkshul, 1926.

———. Review of *Ganovim-lider*, by Shmuel Lehman. *Bikher-velt* 1 (1929): 60.

———. *Yidishe folksretenishen*. Vilne: Di naye yidishe folkshul, 1917.

———. *Yidishe sprikhverter far shul un heym*. Vilne: Di naye yidishe shul, 1920.

Bauman, Richard. "Y. L. Cahan's Instructions on the Collecting of Folklore." *New York Folklore Quarterly* 18 (1962): 284–89.

Ben-Amos, Dan. "The Myth of Jewish Humor." *Western Folklore* 32 (1973): 112–31.

———. "Nationalism and Nihilism: The Attitudes of Two Hebrew Authors toward Folklore." *International Folklore Review* 1: 5–16.

Beregovski, M. *Jidiser muzik-folklor.* Moscow: Meluxiser Muzik-Farlag, 1934.

Bernshteyn, Meyer. "A. M. Bernshteyn: zikhroynes fun mayn bruder." *Di khazonim velt* 1 (1934): 15–17.

Bernstein, Ignaz. *Erotica et Rustica.* Warsaw: n.p., 1908.

———. *Judische Sprichworter und Redensarten.* Warsaw: n.p., 1908.

B[ernstein]., I[gnaz]. "Yidishe shprikhverter." *Hoyzfraynd* 5 (1895). Separate pagination at end of volume, 1–48.

Blumental, Nakhmen. "Dos tsveyte yor funem tsemakh shabad aspirantur." *Literarishe bleter* 13 (1938): 93–94.

Borokhov, Ber. "Di oyfgabn fun der yidisher filologye." In Niger, *Der pinkes,* 1.

———. "Gramatishe frumkeyt." *Di yidishe velt* 12 (1913): 147–53.

———. "Noyekh Prilutskis zamlbikher far yidishn folklor." In Niger, *Der pinkes,* 347–51.

B. Pet [pseud.], and B. Rabinovitch. "Fun di leksikologishe zamlungen fun vilner lerer-seminar." In *Landoy-bukh,* 13–22.

Brock, Peter. "Polish Nationalism." In *Nationalism in Eastern Europe,* ed. Peter F. Sugar and Ivo J. Lederer, 315. Seattle: University of Washington Press, 1969.

Bukhbinder, Avrom-Yitskhok. "Yidisle simonim (zabobones)." In *Hoyzfraund* 2: 249–58.

Cahan, I. L. "Folksgezang un folkslid: bamerkungen tsu *arbet un frayhayt.*" In *Landoy-bukh,* 139–54.

———. "Folkslid un folkstimlekh lid." In Cahan, *Shtudyes vegn yidisher folksshafung,* 194–201.

———. "I. L. Perets vi a zamler fun yidishe folkslider: bamerkungen tsu zayne kolektsyes." *YIVO-bleter* 12, nos. 1–3 (1937): 280–85.

———. *Shtudyes vegn yidisher folksshafung.* Ed. Max Weinreich. New York: YIVO, 1952.

———. "Vegn yidishe folksmayes." In Cahan, *Shtudyes vegn yidisher folksshafung,* 240–61.

———. "Vi alt zaynen undzere libe-lider?" In Cahan, *Shtudyes vegn yidisher folksshafung,* 69–87.

———. "Yidishe folkslider." In Niger, *Der pinkes,* 364–65.

———. *Yidishe folkslider: mit melodien.* 2 vols. New York: International Library, 1912.

———. *Yidishe folksmayses.* Vilne: YIVO, 1940.

———. *Yidishe folksmayses: funem folksmoyl gezamlt.* Vilne: Yidishe folklor bibliotek, 1931.

———, ed. *Yidisher folklor.* Vilne: YIVO, 1938.

Clifford, James. *The Predicament of Culture: Twentieth-Century Ethnography, Literature, and Art.* Cambridge: Harvard University Press, 1988.

Clifford, James, and George E. Marcus, eds. *Writing Culture: The Poetics and Politics of Ethnography.* Berkeley: University of California Press, 1986.

Cocchiara, Giuseppe. *The History of Folklore in Europe.* Philadelphia: ISHI, 1981.

Coleman, Arthur P. "Language as a Factor in Polish Nationalism." *Slavonic Review* 13 (1934): 155–72.

Damesek, A. "Dray naye kindertsaytungen." *Literarishe bleter* 6 (1927): 105.

Danilevitsh, Hershl. "Fun'm folks-moyl: rekrutn un soldatn lider, retenishn, anekdotn." In Vanvild, *Bay undz yidn,* 95–110.

————. *Hersheles lider: ershter zamlung.* Pietrokov, n.p., 1907.

————. "Mi bemayim: poeme fun kantonistn lebn." In *Haynt yoyvl-bukh (1908–1938),* 61. Warsaw: n.p., 1938.

Dawidowicz, Lucy S. *From That Place and Time: A Memoir 1938–1947.* New York: W.W. Norton, 1989.

Dick, Ernst. "The Folk and their Culture: The Formative Concepts and the Beginnings of Culture." In *The Folk: Identity, Landscapes and Lores,* ed. Robert J. Smith and Jerry Stannard, 11–28. Lawrence, Kans.: Department of Anthropology, University of Kansas, 1989.

Dobroszycki, Lucjan, and Barbara Kireshenblatt-Gimblett, eds. *Image Before My Eyes: A Photographic History of Jewish Life in Poland 1864–1939.* New York: Schocken Books, 1977.

Dorson, Richard M. "Is There a Folk in the City?" *Journal of American Folklore* 83 (1970): 185–216.

————. "The Question of Folklore in a New Nation." *Journal of the Folklore Institute* 3, no. 3 (December 1986): 277–98.

Dow, James R., and Hannjost Lixfeld, eds. *German Volkskunde: A Decade of Theoretical Confrontation, Debate, and Reorientation (1967–1977).* Bloomington: Indiana University Press, 1986.

Dowling, Jennifer. "Riddles and Riddle Parodies: Shloyme Bastomskis Yiddishe Folksretenishn." In *History of Yiddish Studies: Winter Studies in Yiddish,* vol. 3, ed. Dov-Ber Kerler. Chur, England: Harwood Academic Publishers, 1987.

Druk, D. *Tsu der geshikhte fun der yidisher prese: in rusland un polyn.* Warsaw: Farlag zikhroynes, 1920.

Druyanov, Alter. "Hahalatsa hayehudit haamamit." *Reshumot* 1 (1918): 303–57.

————. "Jewish Folk Humor." *Reshumot* 2 (1922): 303–57.

————. *Sefer Habedikhah vehakhidud.* 3 vols. 1922. Reprint, Palestine: A. Drujanoff, 1935–38.

Dubnow, Simon. *Nationalism and History: Essays on Old and New Judaism.* Ed. Koppel Pinson. Philadelphia: Jewish Publication Society, 1958.

Duker, Abraham G. " 'Evreiskaia Starina'—A Bibliography of the Russian-Jewish Historical Periodical." *Hebrew Union College Annual* 8–9 (1931–32): 525–603.

Dundes, Alan. *Analytic Essays in Folklore.* The Hague: Mouton, 1975.

Efren, I. "Organizatsye." *Di yidishe velt* 11 (1913): 152–56.

Eisikovits, Max. *Songs of the Martyrs: Hassidic Melodies of Maramures.* New York: Sepher-Hermon Press, 1980.

Elzet, Yehude [Zlotnik]. *Der vunder-oytser fun der yidisher shprakh: davenen.* Warsaw: Levin-Epshteyn, 1918.

————. *Der vunder-oytser fun der yidisher shprakh: der mentshlekher kerper.* Warsaw: Levin-Epshteyn, 1920.

————. *Der vunder-oytser fun der yidisher shprakh: folkstimlekhe rednsartn, glaykhvertlekh un anekdotn.* Warsaw: Levin-Epshteyn, 1918–1920.

————. *Der vunder-oytser fun der yidisher shprakh: malokhes un bal-malokhes.* Warsaw: Levin-Epshteyn, 1920.

————. *Der vunder-oytser fun der yidisher shprakh: yidishe maykholim.* Warsaw: Levin-Epshteyn, 1920.

————. "Idiotizmen: materialen far der frazeologye fun der yidisher shprakh." In Vanvild, *Bay undz yidn,* 189–206.

————. "Miminhagei yisrael: kovetz minhagim shelo nizkeru od o shelo nitbaru adayin kkol tsorham." *Reshumot* 1 (1918): 335–77.

————. "Plinsker kolekotnikes." In Prilutski, *Noyekh Prilutskis zamlbikher far yidishn folklor, filologye un kulturgeshikhte,* vol. 2, 210–12.

————. *Studies in Past Jewish Domestic Life.* Vol. 1 of *One Hundred Years Ago.* Montreal: n.p., 1977.

————. "Zakrutshiner balebatim." In Prilutski, *Noyekh Prilutskis zamlbikher far yidishn folklor, filologye un kulturgeshikhte,* vol. 2, 184–86.

Epshteyn, Nekhame. "Bamerkungen tsu di vitsn un vitsike mayselekh." In Cahan, *Yidisher folklor,* 322–26.

————. Review of *Rosinkess mit Mandlen. Aus der Volksliteratur der Ostjuden: Schwanke, Erzählungen, Sprichwörter und Rätsel,* by Dr. Immanuel Olsvanger. *YIVO-bleter* 4, no. 1 (1932): 73–76.

————. "Variantn un paraleln in yidishe vitsn." Unpublished essay, n.d. Papers of the YIVO *Aspirantur,* YIVO Institute for Jewish Research.

Epshteyn, Nekhame, and S. Z. Pipe. Review of *Games of the Soviet Union,* by V. N. Vsevolodskii-Gerngross, et al., *YIVO-bleter* 11, nos. 3–4 (1937): 287–91.

Etnografishe anketes. Heft 1: yon-toyvim. Vilne: YIVO, 1928.

Fabian, Johannes. *Time and the Other: How Anthropology Makes Its Object.* New York: Columbia University Press, 1983.

Fernandez, James W. "Folklore as an Agent of Nationalism." *African Studies Bulletin* 5, no. 2 (May 1962): 3–8.

Feyn, Khaye. "Yidishe folkslider: gezamlt fun khaye feyn." In Niger, *Der pinkes,* 399–410.

Filologishe shriftn. 3 vols. Vilne: YIVO, 1926, 1928, 1929.

Fishman, Joshua A. "Attracting a Following to High-Culture Functions for a Language of Everyday Life: The Role of the Tshernovits Language Conference in the 'Rise of Yiddish.'" In *Never Say Die!: A Thousand Years of Yiddish in Jewish Life and Letters,* ed. Joshua A. Fishman, 369–94. The Hague: Mouton, 1981.

Fiszer, Dr. Adam. *Zwyczaje pogrzebowe ludu polskietgo.* Lwow: n.p., 1921.

Frankel, Jonathan. *Prophecy and Politics: Socialism, Nationalism, and the Russian Jews, 1862–1917.* Cambridge: Cambridge University Press, 1981.

Friedman, I. "Pinkhes Graubard." In *Pinkes Sochaczew*, ed. A. S. Stein and G. Weissman, 274. Jerusalem: Former Residents of Sochaczew in Israel, 1962.

Frishmans yubileyum-bukh: tsu zayn fuftsik-yorikn geburts-tog. Warsaw: n.p., 1914.

Fuks, Khayim Leyb. "Yitskhok Katsenelsons shtub." *Yidishe shriftn* 2, nos. 5–6 (1947): 12–13.

Gellner, Ernest. *Nations and Nationalism*. Ithaca: Cornell University Press, 1983.

Ginzburg, S. M., and P. S. Marek. *Yidishe folkslider in rusland*. 1901. Reprint, Ramat-Gan: Bar-Ilan University Press, 1991.

Givoni-Pipe, Gershon. "The Life History of My Brother, In View of His Letters." In *Yiddish Folksongs From Galicia*, 23–47. Jerusalem: Hebrew University of Jerusalem, Institute of Jewish Studies, Folklore Research Center, 1971.

Gliksman, Dr. A. "Neo-haskole: a vort vegn undzer folks-universitetn." *Literarishe bleter* 1 (1925): 1–2.

Goldman, Dr. Arthur. "Di vakhnakht bay viner yidn onheyb 15tn yorhundert." In *Landoy-bukh*, 91–94.

Goldshmidt, A. I. "Di historish-etnografishe gezelshaft afn nomen fun S. An-sky." *Literarishe bleter* 46 (1932): 736.

———. "Di Vilner historish-etnografishe gezelshaft un ir muzey." In *Vilner almanakh*, ed. A. I. Goldshmidt, 189–94. Vilne: Ovnt-kurier, 1939. Reprint, New York, 1992.

Goldsmith, Emanuel S. *Architects of Yiddishism at the Beginning of the Twentieth Century: A Study in Jewish Cultural History*. Rutherford, N.J.: Fairleigh Dickinson University Press, 1976.

Gottesman, Itzik. "The Man in the Brimmed Hat: The Fieldwork Narratives of the Warsaw Yiddish Folklorists." *Jewish Folklore and Ethnology Review: Special Issue on Yiddish Folklore* 15, no. 1 (1993): 2–4.

Graubard, Pinkhes. *An ander libn*. Warsaw: Kultur-lige, 1928.

———. "Gezangen fun tom . . . lider fun ganovim, arestantn, gasn-froyen." In Vanvild, *Bay undz yidn*, 17–42.

———. "In yene teg." In *Pinkes Sochaczew*, ed. A. S. Stein and G. Weissman, 330–35. Jerusalem: Former Residents of Sochaczew in Israel, 1962.

———. "Shmuel Lehmans oytser: tsu zayn 30-yoriker folkloristisher arbet." In *Shmuel Lehman: zamlbukh*, 27–31.

———, ed. *Fun nont un vayt: zamlung fun literatur un folklor*. Warsaw: n.p., 1914.

———, ed. *Literarishe shriftn: zamlbukh no. 1*. Warsaw: n.p., n.d.

Graubard, Pinkhes, and Shmuel Lehman. "Folkslider." In *Frishmans yubileyum-bukh*, 205–15.

Greenbaum, Alfred Abraham. *Jewish Scholarship and Scholarly Institutions in the Soviet Union, 1918–1953*. Jerusalem: Hebrew University of Jerusalem, Centre for Research and Documentation of East European Jewry, 1978.

Gromb, M. "Gasn un hoyf reklame." *Filologishe shriftn* 3 (1929): 283–96.

Grunwald, Max. "Aus Hausapotheke un Hexenkuche." *Mitteilungen zur judischen Volkskunde* 5 (1903): 19.

Heine, Heinrich. "The Romantic School." In *The Romantic School and Other Essays*, ed. Jost Jermand and Robert C. Holub, 86. New York: Continuum, 1985.

Heller, (Dov) Bernard. "Tasks of Jewish Ethnography and Folklore in General, and in the Holy Land in Particular." *Tsiyon* 4 (1930): 73.

Heller, Celia S. *On the Edge of Destruction: Jews of Poland Between the Two World Wars.* New York: Columbia University Press, 1977.

Herzfeld, Michael. *Anthropology through the Looking-Glass: Critical Ethnography in the Margins of Europe.* Cambridge: Cambridge University Press, 1987.

————. *Ours Once More: Folklore, Ideology, and the Making of Modern Greece.* Austin: University of Texas Press, 1982.

Herzog, Marvin I. "Grammatical Features of Markuze's *Seyfer Refues* (1790)." In *The Field of Yiddish: Studies in Language, Folklore and Literature,* ed. Uriel Weinreich, 49–62. The Hague: Mouton, 1965.

Hirszhorn, S. *Legendy Zydowdkie o Powstaniu—1863.* Warsaw: Widawnictwo E. Gitlina, 1929.

Hobsbawm, E. J. *Nations and Nationalism since 1780: Programme, Myth, Reality.* Cambridge: Cambridge University Press, 1990.

Hodgen, Margaret T. *The Doctrine of Survivals: A Chapter in the History of Scientific Method in the Study of Man.* London: Allenson, 1936.

Horak, Stephan. *Poland and Her National Minorities, 1919–39.* New York: Vantage Press, 1961.

Hultkrantz, Ake, ed. *International Dictionary of Regional European Ethnology and Folklore.* 2 vols. Copenhagen: Rosenkilde and Bagger, 1960.

Hundert, David, and Gershon C. Bacon. *The Jews in Poland and Russia: Bibliographical Essays.* Bloomington: Indiana University Press, 1984.

Idelsohn, A. Z. *The Folk Song of the East European Jews.* Vol. 9 of *Thesaurus of Hebrew Oriental Melodies.* Leipzig: Friedrich Hofmeister, 1932.

International Conference of the Yiddish Scientific Institute: On Its 10th Anniversary, Held in Vilne from the 14th to the 19th of August, 1935. Vilne: YIVO, 1936.

Kaganovski, Efrayim. *Yidishe shrayber in der heym.* Paris: Oyfsnay, 1956.

Kalmanovitch, Z. Review of *Arkhiv far yidisher shprakhvisnshaft, literaturforshung un etnologye,* by Noyekh Prilutski and Shmuel Lehman. *YIVO-bleter* 5 (1937): 384–87

Katsenelson, Yitskhok. "Di khronik fun Hersheles toyt." In *Yidishe geto-ksovim, Varshe 1940–1943,* 476–78. Israel: Ghetto Fighter's House and Hakibbutz Hameuchad Publishing House, 1984.

————. "Ya mam lidlekh." In *Yidishe geto-ksovim, Varshe 1940–1943,* 479–83. Israel: Ghetto Fighter's House and Hakibbutz Hameuchad Publishing House, 1984.

Katsenelson-Nakhumov, Tsipore. *Yitskhok Katsenelson: zayn lebn un shafn.* Buenos Aires: tsentral farband fun poylishe yidn in Argentina, 1948.

Khayes, Kh. "Gleybungen un minhogim in farbindung mit toyt." In *Filologishe shriftn* 2 (1928): 281–328.

Kiel, Mark W. "The Ideology of the Folk-partey." *Soviet Jewish Affairs* 2 (1975): 75–89.

————. "A Twice Lost Legacy: Ideology, Culture and the Pursuit of Folklore in

Russia until Stalinization (1930–1931)." Ph.D. diss., Jewish Theological Seminary, 1991.

————. "Vox Populi, Vox Dei: The Centrality of Peretz in Jewish Folkloristics." *Polin* 7 (1992): 88–120.

Kipnis, Menakhem. *60 yidishe folkslider mit notn: fun M. Kipis un Z. Zeligfelds repertuar*. Warsaw: A. Gitlin, n.d. [1918].

————. *80 yidishe folkslider: fun Z. Zeligfelds and M. Kipnis repertuar*. Warsaw: A. Gitlin, n.d. [1925].

————. "In a malarusishn dorf." *Der shtral* 1, no. 35 (1910): 17–20; no. 36 (1910): 15–21.

————. *Khelemer mayses*. Warsaw: Cukier, 1930.

————. "Reb Khayem Sholem der toyter geyt shtarbn: a folkstimlekhe ertsteylung." In *Haynt yoyvl-bukh (1908–1938)*, 97–99. Warsaw: n.p., 1938.

Kirshenblatt-Gimblett, Barbara. "Contraband: Performance, Text and Analysis of a *Purim-shpil*." *Drama Review* 3 (1980): 5–16.

————. "The Future of Folklore Studies in America: The Urban Frontier." *Folklore Forum* 16 (1984): 175–234.

————. "Problems in the Historiography of Jewish Folkloristics." Paper presented at conference on "Folklore and Social Transformation: A Dialogue of American and German Folklorists," Bloomington, Indiana. November 1988.

————. "Toward a Theory of Proverb Meaning." *Proverbium* 22 (1973): 821–27.

Kohn, Hans. *Pan-Slavism: Its History and Ideology*. New York: Bantam, 1960.

Krohn, Kaarle. *Folklore Methodology*. 1926. Reprint, Austin: University of Texas at Austin, 1971.

Landau, Dr. Alfred. "Bamerkungen tsum yidishn folklor: vegn S. Bastomskis zamlungun." In *Landoy-bukh*, 13–22.

————. "Bamerkungen tsu Noyekh Prilutskis yidishe folklslider." *Yidishe Filologye* 1 (1924): 151–60.

————. "Kinderratsel aud Galizien." *Mitteilungen zur judischen Volkskunde* 7 (1901): 87–88.

————. "Miluim tso M. Vaynraykhs Shtaplen." *Yidishe filologye* 1 (1924): 55–61.

————. "Spiele der judischen Kinder in Ostgalizien." *Mitteilungen zur judischen Volkskunde* 3 (1899): 40–49.

Landoy-bukh: Dr. Alfred Landoy tsu zayn 75 stn geboyrnstog dem 25stn november, 1925. Vilne: YIVO, 1926.

Lehman, Shmuel. *Arbet un frayhayt: zamlung fun lider vos zenen antshtanen in folk in der tsayt fun der frayhayts-bavegung in tsarish rusland*. Warsaw: Folklor bibliotek, 1921.

————. "Di eyropeyishe milkhome: a zamlung fun yidishe folksvertlekh, anekdotn, rimozim, briv, gramen, lider, mayses un legendes, vos zaynen geshafn gevorn in der tsayt fun krig." In *Lebn: heftn far literatur, kunst, un publitsisdik*, ed. Moyshe Shalit, 3–28. Vilne: 1922.

————. "Di kinder velt: gramen, lidlekh, hamtsoes un shpiln." In Vanvild, *Bay undz yidn*, 113–49.

————. "Elye-hanovi in der folks fantazye: mayses un legendes." In Prilutski and

Lehman, *Arkhiv far yidisher shprakhvisnshaft, literaturforshung un etnologye*, 115–78.

———. *Ganovim-lider: mit melodyes.* Warsaw: Pinkhes Graubard, 1928.

———. "Ganovim un ganeyve: rednsartn, tsunemenishn, shprikhverter, fragn, gramen, anekdotn, un mayses." In Vanvild, *Bay undz yidn*, 43–92.

———. "Libe lider fun ganovim." In *Landoy-bukh*, 291–398. Vilne: Kletskin, 1926.

———. "Sotsyaler moment inem yidishn shprikhvort." *Literarishe bleter* 45 (1935): 728.

———. "Two Cows for a Melody." In Weinreich, *Yiddish Folktales*, 231–32.

———. "Two Songs for Three Hundred Rubles." In *A Treasury of Jewish Folklore*, ed. Nathan Ausbel, 349–53. New York: Crown Publishers, 1948.

Lerer, Moyshe. "An amolike khasene in khelm." *Yidishe filologye* 1 (1924): 392–94.

———. "Miluim tsu N. Prilutskis *Gevet.*" *Yidishe filologye* 1 (1924): 72–74.

Lerner, Yoysef-Yehude. "Di yidishe muze: yidishe folkslider." Ed. Mordkhe Spektor. *Hoyzfraynd* 2 (1889): 182–98.

Lestschinsky, Jacob. "Dubnow's Autonism and his 'Letters on Old and New Judaism.'" In *Simon Dubnow: The Man and His Work: A Memorial Volume on the Occasion of the Centenary of His Birth (1860–1960)*, ed. Aaron Steinberg, 77. Paris: French Section of the World Jewish Congress, 1963.

Levin, Dr. Gershon. *Perets: a bisl zikhroynes.* Warsaw: Yehudia, 1919.

Leybl, Danil. "Shiva shirey am." *Reshumot* 6 (1930): 435–42.

Lilienthal, Regina. *Dziecko zydowkie.* Cracow, 1927.

———. "Eyn hore." *Yidishe filologye* 1 (1924): 245–71.

———. "Przesady zydowskie." *Wisla* 12, 14, 18 (1898, 1900, 1904).

———. "Zycie pozagrobowe w wyobrazeniu." *Lud* 8 (1902).

Lindberg, Yankev. "Tsu dray." *Yidishe filologye* 1 (1924): 397–98.

Litvin, A. *Yidishe neshomes*, 6 vols. New York: Yidishe folksvildung, 1916.

Lomax, John A. *Adventures of a Ballad Hunter.* New York: Macmillan, 1947.

Lorentz, Stanislaw. *Museums and Collections in Poland 1945–1955.* Warsaw: Polonia Publishing House, 1956.

Loyke, Khayim. "Berl Verblunski—der grodner folklor zamler: fartseykhenishn." *Grodner opklangen* (1975): 61–62.

Lunski, Khayim-Khaykl. *Geoynim un gdoylim fun noentn over: sipurim un agodes fun zeyer lebn un shafn.* Vilne: n.p., 1931.

Lunski, Khaykl. "Anecdotes of the Great Rabbi Ayzl Kharif: Rabbi in Slonim." *Yeda Am* 1 (1962): 75–89.

———. "Di yidishe historish-etnografishe gezelshaft." In *Pinkes: far der geshikhte fun vilne in di yorn fun milkhome un okupatsye*, ed. Zalmen Reyzin, 862–63. Vilne: AVJHES, 1922.

———. *Fun vilner geto: bilder un geshtaltn geshribn in shvere tsaytin.* Vilne: Fareyn fun di yidishe literatn un zhurnalistn in vilne, 1920.

———. "Iserlins yidish." *Yidishe filologye* 1 (1924): 288–302.

———. *Legendes vegn vilner goen, reb elye bar shloyme zalmen z'l: geklibn fun menthsn un sforim fun Kh. Lunski.* Vilne: Di naye yidishe folkshul, 1924.

―――. "Olkenik: a shtetl mit legendes." In Shalit, *Af di khurves fun milkhomes unmehumes: pinkes,* 434–43.

―――. "Vilner kloyzn un der shulhoyf." *Vilner zamlbukh* 2 (1918): 97–112.

―――. "Yidish bay r'yankev Vayl." In *Landoy-bukh,* 285–88. Vilne: YIVO, 1926.

Luz, Ehud. *Parallels Meet: Religion and Nationalism in the Early Zionist Movement, 1882–1904.* Philadelphia: JPS, 1988.

Marcus, George E., and Michael M. J. Fischer. *Anthropology as Cultural Critique: An Experimental Moment in the Human Sciences.* Chicago: University of Chicago Press, 1986.

Marcus, Joseph. *Social and Political History of the Jews in Poland 1919–1939.* Berlin: Mouton, 1983.

Matisoff, James A. *Blessings, Curses, Hopes, and Fears: Psycho-Ostensive Expressions in Yiddish.* Philadelphia: ISHI, 1979.

Mayhew, Henry. *London Labour and the London Poor.* 4 vols. 1861–62. Reprint, New York: Dover Publications, 1968.

Mayzel, Nakhmen. "Forgeyer fun der algemeyner entsiklopedye in Yidish." *Literarishe bleter* 12 (March 15, 1935): 170–71.

Meier, John. *Kunstlied und Volkslid.* Halle: M. Niemeyer, 1906.

―――. *Kunstlieder im Volksmund.* Halle: M. Niemeyer, 1906.

Mendelsohn, Ezra. "Aspects of Jewish Politics in Interwar Poland." In *Proceedings of the Conference on "Poles and Jews: Myth and Reality in the Historical Context,"* ed. John Micgiel, Robert Scott, and H. B. Segel, 203–22. New York: Institute on East Central Europe, Columbia University, 1986.

―――. "Jewish Politics in Interwar Poland: An Overview." In *The Jews of Poland between Two World Wars,* ed. Yisrael Gutman, Ezra Mendelsohn, Jehuda Reinharz, and Chone Shmeruk, 9–19. Hanover, N.H.: University Press of New England, 1989.

―――. *The Jews of East Central Europe between the World Wars.* Bloomington: Indiana University Press, 1983.

―――. *Zionism in Poland: The Formative Years, 1915–1926.* New Haven, Conn.: Yale University Press, 1981.

Menes, Avrom. *Fun undzer altn kval: elye hanovi.* New York: CYCO, 1955.

Miron, Dan. *A Traveler Disguised: A Study in the Rise of Modern Yiddish Fiction in the Nineteenth Century.* New York: Schocken Books, 1973.

―――. "Folklore and Anti-Folklore in the Yiddish Fiction of the Haskala." In *Studies in Jewish Folklore: Proceedings of a Regional Conference of the Association for Jewish Studies Held at the Spertus College of Judaica, Chicago, May 1–3, 1977,* ed. Frank Talmadge, 219–50. Cambridge, Mass.: Association for Jewish Studies, 1980.

Mlotek, Eleanor Gordon. "International Motifs in the Yiddish Ballads." In *For Max Weinreich on His Seventieth Birthday: Studies in Jewish Languages, Literature, and Society,* 209–28. The Hague: Mouton, 1964.

Mozes, Mendl. "Der moment (1910–1939)." In *Yidishe prese in varshe.* New York: Congress for Jewish Culture, 1956.

Mukdoni, A. *Oysland: mayne bageginishn.* Buenos Aires: Tsentral-farlag fun poy-lishe yidn in Argentina, 1951.

Naumann, Hans. *Grundzuge der deutschen Volkskunde.* Leipzig: n.p., 1922.

Niger, Shmuel, ed. *Der pinkes: yorbukh fun der geshikhte fun der yidisher literatur un shprakh, far folklor, kritik un bibliografye.* Vilne: Kletskin, 1913.

Nomberg, H. D. *A literarisher dor: vegn I. L Perets.* Warsaw: Levin-Epshteyn, n.d.

———. "Der pedler geyt." In *Dos bukh felyetonen,* 328–33. Warsaw: Kh. Bzozhe, 1924.

Noy, Dov. "The Path of S. Z. Pipe in Jewish Folkloristics." In Pipe, *Yiddish Folksongs from Galicia,* 58.

Noy, Meir, ed. *East Euoprean Jewish Cante Fables.* Israel Folktale Archives, publication series no. 20 (Haifa: n.p., 1968).

Olswanger, Dr. Immanuel. *Rosinkess mit Mandlen. Aus der volksliteratur der Ostjuden. Schwanke, Erzählungen, Sprichwörter und Rätsel.* 2nd ed. Basel: Verlag der Schweizerischen Gesellschaft für Volkskunde, 1931.

Opalski, Magdalena, and Israel Bartal. *Poles and Jews: A Failed Brotherhood.* Hanover, N.H.: Brandeis University Press, 1992.

Opatoshu, Joseph. *1863.* Vilne: Kletskin, 1926.

———. *Roman fun a ferd ganef.* New York: n.p., 1917.

Oyerbakh, Rokhl. "Hershele (Danilevitsh)." *Yidishe shriftn* 2, nos. 5–6 (1947): 15–16.

Papirnikov, Yoysef. "Hersh Danilevitsh." In *Heymishe un noente,* 217–21. Tel-Aviv: Farlag Perets, 1958.

Peretz, I. L. *Briv un redes fun I. L. Peretz.* Ed. Nakhman Meisel New York: YKUF, 1944.

———. "Dos yidishe lebn loyt di yidishe folkslider." *YIVO-bleter* 13, nos. 1–2 (1937): 291–99.

Perlshteyn, Khane, and Borukh Kats. "Tsvey aktuele folkslider." *Yidishe filologye* 1 (1924): 94.

Pipe, Shmuel Zaynvil. "Di zamlungen yidishe folkslider fun I. L. Peretz." *YIVO-bleter* 12, nos. 1–3 (1937): 286–90.

———. "Folklorizatsye fun D. Edelshatats 'der arbeter.' " In Pipe, *Yiddish Folksongs from Galicia,* 333–54.

———. "Napoleon in yidishn folklor." In *Yidn in frankraykh: Shtudyes un materialn: ershter band,* ed. E. Tcherikower, 153–89. New York: YIVO, 1942.

———. Review of *Folklorlider,* by Z. Skuditski. *YIVO-bleter* 14 (1939): 339–67.

———. "S. Z. Pipe's Research Report: 'Art Song Among the Folk—First Report.' " In Pipe, *Yiddish Folksongs from Galicia,* 595–600.

———. *Twelve Folktales from Sanok.* Ed. Dov Noy. Israel Folktale Archives Publication Series No. 15. Haifa: Haifa Municipality, Ethnological Museum and Folklore Archives, 1967.

———. "Yehude Leyb Kahn: fertsik yor folkloristishe arbet." *Literarishe bleter* 4, no. 49 (1936): 1–2.

———. *Yiddish Folksongs From Galicia: The Folklorization of David Edelstadt's Song "Der arbeter"; Letters.* Folklore Research Center Studies vol. 2. Ed. Meir

Noy and Dov Noy. Jerusalem: Hebrew University of Jerusalem, Institute of Jewish Studies, Folklore Research Center, 1971.

———. "Yidishe kinderlidlekh." *YIVO-bleter* 12, nos. 4–5 (1937): 494–507.

———. "Yidishe kindershpiln." *YIVO-bleter* 10 (1936): 39–47.

Pipe, Shmuel Zaynvil, and Oyzer Pipe. "Yidishe folkslider fun galitsye." *YIVO-bleter* 11, nos. 1–2 (Jan–Feb 1937): 53–70; nos. 3–4 (Mar–April 1937): 252–69.

Posern-Zielinski, Alexander. "The Forming of Polish Ethnography as an Independent Discipline of Science (until 1939)." In *Historia Etnografi Polskiej*, ed. Witold Armon et al., 326–32 (Wroclaw: Zaklad narodowy Imienia Ossolinskich Wydawnictwo Polskiej Akademii Nauk, 1973), 326–32.

Prilutski, Noyekh. "Di ershte yidishe shprakh konferents." *Der yidisher gedank in der nayer tsayt*, ed. A. Menes, 261–64. New York: Congress for Jewish Culture, 1957.

———. *Dos gevet: dialogn vegn shprakh un kultur*. Warsaw: Farlag kulturlige, 1923.

———. "Dos yidishe folksvort vegn medines un yeshuvim." In Prilutski, *Noyekh Prilutskis zamlbikher far yidishn folklor, filologye un kulturgeshikhte*, vol. 2, 161–84.

———. "Draysik you literarishe tetikeyt fun noykeh prilutski." *Literarishe bleter*, May 1, 1931: 1–3.

———. "Dr. Moyshe Markuze: a yidishist fun 18tn yorhundert." In Prilutski and Lehman, *Noyekh Prilutskis zamlbikher far yidishn folklor, filologye un kulturgeshikhte*, vol. 1, 1–56.

———. "Grins af shvuos." *Yidishe filologye* 1 (1924): 87–89.

———. *Noyekh Prilutskis zamlbikher far yidishn folklor, filologye un kulturgeshikhte*. Vol. 2. Warsaw: Bikher far ale, 1917.

———. "Polemik—a tshuve eynem a retsenzent." In Prilutski and Lehman, *Noyekh Prilutskis zamlbikher far yidishn folklor, filologye un kulturgeshikhte*, vol. 1, 154–79.

———. "Shpet-loshn." *Yidishe filologye* 1 (1924): 33–45.

———. *Yidishe folkslider*. 2 vols. Warsaw: Nayer farlag, 1911, 1913.

Prilutski, Noyekh, and Shmuel Lehman. *Arkhiv far yidisher shprakhvisnshaft, literaturforshung un etnologye*. Vol. 1. Warsaw: Nayer farlag, 1926–33.

———. *Noyekh Prilutskis zamlbikher far yidishn folklor, filologye un kulturgeshikhte*. Vol. 1. Warsaw: Nayer farlag, 1912.

Rabach, Berl. "Reminiscenes of My Youth from Sonik." In Pipe, *Yiddish Folklore from Galicia*, 50–52.

Radoshitski, I. "Hershele-der lodzher trubador." In *Lodzer Yisker-bukh*, 119–21. New York: Fareynikte reytungs komitet far der shtot lodzh, 1943.

Ranke, Kurt. "Walter Anderson (1885–1962)." *Fabula* 5 (1962): unpaginated first page.

Ranke, Otto. "Hans Naumann: Mann und Werk." *Hessische Bletter fur Volkskunde* 46 (1955): 1–7.

Ravitch, Melekh. *Mayn leksikon*. Montreal: n.p., 1941.

———. "Shmuel Lehman." In Ravitch, *Mayn leksikon*, vol. 2, 36–38. Montreal: A Committee in Montreal, Canada, 1947.

Ravnitski, J. Ch. *Yidishe vitsn*. 2 vols. 1922. Reprint, New York: Moyshe Shmuel Shklarski, 1950.

Report of the Conference of the Yiddish Scientific Institute: Held in Vilne From the 24th to the 27th of October 1929. Vilne: YIVO, 1930.

Ringleblum, Emanuel. *Ksovim fun geto*. 2 vols. Tel-Aviv: Farlag I. L. Peretz, 1985.

Rivkind, Isaac. "Der bal-malokhe in an alt yidish lid." In *Landoy-bukh*, 42–50.

Roskies, David G. *A Bridge of Longing: The Lost Art of Yiddish Storytelling*. Cambridge: Harvard University Press, 1995.

———. "Ideologies of the Yiddish Folksong in the Old Country and the New." *Jewish Book Annual* 50 (1992–93): 143–66.

———. "S. Anski and the Paradigm of Return." In *The Uses of Tradition: Jewish Continuity in the Modern Era*, ed. Jack Wertheimer, 243–60. New York: Jewish Theological Seminary, 1992.

Rozen, Ber I. *Portretn*. Beunos Aires: Tsentral farband fun poylishe yidn in Argentina, 1956.

Rozentsvayg, Ayzik. *Sotsyale diferentsiyatse inem yidish folklor-lid*. Kiev: Farlag fun der alukraynisher visnshaftlekher akademye, 1934.

Rubin, Dr. I. "Akshonim (S. Bastomski)." *Literarishe bleter* 29 (1929): 568.

Rubin, Ruth. "Y. L. Cahan and Jewish Folklore." *New York Folklore Quarterly* 11 (1955): 34–45.

Rubinshteyn, Shmuel. "Shprikhverter un rednsartn." In *Landoy-bukh*, 411–26.

Sadan, Dov. "Araynfir tsu Khayim Zeltsers khelmyade." In *Chaim Zeltser, Shtern afn yarid oder khelm: di festung fun khokhme*, 7–18. Tel Aviv: Farlag Yisrol Bukh, 1985.

———. "Khokhmey khelm." *Yeda-Am* 2 (1954): 229–32.

Schaechter-Widman, Lifshe. *Durkhgelebt a velt*. New York: Lifshe Vidman Bukh Komitet, 1973.

Schwarzbaum, Haim. *Studies in Jewish and World Folklore*. Berlin: Walter De Gruyter, 1968.

Segalovitch, Z. *Tlometske 13: fun farbrentn nekhtn*. Buenos Aires: Tsentral farband fun poylishe yidn in Argentina, 1946.

Segel, B. W. "Elijah der Prophet: eine Studie zur juddischen Volks- und Sagenkunde." *Ost und West* 1904: 477–88, 675–80, 807–12.

Senn, Henry. "Folklore Beginnings in France, The Academie Celtique: 1804–1813." *Journal of Folklore Institute* 18, no. 1 (January–February 1981): 23–31.

Shalit, Moyshe. *Af di khurves fun milkhomes un mehumes: pinkes*. Vilne: Gegntkomitet YEKOPO, 1930.

———. "Der An-ski arkhiv—Zayn inhalt un vert." *Literarishe bleter* 16 (1929): 313.

———. Foreword to *Muzikalisher Pinkes: nigumim-zamlung fun yidishn folkoytser*, by A. M. Bernshteyn. Vilne: Vilner yidisher historish-etnografishe gezelshaft af dem nomen fun S. Ansky z'l, 1927.

———. "Vegn fareynikn di historish-etnografishe gezelshaft mit dem yidishn visnshaftlekhn institut." *Literarishe bleter* 39 (1928): 763.

Shatsky, Jacob. "Di naye dershaynungen in der yidisher folklor-literatur." *Dos naye lebn* 1, no. 11 (1923): 44–48.

———. "Peretz-shtudyes." *YIVO-bleter* 28 (1946): 63.

———. "Samuel Lehman: 1886–1941." *YIVO-bleter* 18 (1941): 80–83.

———. *Yehuda Leyb Cahan*. New York: YIVO, 1938.

———. "Yehude Leyb Kan (1881–1937): materialn far a biografye." In *Yorbukh fun Amopteyle,* eds. A. Mukdoni and Jacob Shatsky, 16–18. New York: Yiddish Scientific Institute—American Section, 1938.

Sherman, P. "A. M. Bernshteyn: tsu zayn tsveyter yortsayt, dem tsentn siven." *Di khazonim velt* 1 (1934): 1–4.

Shiper, Yitskhok. "Araynfir verter in der folkskentenish." *Landkentnish* 1 (1933): 61–71.

———. "Di nayste matone funem yidishn visnshaftlekhn institut." *Literarishe bleter* 5, no. 9 (March 2, 1929): 187.

———. *Geshikhte fun yidisher teater-kunst un drama*. 3 vols. Warsaw: Kultur-lige, 1927.

Shmeruk, Chone. "Aspects of the History of Warsaw as a Yiddish Literary Centre." *Polin: A Journal of Polish Jewish Studies* 3 (1998): 142–55.

"Shmuel Lehman." In *Doyres bundistn, tsveyter band,* ed. J. S. Hertz, 252–53. New York: Undzer tsayt farlag, 1956.

"Shmuel Lehman—the man—the institution." In Ringleblum, *Ksovim fun geto,* vol. 2.

Shmuel Lehman: zamlbukh. Warsaw: Published with the aid of the Union of Yiddish Writers and Journalists in Warsaw, 1937.

Shpirn, Tsvi. "Di role fun nemen in undzer mame-loshen." *Filologishe shriftn* 2 (1928): 175–86.

Shtif, Nokhem. "Ditrikh fun bern: yidishkeyt un veltlekhkeyt in der alter yidisher literatur." *Yidishe filologye* 1 (1924): 1–11; 112–22.

———. "Vegn a yidishn akademishn institut." In *Di Organizatsye fun der yidisher visnshaft,* 1–10. Vilne: Tsentraler Bildung Komitet and Vilbig, 1925.

Singer, Isaac Bashevis. "Vanvild Kava." In *Collected Stories of Isaac Bashevis Singer,* 580–86. New York: Farrar Strauss Giroux, 1982.

Siporin, Steve. Review of *Avanti Popolo! Revolutionary Songs of the Italian Working Class. Journal of American Folklore,* 389: 373–74.

Skuditski, Z. "Araynfir." In *Folklor-lider: naye materialin-zamlung.* Vol. 2. Moscow: Emes, 1936.

———. "Vegn folklorishn arbeter-lid." In *Problemes fun folkloristik,* ed. Meyer Viner. Kharkov-Kiev: Melukhisher natsmindfarlag bam erezidium fun vutsik, 1932.

———. "Vegn folksiberarterungen fun Gotlobers lider." *Tsaytshrift* 5 (1931): 245–55.

Slobin, Mark. *Chosen Voices: The Story of the American Cantorate.* Urbana: University of Illinois Press, 1989.

Slotnick, Susan A. "The Contributions of the Soviet Yiddish Folklorists." *Working*

Papers in Yiddish and East European Jewish Studies. Vol. 20. New York: YIVO, 1976.

Soifer, Paul. "Soviet Jewish Folkloristics and Ethnography: An Institutional History, 1918–1948." *Working Papers in Yiddish and East European Jewish Studies.* Vol. 30. New York: YIVO, 1978.

Sosnovik, Eli. "Dem raboyne shel oylems tanoyim." In *Landoy-bukh,* 97–42.

Sosnovik, Elye. "Materialn tsu der yidisher folksmeditsin in vaysrusland." *Yidishe filologye* 1 (1924): 160–62.

Stewart, Susan. *Crimes of Writing: Problems in the Containment of Representation.* Oxford: Oxford University Press, 1991.

Stocking, George. *Race, Culture and Evolution.* New York: Free Press, 1968.

Suilleabhain, Sean O. *A Handbook of Irish Folklore.* 1942. Reprint, Hatboro, Pa.: Folklore Associates, 1963.

Sutskever, A. "Dov Sadan: 1902–1989." *Goldene keyt* 128 (1990): 5.

Szajkowski, Zosa. *YIVO and Its Founders: Catalogue of the Exhibition On the Occasion of the Fiftieth Anniversary of the YIVO Institute for Jewish Research.* New York: YIVO, 1975.

Taylor, Archer. "Characteristics of German Folklore Studies." *Journal of American Folklore* 74 (1961): 297.

———. "Precursors of the Finnish Method of Folk-lore study." *Modern Philology* 25 (1927–28): 481–91.

Terras, Victor, ed. *Handbook of Russian Literature.* New Haven, Conn.: Yale University Press, 1985.

Thompson, Stith, ed. *Four Symposia on Folklore: Held at the Midcentury International Folklore Conference, Indiana University, July 21–August 4, 1950.* Bloomington: Indiana University Press, 1953.

Trunk, Isaiah. "Homer bilti-yada shel 'mishlahat An-ski' ba-shanim 1912–1916." *Gal-Ed* 6 (1982): 229–45.

———. "Shumel Lehman." In *Geshtaltn un gesheenishn,* 47–50. Buenos Aires: Tsentral Farband fun poylishe yidn in Argentina, 1962.

Trunk, J. *Poyln: zikhroynes un bilder.* New York: Undzer tsayt, 1953.

———. "Yidishizm un yidishe geshikhte: polemishe shrift." *Amol in a yoyvl: zaml-bukh* 2 (1931): 155–208.

Trzeciakowski, Lech. "The Role of Learned Societies in the Development of Polish Culture during the Period of the Partitions." *East European Quarterly* 22 (1988): 291–303.

Tsoller, Dr. I. "Lilit." *Filologishe shriftn* 3 (1929): 121–42.

Turkow, Janus. *Farloshene shterns.* Vol. 1. Buenos Aires: Tsentral farband fun poylishe yidn in Argentine, 1953.

Tylor, E. B. *Primitive Culture.* 2 vols. London: J. Murray, 1871.

Vanvild, M. "An ideal fun a folklorist." *Literarishe bleter* 7 (1932): 107.

———, ed. *Bay undz yidn: zamlbukh far folklor un filologye.* Warsaw: Farlag Pinkhes Graubard, 1923.

Vaynig, Naftuli. "Dos poylishe folkslid 'Wojna zydowska.'" *Filologishe shriftn* 3 (1929): 411–66.

―――. "Geshikhte un problemen fun der yidisher paremiologye." *YIVO-bleter* 8 (1935): 356–70.

―――. "Khaykl Lunski." *Literarishe bleter* 12 (1933): 188.

―――. "Mageyfe-khasenes." *Sotsyale Meditsin* 10, nos. 9–10 (1937): 24–32.

―――. "Organizatsye un arbet fun an etnografishn krayz." *Landkentnish* 2 (1934): 5–17.

―――. "Parekh-krankkayt in yidishn folklor." *Sotsyale meditsin* 11 (1938): 22–27.

―――. "Refues un sgules bay yidn in tsaytn fun epidemyes." *Sotsyale meditsin* 10, nos. 11–12 (1937): 25–31.

Veykhert, Mikhl. *Zikhroynes.* Vol. 2. Tel-Aviv: Menora, 1961.

Vilenski, L. [I. L. Cahan]. "Yidishe folkslider." In Niger, *Der pinkes,* 356–65.

Vos iz azoyns yidishe etnografye: hantbikhl farn zamler. Vilne: YIVO, 1929.

Wachstein, Dr. Bernard. "Di oysbreyterung fun Ignats Bernshteyns lebensverk." In *Landoy-bukh,* 28–38.

Wehrhan, Karl. *Kinderlied und Kinderspiel.* 1909. Reprint, Gloucester, Mass.: Peter Smith, 1970.

Weiner, Leo. "Aus der Russisch-Judischen Kinderstube." *Mitteilungen zur judischen Volkskunde* 2 (1898): 40–49.

Weinreich, Beatrice Silverman. "Four Yiddish Variants of the Master-Thief Tale." In *The Field of Yiddish: Studies in Yiddish Language, Folklore, and Literature,* ed. Uriel Weinreich, no. 3, 199–213. New York: Publications of the Linguistic Circle of New York, 1954.

―――. "Genres and Types of Yiddish Folk Tales about the Prophet Elijah." In *The Field of Yiddish: Studies in Language, Folklore and Literature, Second Collection,* ed. Uriel Weinreich, 202–31. The Hague: Mouton, 1965.

―――, ed. *Yiddish Folktales.* Trans. Leonard Wolf. New York: Pantheon Books, 1988.

Weinreich, Max. Afterword to Cahan, *Shtudyes vegn yidisher folksshafung.*

―――. "Der yidisher visnshaftlekher institut." In *Vilne,* ed. J. Jeshurin, 323. New York: Workmen's Circle—Branch 367, 1935.

―――. *History of the Yiddish Language.* Trans. Shlomo Noble. Chicago: University of Chicago Press, 1980.

―――. "Lantukh: di geshikhte fun a heymishn nitgutn." In *Landoy-bukh,* 217–36.

―――. *Mekhires yoysef.* Berlin: Vostok, 1923.

―――. Review of *Bay undz yidn,* by M. Vanvild. *Bikher-velt* 2, no. 6 (1923): 480.

―――. "Tsu: lantukh, di geshikhte fun a heymishn nitgutn." *Filologishe shriftn* 2 (1928): 494–500.

―――. "Tsu der kharakteristik fun undzere folksgleybenishn: onmerkungen tsu E. Sosnoviks artikl." *Yidishe filologye* 1 (1924): 168–76.

―――. "Vilner tezisn vegn yidishn visnshaftlekhn institut." *Di organizatsye fun der yidisher visnshaft.* Vilne: Tsentraler Bildung Komitet and Vilbig, 1925.

Weinreich, Max, and Zalmen Reyzin. "A briv tsu ale yidishe filologn." *Teolit: teater un literatur* 1 (1923): 48.

Weinreich, Uriel. "Di forshung fun 'mishshprakhike' yidishe folkslider." *YIVO-bleter* 34 (1950): 282–88.

Weinreich, Uriel, and Beatrice Weinreich. *Yiddish Language and Folklore: A Selective Bibliography for Research.* The Hague: Mouton, 1959.

Weissenberg, Dr. Shmuel. "Das purimspiel van Ahasverus und Esther." *Mitteilungen zur judischen Volkskunde* 7, no. 1 (1904): 1–26.

———. "Di tsunemenishn fun yidn in yelisavetgrader krayz." In *Landoy-bukh*, 79–90.

Wilson, William. *Folklore and Nationalism in Modern Finland.* Bloomington: Indiana University Press, 1975.

———. "Herder, Folklore and Romantic Nationalism." *Journal of Popular Culture* 6 (1973): 819–35.

Wisse, Ruth R. *I. L. Peretz and the Making of Modern Jewish Culture.* Seattle: University of Washington Press, 1991.

Yashunski, Y. "Pruvn fun yidishe entsiklopedias." *Bikher-velt* 1 (1922): 127–32.

The Yiddish Scientific Institute, Account of Two Years Organizing Work [sic] (1925–1927). Vilne: YIVO, 1927.

Zak, Avrom. *In kenigraykh fun yidishn vort: eseyen un dermonungen.* Buenos Aires: YIVO, 1966.

———. *In onheyb fun a friling: kapitlkhe zikhroynes.* Buenos Aires: Tsentral farband fun poylishe yidn in Argentina, 1962.

Zinberg, Israel. "Vanderendike motivn in yidishn folklor." *YIVO-bleter* 3 (1932): 330–36.

Zipperstein, Steven J. *The Jews of Odessa: A Cultural History, 1794–1881.* Stanford, Calif.: Stanford University Press, 1985.

Zlotnik, Rabbi Yeshaye. *Khumesh-folklor.* 3 vols. Warsaw: n.p., 1937–38.

———. *Leksikon fun yidishe khokhmes: gute verter fun kluge yidn.* Warsaw: n.p., 1930.

———. *Yomim-toyvim folklor: ershter teyl.* Warsaw: n.p., 1930.

Index

of, 107; David and Goliath story, 45; Ethnographic Commission's questionnaires and, 122; folklore informants and, 20; psychological folklore analysis and, 48–49; as share of collected material, 136; in Shiper's history of Yiddish drama, 55; as vanishing custom, 123; in *Yidisher folklor,* 162, 165

Purim songs, 41

questionnaires, 123–28, 124, 135, 147; about Napoleon-related genres, 157; compilation of, 137–38; on folk medicine, 136

Rabbi of Lubomir story, 65
rabbis, 79, 80, 127, 136, 142
Rabinovitsh, S. *See* Sholem Aleichem
Radom, Poland, 64
Radoshitski, I. H., 52, *95*
Rapaport, I., 28
Rapaport, Shloyme Zayvnil. *See* Ansky, S.
Rashi, 130
Rashke iz a moyd a voyle (Rashke is a good girl) (Hershele), 53
Ravitch, Melekh, 12
Ravnitzki, J. Ch., 160
"*Reb Getsele Din*" (Mr. Getsele Din), 10
rednsart expression, 143
Reisin, Avrom, 59
rekrutn (recruit) songs, xix
religion, 38, 174
Renaissance humanists, xii–xiii
Reshumot (journal), 55, 66
revolutionaries, 43
revolutionary songs, 153
reyzelekh, 124
Reyzen, Zalmen, 57, 86, 89, 105, 113; *aspirantn* (young scholars) and, 146, 151; *Filologishe shriftn* and, 133, 134–35; founding of YIVO and, 116

riddles, 44, 47, 54, 76, 92, 143; Bastomski's collection of, 87; Cahan's collection of, 156; as genre of "folk creation," 121; primitive sources of, 207n143; relating to Napoleon, 157
Ringelblum, Emanuel, 12, 24, 25, 58
Rivkind, Isaac, 131
Riz, Noyekh, 20
romanticism, xiii, xxii, 156, 173
Roman-tsaytung, Di (newspaper), 56
Rosen, Ber, 30
Roskies, David, 20
Rothschild family, 120, 125, 164
Rovner, Cantor Zeydele, 56
Rozentsvayg, Ayzik, 16–17
Rubinshteyn, Shmuel, 130
Rubshteyn, Ben-Zion, 77
Rumania, 123, 157
Russia, xvi, xix, 46, 157; czar of, 18, 19, 54; Jewish assimilationists in, xviii; Yiddishists in, xv
Russian language, xxi, 31; banned in Vilne (1915), 75; education in, 88; encyclopedias in, 112; folk poetry in, 52; press in, 35
Russian Revolution, 18, 101
Russians, xxii, 30, 115
Russo-Japanese War, 18

S. Ansky Vilne Jewish Historical-Ethnographic Society, 19, 44, 75–78, 173; Bastomski and, 86–92, 101–8; Bernshteyn and, 81–86; history of, 195n2; Lunski and, 78–81; YIVO Ethnographic Commission and, 120
Sabbath, 83, 114, 125, 137, 206n123
St. Petersburg Ethnographic Society, 57, 75, 76, 195n2
Samber, Ayzik, 62
sayings, 89, 90, 92, 105, 136; collected by children, 125; folk knowledge

Warsaw (*continued*)
Council, 36; folk songs in, xx;
Jewish underworld in, 8
Warsaw Ghetto, 6, 22, 58; Hershele in,
52; Lehman in, 11, 12, 19, 184n88
weddings, 125, 127, 154, 168
Wehrhan, K., 150
Weiner, Leo, 39
Weinreich, Max, xvi, 21, 22, 113;
aspirantn (young scholars) and,
146, 150–51, 153, 159; criticism
of Hershele, 54–55; *Filologishe
shriftn* and, 130, 131, 132, 133,
134–35; founding of YIVO and,
116, 117; as historical linguist, 173;
Jewish Historical-Ethnographic
Society and, 78; notes on folk
medicine, 114–15; *Purim-shpiln*
(Purim plays) and, 107; on "Songs
of the Abyss," 34; YIVO Folklore
Commission and, 118, 119, 122; as
YIVO policy maker, 137
Weissenberg, I. M., 62
Weissenberg, Shmuel, 123, 130
White Russia (Belarus), xv, 75, 82, 128
White Russians, 115
"Who [Shall Die] by Water: Poem
on the Life of the Cantonists"
(Hershele), 53
wishes, 131
Wisla (journal), 5, 47
witches, 48, 136
women, xix, xx, 41–42, 105
wonder tales, 127
wordplays, 49, 54, 70
working class, 29, 157

YEKOPO (social welfare organization),
81
Yeshiva students, 83, 140
Yiddish Folksongs in Russia (Ginzburg
& Marek, eds.), xxi, 60
Yiddishism, xiv–xv, 48, 50; de-
Judaization and, 124; humanism

and, xii–xiii, 172; ideology of,
142, 144; modern orientation of,
174; origin of term, 177n27; post-
Holocaust, 172; roots of folklore
study and, xvii–xxiii; scholarship
before founding of YIVO Institute,
111–15; schoolteachers and, 119;
theoreticians of, xv–xvii; Vilne
as center of secularism, 107,
108
Yiddish language, xi, 28, 173; alphabet
of, 45, 69, 84; education in, 88;
Jewish identity and, xii; leftist
politics and, 186n2; *maskilic*
period in literature, 67; as
national language of Jews, 4,
35; in old rabbinical texts, 80;
poetry in, xviii; press in, xiv, 57;
relation to German language, 129,
130; Romance component of,
130; scholarship in, 50; secular
literature in, 66; Slav roots
and, 157; status in Israel, 150;
uniqueness of, 112; variants of,
174; wonders of, 128; Yiddishism
and, xiv–xv; Zionism and, 29. *See
also* dialects, Yiddish
Yiddish Philology (journal), 5
Yiddish Proverbs and Expressions
(Bernstein, ed.), xxi
Yiddish school movement, 44
Yiddish (Soviet journal), 113
Yiddish-Ukrainian songs, 59, 60, 61
Yidishe filologye (journal), 47
Yidishe folksmayses (Cahan, ed.), 20
Yidishe folksretenishn (Bastomski, ed.),
87
Yidishe gezelshaft far landkentnish
(Jewish Geographic Society), 24,
26, 166, 167
Yidisher folklor (journal), 86, 120, 160,
162–66
Yidishes filologye (journal), 113–15, 158
Yidishes folksblat (journal), xix, xx

www.ingramcontent.com/pod-product-compliance
Lightning Source LLC
Chambersburg PA
CBHW070439100426
42812CB00031B/3333/J